Soundings in
SATANISM

Soundings in
SATANISM

ASSEMBLED BY

F. J. Sheed

Introduction by John Updike

SHEED AND WARD · NEW YORK

ACKNOWLEDGMENTS

"The Devil and Cotton Mather," from *The Devil in Massachusetts* by Marion L. Starkey. Copyright © 1949 by Marion L. Starkey. Reprinted by permission of Collins-Knowlton-Wing, Inc.

"Satanism Today," adapted from *The Occult Revolution* by Richard Woods, O.P. Copyright © 1971 by Herder and Herder, Inc. Reprinted by permission of Herder and Herder.

"The Hint of an Explanation," from *Twenty-one Stories* by Graham Greene. Copyright 1947 by Graham Greene. Reprinted by permission of The Viking Press, Inc.

Library of Congress Cataloging in Publication Data

Sheed, Francis Joseph, 1897-   comp.
    Soundings in Satanism.

    Includes 11 articles from an earlier volume published in 1951 under title: Satan.
    1. Devil—Addresses, essays, lectures. 2. Devil—Art—Addresses, essays, lectures. 3. Devil in literature—Addresses, essays, lectures. I. Satan. II. Title.
BT 981.S5   133.4'22   72-6688
PAPER ISBN: 0-8362-0512X
CLOTH ISBN: 0-8362-0507-3

Contents

ASSEMBLER'S NOTE

Twenty years ago we published *Satan*, a translation of a volume of the same name in the series Etudes Carmélitaines, edited by Father Bruno, O.C.D. The present book is not about Satan but about Satanism. The eleven articles used here, roughly one-third of the original work, treat of the ways in which throughout the ages Satan's devotees have expressed their devotion.

We have added two studies of witch burning—"The Trial of Anne de Chantraine" (early-seventeenth-century Belgium) and Marion L. Starkey's "The Devil and Cotton Mather" (late-seventeenth-century America); two stories about the craving to profane the Eucharist—"Black Mass in Paris," from J.-K. Huysmans's *Là-Bas*, and Graham Greene's "The Hint of an Explanation"; "Satanism Today," by Father Richard Woods, O.P.; and "Variations on a Theme," by me.

John Updike's Introduction theorizes on what Satan might be if he is, and on what nerve he touches when he does.

F. J. S.

Introduction

John Updike

Most of the contributors to this volume are Catholic or European or both; an American Protestant feels an understandable diffidence at leading such a parade, as it confidently marches from the mustering ground of biblical exegesis into the weird marshes of possession, exorcism, and witchcraft and onward to the familiar firm terrain of psychopathology and literary criticism. To be honest, most of us Americans who out of reasons quixotic and sentimental and inertial persist in playing disciple to Calvin and Luther and Henry VIII have trouble enough conceiving of a deity, without dabbling at diabolism. Can evil be a personal, dynamic principle? The suggestion seems clownish; instinctively we reject it. If we must have a supernatural, at the price of intellectual scandal, at least let it be a minimal supernatural, clean, monotonous, hygenic, featureless—just a *little* supernatural, as the unwed mother said of her baby. There is no doubt a primitive resonance in the notion of God battling, across the surface of the universe, with a malevolent near equal. But can we morally tolerate the God who would permit such an opponent to arise, who would arm him with death and pain, who would allow suffering Mankind to become one huge Job, teased and tested in heavenly play? Alas, we have become, in our Protestantism, more virtuous than the myths that taught us virtue; we judge them barbaric. We resist the bloody legalities of the Redemption; we face Judgment Day, in our hearts, much as young radicals face the mundane courts—convinced that acquittal is the one just verdict. We judge our Judge; and we magnanimously grant our Creator his existence by a "leap" of our own wills, incidentally reducing his "ancient foe" to the dimensions of a bad comic strip.

Yet these grand ghosts did not arise from a vacuum; they grow (and if pruned back will sprout again) from the deep exigencies and paradoxes of the human condition. We know that we live, and know that we will die. We love the creation that upholds us and sense that it is good, yet pain and plague and destruction are everywhere. It is not my province to discuss the shadowy Old Testament Satan so well evoked by Father Valensin; nor the demons swarming through all cultures, touched upon by M. Bazin in his essay on art; nor the disturbing boundary area where sexual hysteria and Christ's ministry of healing and the (to a Protestant) incredible rite of exorcism intertwine. I would, timidly, in my capacity as feeble believer and worse scholar, open the question of the devil as metaphysical possibility, if not necessity. For the assertion "God exists" is a drastic one that imposes upon the universe a structure; given this main beam, subordinate beams and joists, if reason and logic are anything, must follow. But let a true theologian speak. Karl Barth somewhere, coping with the massive—nay, central—theological problem of evil, speaks of God "turning his back" upon a section of the cosmos. Unable to locate this frightening metaphor, I found instead, in *Church Dogmatics*, a systematic portrait of "nothingness," which I here abridge:

Only God and His creature really and properly are. But nothingness is neither God nor His creature. . . . But it would be foolhardy to rush to the conclusion that it is therefore nothing, i.e., that it does not exist. God takes it into account. He is concerned with it. He strives against it, resists and overcomes it. . . . Nothingness is that which God does not will. It lives only by the fact that it is that which God does not will. But it does live by this fact. For not only what God wills, but what He does not will, is potent, and must have a real correspondence. . . . The character of nothingness derives from its ontic peculiarity. It is evil. What God positively wills and performs in the *opus proprium* of His election, of His creation, of His preservation and overruling rule of the creature revealed in the history of His covenant with man, is His grace. . . . What God does not will and therefore negates and rejects, what can thus be only the object of His *opus alienum*, of His jealousy, wrath and judgment, is a being that refuses and resists and therefore lacks His grace. This being which is alien and adverse to grace and therefore without it, is that of nothingness. This negation of His grace is chaos, the world which He did not choose or will, which He could not and did not create, but which, as He created the actual world, He passed over and set aside, marking and excluding it. . . . And this is evil in the Christian sense, namely, what is alien and adverse to grace, and therefore without it. In this sense nothingness is really privation, the attempt to defraud God of His honour and right and at the same time to rob the creature of its salvation and right. For it is God's honour and right to be gracious, and this is what nothingness contests. . . . In this capacity it does not confront either God or the creature neutrally. It is not merely a third factor. It opposes both as an enemy, offending God and threatening His creature. From above as well as below, it is the impossible and intolerable. By reason of this character, whether in the form of sin, evil, or death, it is inexplicable as a natural process or condition. . . . It "is" only as the disorder at which this counter-offensive is aimed, only as the non-essence which it judges, only as the enemy of God and His creation. We thus affirm that it is necessary to dismiss as non-Christian all those conceptions in which its character as evil is openly or secretly, directly or indirectly, conjured away, and its reality is in some way regarded or grouped with that of God and His creature.

(Church Dogmatics, 3, 3)

Pantheism on one side, Manichaeanism on the other, clutch at the theologian's skirts. A potent ''nothingness' was unavoidably conjured up by God's creating *something*. The existence of something demands the existence of *something else*. And this same ontic inevitability serves Barth to explain man's strange capacity, under God, to choose evil.

Without this possibility of defection or of evil, creation would not be distinct from God and therefore not really His creation. The fact that the creature can fall away from God and perish does not imply any imperfection on the part of creation or the Creator. . . . A creature freed from the possibility of falling away would not really be living as a creature. It could only be a second God—and as no second God exists, it could only be God Himself.

Are there not tendencies in our private psychologies that would give these cosmic propositions credence? Is not destructiveness within us as a positive lust, an active hatred? Who does not exult in fires, collapses, the ruin and death of friends? Who has seen a baby sleeping in a crib and not wanted, for an instant of wrath that rises in the throat like vomit, to puncture such innocence? What child is not fascinated by torture and monstrosity? What man can exempt, from his purest sexual passion and most chivalrous love, the itch to defile? What man or woman does not carry within, as tempter and last resort, the thought of suicide? After satisfaction, revulsion. Into the most ample contentment rushes, not an impulse to sing gratitude, but a frightful impatience that would, like Lucifer, overthrow the tyranny of order, however benign. Indeed, the more fortunate our condition, the stronger the lure of negation, of perversity, of refusal. For the more completely order would enclose us, the greater the threat to our precious creaturely freedom, which finds self-assertion in defiance and existence in sin and dreads beyond hell a heaven of automatons forever "freed from the possibility of falling away." Thus the devil—to give "nothingness" his name—thrives in proportion, never falls hopelessly behind, is always ready to enrich the rich man with ruin, the wise man with folly, the beautiful woman with degradation, the kind average man with debauches of savegery. The world always topples. A century of progressivism bears the fruit of Hitler; our own supertechnology breeds witches and warlocks from the loins of engineers.

We resist what is good for us; humanity cannot be imagined doing otherwise and remaining human. Barth's formulas fit:

man is a battlefield, and Satan at best is "behind" one. But what of creation in general? Does a black-and-white *opus proprium* and *opus alienum* really satisfy our perception of the universe as a curious explosion, a chaos wherein mathematical balances achieve momentary islands of calm? Man as organism is beset not by "nothingness" but by predators and parasites themselves obeying the Creator's command to survive and propagate. Disease is a clash of competing vitalities. And what of those shrugs, those earthquakes and floods and mudslides, whereby the Earth demonstrates her utter indifference to her little scum of life? Nature—Nature, whom we love more than our own bodies, from whose face we have extracted a thousand metaphors and affectionate messages—cares nothing for us. Is this the Satanic nothingness? In fact, it has been taken as such; the Christian West, with its myth of the devil, has taken the fight to Nature with a vengeance, has sought out the microbe and dammed the river and poisoned the mosquito in his marsh and gouged the mineral from its hidden vein and invented the machines that now threaten to scrape Nature into the infernal abyss as Lucifer's angels were scraped from Heaven. Oriental fatalism, which would see death and nothingness as limbs of God, could not have done this. Yet we wonder, as now our human species like some big *bacterion* fills every vacuum and re-creates chaos artificially, if this was intended. Or if the essence of our creaturehood is cooperation, with even the devil.

I do not know. I call myself Christian by defining "a Christian" as "a person willing to profess the Apostles' Creed." I am willing, unlike most of my friends—many more moral than myself—to profess it (which does not mean understand it, or fill its every syllable with the breath of sainthood), because I know of no other combination of words that gives such life, that so seeks the *crux*. The Creed asks us to believe not in Satan but only in the "Hell" into which Christ descends. That Hell, in the sense at least of a profound and desolating absence, exists I do not doubt; the newspapers give us its daily bulletins. And my sense of things, sentimental

I fear, is that wherever a church spire is raised, though dismal slums surround it and a single dazed widow kneels under it, this Hell is opposed by a rumor of good news, by an irrational confirmation of the plenitude we feel is our birthright. The instinct that life is good is where natural theology begins. The realization that life is flawed admits the possibility of a Fall, of a cause behind the Fall, of Satan. How seriously we must take this possibility, and under what forms we might imagine it, the following pages will elucidate.

Soundings in
SATANISM

Diabolic Possession:
The Devils of Loudun

Jean Vinchon

When studied from a purely natural point of view, accounts of possession are found to have many traits in common, though the possessions may occur in different places, at different times, in different civilizations. The possessed in the Gospel seem to differ very little from those observed by missionaries in Africa or Asia, where, according to legend, certain countries—such as Mongolia—are still haunted by demons. The possessed of antiquity resemble the possessed of modern times, except that, before the coming of Christ, the spirits of the dead fulfilled the role later attributed to the devils. Again, the possessed, admitted as such by the Church, appear to suffer and to behave in many ways like sick people who have a fixed delusion of possession. Such possessions can, however, be distinguished from these delusions by certain characteristics which mark them as preternatural and by the frequency with which exorcism brings about a cure.

Environment can multiply cases of possession, but it cannot be their sole origin. Interior tendencies, sometimes almost trivial ones, may play a very important part. The observer who traces the complete curve—beginning in scrupulosity and mental unrest, and continuing through the successive stages which end up in full possession—will form the hypothesis that each of us carries a devil within him, but that happily not everyone becomes his prey. The study of this filiation of mental states reveals the diverse actions of the devil on the body and soul of the possessed, which they transform to such a degree that, in extreme cases, one can see in them aspects of the devil himself—or, if one prefers, of the forces of evil whose existence even unbelievers do not deny. The articles published in many papers on Hitler and his doctrine have not hesitated to describe them as demoniacal, even when addressing an audience indifferent to all religious dogma.

A certain kinship of disposition before the personality has been invaded by the forces of evil explains both the resemblances of the possessed to one another and the contagious nature of possession. This must not, however, be taken as a proof that possession is a natural phenomenon. The Church holds that sickness does not exclude demoniacal action. In the old manuals of exorcism, she combined with her rites *Remedia Corporalia;* today, her priests see that the possessed receive proper medical attention while they themselves pray for them.

The interior dispositions that pave the way for possession reveal themselves by physical, intellectual, and emotional signs, which are present in their fullness when the possession is complete.

The physical signs consist, in the first place, of bodily and facial changes. The possessed becomes unrecognizable, so different from his former self that at Loudun both great lords and commoners came to see the nuns whose faces had been changed to that of the devil. If the possession is long established, the change is completed by the wasting of the frame and the distention of the stomach. The features express anger, hatred, mockery, and insult; at the same time, the organic functions are affected by contractions and spasms of the entrails. The complexion alters; there are distressing symptoms of nausea—vomiting, a furred tongue, and foul breath. The action of the entrails, which in a normal, healthy body is not noticed, here causes sensations of great pain and anguish, further aggravated by irritations of the skin and of the mucous membrane. The victim explains his anguish by the presence of an animal or a devil which is constantly moving inside his stomach, biting, pinching, burning, torturing him in every possible way. The list of his sufferings is completed by dizziness, headaches, and various sensations which seem to have some exterior cause, such as violent pains in the nape of the neck, which the victim imagines to have been occasioned by a blow, and pains in the spine, which he attributes to the same cause. To this must be added twitchings, cramps, impressions of swelling, and varying states of tension, which the victim interprets as marking the entrance of the devil into his body or the moment of his leaving it.

The voice also changes. It no longer has the same quality, but becomes deep, menacing, or sardonic, mocking the most respectable persons, and using, quite against the victim's usual practice, erotic or filthy words. Automatic writing will appear suddenly in the middle of a page of ordinary writing; sometimes, too, the pen will be snatched away and flung into the middle of the room. At other times, the page is angrily slashed by an unseen hand that tears the paper or splashes it with ink. The automatic writing of the possessed is of a violent character, which distinguishes it from that of mediums.

The possessed imagine that the devil who lives in them has a smaller body than their own. This supposed smallness of the devil's body explains the great tribe of little devils in Gothic cathedrals, and surrounding certain statues of Buddha. Because of his smallness, the devil, always bent on evil, can change his character, so as to become a sort of perverse child or formidable yet alluring animal, thus revealing in symbolic forms the emotional ambivalence of which we shall treat very shortly.

The reactions of the possessed have one characteristic in

common, namely, aggressive impulsiveness, which can be replaced by its contrary, inhibition. Insults, menacing gestures, words written by a hand which has lost all control—these symptoms, together with cramps, contortions, and convulsive crises, appear suddenly, without the slightest warning. The violent impulses noted above are a sign of the "occupation" of the personality, and the emotional character of this new personality is shown by its aggressiveness toward God and men. Such reactions, though they seem to be beyond psychic control, are not unconscious. The possessed person knows that another thinks, speaks, and acts through him, and he suffers cruelly as a result. He suffers also from the knowledge of his inhibitions.

One sensation recurs frequently, both in accounts of demoniacal possession and in those of metapsychical experiences. The subjects and the assistants experience a sudden feeling of glacial cold, which often seems to emanate from the walls. At a Sabbath, the devil's arrival is signalized by an icy chill and a sensation of freezing physical contact. Cold hands close about the neck of the possessed; a cold wind blows suddenly. Fear, making the flesh creep, and the chill of the extremities, partly explain this sensation of cold; but sometimes it seems inexplicable. It is generally accompanied by sexual frigidity. The witches had this frigidity, and this was regarded by the Inquisitors as one of the signs of the devil's presence. Cold and frigidity are accompanied by insensibility to pain: in states of possession, the subjects can be burned or pinched without complaining, making the least movement, or changing color.

Possession upsets feminine functions, causes false impressions of pregnancy by distending the stomach, and brings about its effects mingled with the symptoms of the menopause. It throws all the instincts into disorder, destroys the appetite or causes bulimia, and at times brings on an overpowering wish for strange or repugnant forms of food.

Different intellectual signs are mentioned in the manuals

of exorcism, such as the faculty of reading the thoughts of others, the knowledge of future or far-off events or of languages which the subject had never learned; acts contrary to the laws of nature—levitation, or instantaneous removals to far-off places—were also recognized marks of possession. These latter manifestations are rare and constitute the preternatural part of possession with which we are not concerned here. We shall confine ourselves to the facts grouped by metaphysicians under the name paranormal knowledge, which may sometimes appear to be preternatural and at other times to belong unquestionably to the natural order.

This knowledge is limited in the case of mediums. In some cases which are beyond the possibility of fraud, they give dates and proper names which inevitably carry conviction. On the other hand they are often wrong. A state of great tension increases paranormal knowledge, but up to a certain point only. The possessed also have this faculty, but they usually limit themselves to remarks on the character and defects of those present. Such remarks are often very pointed and greatly impress their hearers; in fact, they can lead to the exorcist himself becoming possessed, as happened with Père Surin after he had received numerous paranormal communications from a nun whom he was exorcising.

In the majority of cases, however, the possessed plays the part of a false prophet. He is the instrument of the devil, that is, of a personified *lie*. He is apt to bring to his absurd prophecies the exuberance of an imagination out of touch with all reality.

The emotional signs we are about to study are less evident, less well known, and less classic than the physical and intellectual signs. They are at the root of neuroses and psychoses, which Msgr. Catherinet has described as "the chosen soil" of demoniacal possession.

In his *Demonomania*, published in 1814, Esquirol has shown that possession develops by fits and starts. He tells the story of an unmarried woman of thirty, in love with a man whom her parents would not allow her to marry. She fell into a state of depression during which she decided to take a vow of chastity, but this did not prevent her from having a lover some time later. Seized with remorse, she was obsessed with ideas of damnation that lasted for six years, throughout which time she had to be kept in confinement. She came out again, uncured, and with her intelligence impaired. Shortly after this, she became the dupe of a young man who declared he was Jesus Christ; she succumbed anew and believed herself to be possessed. The devil inhabiting her body prevented her from eating, gnawed at her heart, tore at her entrails. Before very long, she died of tubercular peritonitis.

From this example, we can distinguish two fundamental obsessions of the possessed. There is the obsession of moral solitude to which is joined the obsession of inferiority, frequent with spinsters, with widows, with people who live on the fringe of life, having neither family nor home, with certain religious and nuns ill-adapted to the cloister, which they have entered, not by vocation, but as a result of some previous disappointment. Such morally isolated beings make up a fairly high percentage of the cases of diabolical possession. In fact, obsessions of solitude and inferiority prepare the ground for possession.

Obsessions of guilt determine it. The obsessive idea that one has been guilty of a fault and must suffer for it can exist altogether apart from any fault known to the intellect. It is the expression of a deep-rooted suffering of the unconscious. In illness or possession, it can be so intense as to invade the whole psychic being. It is the cause of ordinary scruples, of childish fears, of sheer funk, and of a thousand other states which appear to be incidents of ordinary psychological life. The dogma of original sin explains, from the religious point of view, the universality of the feeling of guilt.

It must be observed that this feeling, when it lasts for a long time and is entertained with a certain complacency, can become dangerous. Christ said to the sinner he had absolved: "Go in peace" or "Go and sin no more." He did not make long speeches to show in detail the horror of sin; he was content to lift up the sinner and show him the way of life. We should remember his teaching. In fact, when the feeling of guilt becomes an obsession, it paves the way for further falls into the same sins. It may be held, indeed, that the obsession itself becomes part of the temptation by ceaselessly filling the mind with the remembrance of the sin, thus weakening it and draining its resistance.

The obsession of guilt has been described by Père Surin in his "Histoire des diables de Loudun," and in "Science Expérimentale" (*Revue d'ascétique et de mystique*, Toulouse, 1928). Père Surin, who could not reproach himself with any grave sin, ended by believing that he "had desired overeagerly to exalt himself, and that God by a just judgment had willed to humble him." Unable to endure this obsessive idea and believing himself to be damned, he went through the usual sequence: his guilt feeling was followed by attempts at self-punishment, and he tried to commit suicide. Even in the periods when he was not possessed, he was in a state very like guilt obsession, which occasioned crises in which all movement and all thought were either impossible or very difficult. Later, when he was better, these inhibitions became less overwhelming, but he was still unable to give more than a few minutes to the preparation of his sermons. In 1635, the year in which cases of possession in Loudun were most numerous, Surin described his sufferings as "a torment of the spirit." To a certain degree, he recognized that he was suffering from some malady which appeared strange to him. During the crises of possession, he described the cleavage within him in a striking phrase, saying that "his soul became as it were separated." Almost in the same moment he experienced a profound peace, which was immediately succeeded by furious rage. The devil then urged him on to violent words and movements. In his periods of calm, good works no longer gave him their customary joy but aggravated his guilt obsessions, so that he reproached himself with disobeying God "by leaving the ranks of the damned into which he was born."

Père Surin's impulsions arose from obsessions of contrariety which forced him into actions entirely against his will and his desires; he was led, though protesting, to hate Christ, to invent heresies, to approve of Calvin's ideas on the Eucharist.

The signs were present in their fullness a month after Père Surin's arrival at the Ursuline convent of Loudun; throughout that month the prioress, whom he was exorcising, had revealed to him more than two hundred times "very secret things, hidden in his mind or on his person."

This prioress, Soeur Jeanne des Anges, analyzed her own guilt obsessions with considerable perceptiveness. She was "nearly always suffering from remorse of conscience, and with good reason. . . . The devil acted in me only in proportion as I allowed him entry. . . . They took possession of all my exterior and interior faculties to do their will with them, not because I believe myself guilty of blasphemy and other disorders into which the devils often cast me, but because in the beginning I listened to their suggestions." In her crises, Soeur Jeanne des Anges insulted God and blasphemed his goodness and love, expressed her hatred of the religious life, tore and chewed her veil, and spat out the Host into the priest's face.

She sometimes found it possible to resist, and then she did not allow herself to blaspheme or to commit sacrilege, even though the thought of doing so came to her. She even admitted to a certain pleasure, astonishing in a nun, in submitting to possession. "The devil often tricked me by a little feeling of pleasure that I had in the disturbances and other extraordinary things he occasioned in my heart."

Père Surin and Soeur Jeanne des Anges represent types of possession which apparently differ, but which are found to have the same origin in guilt obsessions, split personality, spirit of contrariety, and emotional ambivalence. They are an exact parallel, as we have said, to modern cases of possession, but they had a greater gift of self-analysis; they had, if one may say so, the time to give to it. The more methodical and more restrained practice of exorcism today limits suggestion and prevents the development of those mental states, highly colored and full of detail, which abounded up to the beginning of the seventeenth century. Again, exorcisms are no longer performed in public, and this eliminates the element of mass suggestion traceable in former exorcisms.

Pride, the sin of the devil, plays only a secondary part in cases of possession, as when, for example, it serves to justify guilt obsessions. It was so used by Père Surin when he believed himself to be damned, as St. Teresa and certain other saints had done before him.

We have now considered the signs of the states of possession—signs physical, intellectual, and emotional, with special emphasis on guilt obsessions. Perhaps it is possible to deduce from these signs a knowledge of certain aspects of the devil.

The countenance of the devil, as it is represented by the sculptors of the Gothic cathedrals and by the artists of the Far East, can be seen during crises in the faces of the possessed, who also reproduce with varying degrees of skill and richness of imagination the gestures and conduct of their model. But the physical aspect, even if the resemblance is a very close one, remains secondary.

In the moral sphere, the aspects of the devil are more closely fitted to the individual characters of the possessed. The tempter who multiplies his wiles and varies his dialectic to seduce a Faust is as different from the devil who tempts the possessed as is the pride-intoxicated Lucifer who led his legions against God. The devils of the possessed are more ordinary and commonplace. They are, so to speak, the devil-in-the-street, designed for the man-in-the-street.

Thus, these devils do not appear as new guests but as old guests who have come to be more and more sure of themselves, until they finish up by being masters of the house. They keep the deceit and the pride, the subtlety of insinuation, the malignity and aggressiveness of the classic devil, but they are more intimately mingled with the personality of their host. It often happens that, during impulsions of contrariety, they attack objects or persons who, at some time or other, have had their share in the formation of personal complexes. These impulsions then appear as attempts to cut free from the conflicts which arise from these complexes. The insults to God, to the Church, and to the Host thus take on an especial meaning. The possessed attack them as obstacles which have opposed some of their desires.

The history of Soeur Jeanne des Anges proves the reality of the psychoanalytic mechanism of her impulsions of contrariety. She makes this clear when she speaks of the "little feeling of pleasure" she felt when she yielded to her aggressiveness. Her demon, we recognize, was that of the Marquis de Sade.

That of Père Surin, on the other hand—Père Surin, who said he was born "damned"—is a perfect example of the guilt obsession which has no sin as its cause, but is constantly on the lookout for sins with which to justify its existence. The mission of this devil seems to be to witness to the reality of original sin, which has transmitted the inborn sense of guilt from our first parents down to us.

Let us now turn from the demoniacs of Loudun to the sick of our own day. Another demon, in the form of a little animal, took up his abode in the body of an elderly spinster, and remained there through a certain "consent" on her part, as Soeur Jeanne des Anges put it. He peopled the solitude which obsessed her, answered her questions, conversed with her; then after a certain time tormented her so much that she had recourse to a priest, who, in turn, sent her to a doctor.

Another devil installed himself in a girl who was honest

and decent to the point of scrupulosity, and obsessed her with images of thefts which she had never committed. He recognized the chastity of his hostess and used these theft images as symbolic equivalents of the erotic thoughts which he knew she would not entertain.

These humanized devils belong to every age and every country. They came with the first man and will leave with the last. Notwithstanding their lack of dignity, and because they are so well adapted to our condition, they represent the most dangerous forms of the forces of evil, the forms which haunt the precincts of the common day.

Pseudo-Possession

Jean Lhermitte

As the trial of Anne de Chantraine (see pp. 46-54) shows, it was decidedly dangerous to be suspected of holding intercourse with the devil, and those who were so suspected were threatened by the most dire tortures. In this respect, at least, we have grown more compassionate and humane.

It must be admitted that the science of psychiatry takes a very humble place among the other biological disciplines, for psychiatry operates on a plane where soul and body meet, and we still do not know how that "seam of soul and body" is made. In spite of this, however, we must admit that our knowledge of mental disorders began greatly to improve from the time when spiritual disturbances ceased to be regarded purely as an expression of supernatural influence and were seen as evidence of modifications in the development or the adjustment of psychophysiological functions. There is no psychiatrist today who could not with the greatest ease discover under the mask of witchcraft in the past the most significant symptoms of psychoses, such as come up for treatment every day.

The sole aim of any doctor investigating the matter must be to trace the origin and source of demonopathy, to unravel its strands, often much entangled, to identify the process at work, whether psychic or organic, and finally to cure or at least diminish the pathological deviations of the mind. This is his task, and one may if one wishes consider it a humble one, since it must not transgress the frontiers of natural phenomena, but has to remain aloof from the far loftier problems which call for the notice and powers of discernment of the philosopher and theologian.

Our discussion, therefore, is limited to precisely this: can we discover, in certain persons supposedly possessed by the devil, any signs which would permit us to relate the idea of demonopathic possession to a morbid process—that is to say, to an illness properly so called?

It is, of course, true that the diagnosis of mental disturbances differs somewhat from that of organic physical diseases, for the latter produce not only objectively obvious symptoms, but also evidence of a still more positive nature in the alterations of the organic texture.

This is not so in the case of the psychopathies; for most of them, the anatomical basis is wanting, which does not mean it is nonexistent. Still, even if the anatomical control fails us, we are entitled to diagnose illness in those cases where the deviation of the mind is accompanied by certain features which remain constant whatever the education or social conditions of the affected persons. Moreover, given a psychopathological syndrome, its development can be foreseen, together with its social and medicolegal consequences. It is strange, too, to observe that the pathopsychological reactions of man at his most highly civilized are not very numerous; it is the coloring, the content of the delirium, rather than its inner structure, its foundation, its essence, which has the most varied (and often picturesque) aspect. Whether a paranoiac feels himself persecuted by waves from "the other side," by the Freemasons, by the Jesuits, by this or that imaginary person or group of persons, or by the devil makes no difference. The disease will reveal itself as being more or less complex, more or less interesting in its details: the patient's complaints and recriminations will be more or less plausible or completely unlikely; but the development and prognosis will not be modified, any more than the preventive treatment or the attempted cure.

Indeed, it would be too much to ask of the doctor more than a careful diagnosis, accompanied by an accurate prognosis and efficient treatment.

This said, we will attempt to present an analysis of the facts relevant to the demonic possessions with which the psychiatrist has to deal.

Let us first examine the way in which a possessed person is represented in popular works on the subject. It is, I think, the moral transformation of the victim which has most struck the nonscientific observer.

The patient does, indeed, appear to be transformed, penetrated by a new personality which is superimposed on or juxtaposed to the individual's real personality. In those accounts which can be found in M. Oesterreich's interestingly documented collection, *Les Possédés*, the possessed person not only gives the impression of being invaded by another soul, but even his physiognomy, his bearing, and his social behavior seem transformed.

It goes without saying that this apparent metamorphosis is not continuous but is visible only during those periods when the state of possession is at its most acute—that is to say during moments of trance; but this corporeal change, essentially dynamic, becomes extremely personal in each possessed subject, so that he gives the impression that his physical personality is truly transformed into an alien personality.

"Every time the devil seized her," says Eschenmayer of a woman who believed that she was possessed by the spirit of a dead person, "her face assumed the features which distinguished the dead man during his life, and as these were very pronounced, it was necessary at every attack to keep the woman away from people who had known the dead man, for they at once recognized him under the features of the demonic woman.''

Another point of interest is that the new character or attitude, the change of conduct which marks the person in a state of trance or possession, is opposed in every detail to the possessed person's own primary personality. Witnesses of these scenes are astonished, indignant even, at hearing the foulest insults, the most obscene words, from the mouth of a young girl whose education and morals might have been thought irreconcilable with such an outburst of the lowest passions and the coarsest possible language.

It was said of the young girl of Orlach described by Eschenmayer that ''during the attacks, the spirit of darkness speaks through her mouth like a mad devil, saying things which a young girl of upright heart should not know—maledictions of Holy Writ, of the Savior, of all that is sacred.''

I have myself observed cases of this kind which are indeed astonishing, for one wonders where these well-brought-up and sheltered young girls could have learned the vocabulary they pour forth with such violence during their attacks.

In all the numerous examples of demoniacal possession found in the abundant literature devoted to the subject, invasion by the demonic personality is evident only in certain states, called attacks or trances, during which the possessed person no longer controls himself and even loses consciousness of his own natural personality. It cannot therefore be said that a splitting of the personality occurs, but rather, as Eschenmayer and Oesterreich maintain, that the loss or lapse of consciousness becomes an essential characteristic of demonic possession; to this suspension of the functions of consciousness can be added the subsequent total forgetfulness of what has occurred during the attack.

It is incontestable that such phenomena have occurred

and continue to occur in our times, but we are better equipped to understand their nature and origin than were our predecessors. Indeed, there is a disease of frequent incidence which is characterized by the temporary loss of consciousness and the transformation of its victim into an automaton controlled by ideas, sentiments, and memories entirely alien to those he normally entertains—even entirely opposed to his true personality. This disease is epilepsy; it is the *morbus sacer*, the sacred ill, the "high ill," the "comitial ill" of the ancients.

Contrary to general belief, epilepsy does not manifest itself only by convulsions, which animals, too, can suffer, but also very frequently by sudden changes of the moral personality—catastrophic upheavals which may last any length of time from a few moments to several hours or days. The sick person remembers nothing of what occurred during these attacks. Yet today it is possible for us not only to define the epileptic disease with absolute precision from the features of the clinical context, but also to specify the nature of the mental disorder, thanks to the detection of special waves shown by the electroencephalographic apparatus.

But if epilepsy can simulate a state of demonic possession, there is another morbid state, also very common, which is found underlying the manifestations examined in these pages: this is the "great neurosis" of Charcot—hysteria. Most of the cases of possession characterized by trances during which the victim's personality appears transformed, and by stormy, theatrical manifestations, whose violence is proportioned to the audience available, can undoubtedly be related to this neurosis. It is true that the hysterical person's state of consciousness is very different from that of the epileptic, and that if it does become to some extent clouded, this clouding does not reach the degree of utter annihilation of the consciousness which characterizes the disease of epilepsy. Nevertheless, the "great neurosis" of Charcot is not made up solely of deceit, theatricality, mockery, mythogenesis, and pathogenesis, as some doctors have maintained. There is also a genuine disorder of the mind and of the consciousness, shown by the curious reactions of the electroencephalographic apparatus, as revealed in the remarkable studies of Titéca (Brussels).

In a hysterical attack, the consciousness does not suffer total annihilation, in the Jacksonian sense, as it does in the case of epilepsy; but there is too much evidence for us to doubt that some suspension or considerable weakening of certain psychic functions does take place. It is thus easy to understand why psychologists, and in particular M. Oesterreich in his important work devoted to the study of the possessed, feel that all states of possession during which the normal individuality is suddenly replaced by another temporary personality, and which leave no memory when the victim returns to a normal state, should be known as somnambulant. If we put on one side for a moment the factor relating to complete loss of memory, which disregards the difference between epilepsy and hysteria, the author's thesis is one which we may accept.

As I have indicated above, the "great neurosis" is essentially contagious, a fact of which the experiments at the Salpêtrière under Charcot, are a striking proof. It is then to hysterical demonopathy that we should relate the great majority of, if not all, epidemics of possession. Such epidemics were extremely numerous in the days when the manifestations of "the great deceiver," hysteria, were but imperfectly known.

Everyone remembers the epidemics of possession which raged in the world at a time when psychiatry had barely come into being; the examples produced by these epidemics showed most clearly the symptoms of hysterical psychoneurosis, or of pithiatism, that is to say, of that neurosis where simulation and mythomania act together. It must not, however, be thought that our forerunners knew nothing of pithiatism. Take the case of Marthe Brossier, whose trial took place in the reign of Henri IV. Marthe was a young girl of poor circumstances, the eldest of four, with an unaffectionate, mediocre father. Eager to get married and seeing her project miscarry, she cut her hair short and wore men's clothes, like Joan of Arc. One day in the year following she suddenly set on a friend of hers called Anne Chevion, scratched her face, and accused her of having ruined all her hopes. She was thought to be possessed by the devil, on account of the violence of her reactions and of the "marvelous things she uttered against the Huguenots"—for this occurred in 1599, the very year of the Edict of Nantes—and she was solemnly exorcised. One reads that Beelzebub swelled her belly, then, several times, bent her body so far back that her head touched her feet, while she shouted: "I am more tormented than if I were in hell"; then submitting to the exorcist's commands, she said, "You will make me to lose my Huguenots."

Confronted with this scandal, Henri IV decided to have Marthe interned in the great Châtelet, where she was visited by doctors and clerics. The experts affirmed that there was no question of a genuine possession, and Henri IV ordered Marthe to be sent back to her father in Romorantin. What, then, had occurred? We have the documents of the trial, and nothing could be more instructive. Dr. Marescot, helped by three of his colleagues, examined the "possessed" girl.

Was she able to understand languages which she had never learned, as was maintained? No; directly questioned in Greek, in Latin, she remained silent. When exorcised, she indeed fell into a fainting fit, her thighs quivering like the flanks of an exhausted horse (which is easy enough to imitate). Marthe mocked the exorcist, but, taken to task by Marescot, confessed that the devil had left her. And Marescot concludes: "Nothing demonic, not much illness, a great deal of acting."

Pursuing his demonstration, Marescot wonders on what criteria one may depend to decide on the genuineness of a possession. Convulsion? But charlatans and grooms can imitate them. Insensibility to the insertion of a needle? But the same rogues can bring this off with great success. The absence of blood when the skin is punctured? But this shows only that the veins have not been touched. Ventriloquism? But Hippocrates had already discovered the gift in persons who were beyond any suspicion of witchcraft. The discerning of objects? But Marthe made serious mistakes: for example, a wrapped key was presented to her as a fragment of the true cross, and Marthe responded with every conceivable diabolic symptom. Levitation? But if a few persons thought they had seen Marthe suspended in the air without support, it was in the afternoon, when their intelligence had been somewhat dimmed by a hearty meal; nothing similar had occurred in the mornings.

Marescot, whose analytical powers are so remarkable, does not stop there; our colleague wonders what can be the cause of this pretended possession. And he discovers it in the cupidity of Marthe and her father, for the latter had been given sums of money to get his daughter cured. But, Marescot finally asks, how could this Marthe, whose education was scanty, be capable of so many tricks? Here the inquiry shows that Marthe had in point of fact read many books describing deeds attributed to the devil, and that, moreover, she was always being told that she had "*le diable au corps.*"

The part played by suggestion, which has been so vigorously denied by Bernheim and Babinsky, is seen again in another patient whom, among others, I had occasion to observe. The case is that of a young nun who from the age of fifteen was assailed by sexual trials: obsessions and perhaps compulsions. Her director unwisely told her that the devil was at work, and the girl suddenly felt her personality divided and spellbound by the evil spirit. From then onward, exorcisms were multiplied until they were performed daily; during these exorcisms the girl threw herself into a thousand contorted attitudes and gave way to the wildest and most fantastic tricks. Worse still, in between the periods of exorcism she began to smash things and to utter prophecies, so that the peace and composure of the convent were exceedingly disturbed.

We proceeded to examine this patient in the presence of a qualified exorcist, refraining, however, from applying the ritual which had been somewhat immoderately used. We merely asked her to read the prayer to St. Michael usually recited at the end of low mass. As soon as she reached "*defende nos in praelio*," she leaped to her feet, glared at us, overwhelmed us with filthy insults, tore off her wimple and veil and flung them at us. Then she began to twirl and dance and to assume innumerable fantastic postures similar to those observed at the Salpêtrière, in the time of Charcot and Paul Richer.

In a second examination, the same phenomena were repeated, and we decided to apply electric-shock treatment and to isolate the patient. After one month of this, she was completely free from all idea of demonic possession.

Here is another example: a young girl of twenty drew attention to herself by her conduct and went along to consult a priest because, she said, on Friday afternoon her forehead became covered with blood; to prove this allegation she produced a handkerchief soaked in blood; which turned out, on examination, to be indeed human blood unmixed with any extraneous matter. Her mother was interrogated and reported that for some time past her daughter had become somewhat self-absorbed. "She believes herself to be a saint," she said. "It is just as if there were two persons in her; she keeps vigils, has all sorts of odd ideas."

Then one night, between eleven and midnight, the girl, according to her story, was assaulted by the devil. A man leaped up before her bed; simultaneously the lights went out, while a red glow shone everywhere. The vision of this being, appearing in the shape of a man, filled her with disgust. "I noticed a curious thing," she remarked. "His eyes followed me and his body moved only according to my own movements." This disturbing person tried to kiss her on the forehead and the cheeks, to overpower her, but without success. At times she seemed to hear the devil.

These strange phenomena often drove her, she said, to consult her spiritual director, but he did not understand her, and this completely unstrung her. In an attempt to verify, as far as possible, the truth of her allegations, one of her companions, whose honesty was beyond suspicion, was asked to keep a particularly attentive watch on Ma (this being the patient's first name), day and night, for a fortnight. Her report was as follows:

"I saw openings form on her forehead and blood flow, even while we were walking arm in arm, several Fridays running. I also saw Ma's shoes taken off without her moving; the seat of her chair burned while she was on it, without her being hurt. At the chapel of the Benedictines, the chairs moved behind Ma, yet nobody could be seen. I have also touched," the watcher continued, "the end of one of her ribs, jutting out under her right arm; Ma herself brought the pieces together again, after a burst of laughter. Sometimes, without apparent cause, she fell out of bed. One night, something very strange occurred: suddenly I heard Ma scream, she switched on the light, picked up a parcel, and then put out the light again; there was a smell of burning and Ma handed me an undershirt, partly burned and charred. Sometimes her dress was stained with blood, but I cannot tell where it comes from."

In spite of these extraordinary features in Ma's behavior, our watcher declared that she believed these phenomena to be quite authentic. "There are sufficient elements," she said, "which do not allow of any doubt about her."

During these observations we had been carrying out an inquiry into Ma's family and its history. We learned that Ma's father was an alcoholic, as was her grandmother on the mother's side. Ma, it turned out, had received sufficient education to obtain an elementary certificate. But what was more interesting was that Ma was a proved liar, and evidently a mythomaniac; that, after a pilgrimage to Lourdes, her mother had said to the headmistress: "That was a nice trick you played on us in taking my daughter to Lourdes; you have brought back a devil."

Before manifestations thus equivocal, we asked Ma to come to my consulting room, so that we could ourselves observe the flow of blood which was supposed to cover her forehead every Friday.

We were disappointed in this, for on the morning when she was due to present herself she sent us a letter, the essential passages of which are given here:

I would like to be open with you, but feel as if paralyzed and cannot speak.

For over six months I have had an interior struggle with the devil; it is like a relentless war within me between the spirit of God pushing me toward good and another spirit drawing me, thrusting me toward evil.

All these stories you have heard are only one long lie, and I wish I could attempt to tell you of my state of misery.

I felt driven to lie from the beginning . . . I let myself be dragged further and further, often forced to speak and to act, in spite of myself.

I have never had terrible visions of the devil, but at certain moments I feel him very close to me. It is he who made me set fire to my underwear in spite of myself. I don't remember doing it.

I have invented all these stories, I do not know why, and I feel more and more unhappy, I cannot speak, however much I should like to. . . .

Yet there are a few visible, real signs of this devil's presence—odors smelled in various places, noises in church, a few other minor incidents at my friend's house. . . .

It is only in the last few days that I have understood the gravity of the wrong I have been doing.

What I do not understand is that in the midst of all my darkness, with God remaining hidden as my sins have deserved he should, I feel more and more called to a life of reparation. I sometimes end up by wondering if it isn't just another trick of the devil, and I feel ill; you cannot conceive how much I suffer with the headaches I have on Fridays.

This case certainly looks more complex than many others of the same kind, yet it has certain ostentatious, theatrical features that perfectly characterize the pseudo-possession of the hysterical subject; if to this is added lying, duplicity, and mythomania, it will be seen that identification is easy enough. What should be noted as far more important in this case is the enlightenment offered by Ma on her own psychological state: she had been driven to lie, to invent all manner of stories, and she would repent. Many hysterical people have confessed to this inner compulsion, but in their consciousness the notions of true and false, which seem to us so clear and distinct, are usually blurred as in a mist, or else are so unstable that it would be most imprudent to accept such allegations with any measure of conviction.

A last example of this kind: a nun belonging to a teaching order, inclined, from the age of eight, to morbid sexual practices and a prey to obsession and scruples, managed by force of will power to pass through the stages of the novitiate which lead to the final vows.

Toward her thirtieth year, however, the obsession of the devil began to haunt her; she could no longer bear the sight of the crucifix or of a holy image. Becoming convinced that she was possessed by the evil spirit, she asked to be exorcised. In spite of the exorcism, the demonopathic phenomena continued and grew out of all proportion. Yes, the devil was there; he lay in wait for her during the night, bound her to her bed, sometimes undressed her, and left her there naked. Wishing to make an end of it, she signed a pact with the devil, writing these words on a piece of paper, with a pen dipped in her own blood: "O Satan, my Master, I give myself to you forever." And just as Pascal carried his touching Memorial against his heart, she wore this diabolical talisman day and night; then, seized with remorse, she went through the motions of suicide by taking several tablets of gardenal.

In this case, as in those preceding, the exorcism was vain because the question was one of psychosis and not of possession; and we must add that in such cases, where suggestibility assumes such a powerful role in the development of morbid phenomena, not only should exorcism be avoided, but also any action which might tend to maintain the idea of possession in the mind of the subject. Moreover, as Marescot recalled, the Roman ritual commands that possession should not be too easily believed in, and he adds: "For often the overcredulous are deceived, and frequently melancholics, lunatics, and those bewitched deceive the exorcist, saying that they are possessed and tormented by the devil, when in fact they are more in need of the remedies of the doctor than the ministration of the exorcist."

Besides the type of demonopathy which manifests itself in crises or trances, accompanied by a more or less complete dissolution of consciousness, we must now examine a very different species, deserving of even more attention. I have in view here what has been called the "lucid" form of possession. The expression is not a very happy one and has too much of a flavor of the time when people spoke of "lucid madness"; I feel it is preferable to call the phenomenon in question "delirium of possession" or "demonopathic delirium."

What are the characteristics which enable us to differentiate between this form of possession and those we have already discussed? The most important one is that the patients we are now examining are not affected by attacks, crises, or trances; their consciousness remains lucid in that they are fully aware of what is happening within them, bodily and spiritually, and they give minute, picturesque, and singularly revealing descriptions of it. One of the most significant examples of this state of mind is that of Père Surin, exorcist of the possessed of Loudun (see pp. 1–11). This priest, whose mystical life was highly developed, vital, and of great sanctity, was afflicted by strange disturbances which he describes in a letter to a friend:

I am in perpetual conversation with devils, and have had

adventures which it would take too long to describe. . . . So much so that for three and a half months I have never been without a devil hovering about me. . . . The devil passes from the body of the possessed person and, entering mine, overthrows me, agitates me, and passes through me visibly, possessing me for several hours like a demoniac. It is as if I had two souls, one of which is dispossessed of its body and of the form of its members and holds itself aloof, watching the other which has usurped its place. The two spirits fight on the one battlefield, which is the body, and the soul seems to be divided.

He adds by way of postscript:

The devil had said to me: I shall deprive you of everything, and you will indeed need to keep your faith; I shall stupefy you . . . so I am obliged, in order to retain some kind of clear thought, to hold the Holy Sacrament frequently to my head, using the Key of David to open my memory.

In his work entitled *Studies in the History and Psychology of Mysticism*, Delacroix reports several other characteristics relevant to the condition of Père Surin, found in the manuscript in the Bibliothèque Nationale. It is there stated that the sufferings of the unfortunate Père Surin lasted no less than two years.

He was so worn out that he was unable to preach or carry on a conversation. He even became dumb for seven months, was incapable of dressing and undressing himself, and finally, of making any movement whatever. He fell into an unknown illness against which all medicines were ineffectual. Several times he had impulses to commit suicide and made one serious attempt to do so. In spite of all this, his soul did not entirely lapse from attention to God; often, in the midst of his infernal torments, he was strongly moved to unite himself with Christ. . . . In his trials, he was conscious at one and the same time of despair and the desire to act in accordance with God's will.

As it was impossible at that time to analyze the nature of the psychic troubles afflicting Père Surin, he was regarded as insane and classified in the registers of his order as mentally disordered.

Nothing could have been more judicious, and we should have extreme compassion for such unfortunates, whose incessant suffering is inexpressible and, quite often, leads them to suicide.

For many reasons, the case of Père Surin deserves close attention from any medical psychologist: the progressive nature and incurability of the illness, the general disorders which overwhelmed both mind and body, the inhibitions, impulsions, contradictions, aural hallucinations, the spoken words attributed to the devil, the sensation of a splitting of the personality, or of the mind's having been taken captive by a force stronger than that of the will, the continuous feeling of constraint—all these abnormal or unusual psychological elements have seldom been better described and analyzed than by Père Surin.

It would be easy to find examples of similar cases in the literature devoted to demonopathy, but, since space is restricted, I think it better to offer a few observations on cases I myself have studied—cases answering to the type of possession we have here in mind.

I received one day a visit from a man of sixty, a retired official from some ministry, who told me that for a considerable time he had been suffering the onslaughts of the devil, who had forced him to undergo strange affronts and who never left him, day or night; to put it briefly, he was possessed. This man had been brought up in a religious college; from his childhood he had been haunted by the problems of sex and had given himself up to solitary sexual practices, with some tendency to homosexuality. He married, however, and if he afterward had some lapses, they were not numerous, and never homosexual. Nevertheless, he was incessantly tormented by certain obsessions, and in the effort to counter them he took refuge increasingly in prayer, in spiritual struggle, and in penance. In fact, he was drawn more and more to prayer until the day came when he felt that a strange transformation had taken place within him. Everything that happened around him became symbolic: thus the crow of a cock meant moral deliverance; dark objects and colors, dirty linen, mud, the grills of drains, dark corners in apartments, cigarette ash, gravel, scrap-iron dumps, tree trunks, the bottoms of saucepans, all these represented evil spirits; while good spirits were symbolized by gold, silver, golden frames, mirrors, anything blue, lights, brightly colored flowers.

However, in spite of this irrational symbolism, the man continued to lead a fairly calm life until one day when, walking near the lake in the Bois de Boulogne, he heard a voice address him in words which are quite unrepeatable. He hailed a taxi and returned home in a state of extreme anxiety. When he reached home, he said to his wife: "This time the devil *is* with me; I am possessed." Ever since this episode, which had taken place many years before, the evil spirit had never left him. He felt his presence unceasingly; all day long the devil spoke to him, insulted him, pursued him with the most filthy obscenities or with the most incongruous words. Often, too, the devil would defy or command him and remind him of past faults, which he called "culpae." One day, on the way to Ville-d'Avray, the devil threatened him with the words: "If you go any farther, you are a dead man." The evil spirit not only assailed him with filthy expressions and tried to anger him by repeating his thoughts, but also brought before his eyes the most startling pictures of lust—scenes of utterly unbridled eroticism reminiscent of the temptations of St. Anthony, but with one specific and individual feature. All those orgies, which were of an unimaginable erotic splendor, were characterized by a brazen homosexuality. The devil would also often appear to him in the shape of a hybrid monkey and wolfhound, and stand before him, jeering or threatening him, raising himself on his hind paws, putting out a red tongue at him, and showing his sharp teeth. The wretched man would hurl himself in fury on this simulacrum, fling stones at it, scourge it, or nail it to the pillory. Fortunately the good spirits brought their consolations to make up to him for all his sufferings. These good spirits spoke through a statue of the Virgin and through the crucifix, or else in the shape of sinuous blue snakes. The possessed man had within him two opposing influences: that of the devil, which remained dominant, and that of the good spirits, to which he often appealed for help. Knowing the thousand-and-one tricks of the devil, he used to make experiments and employ a series of spiritual and material means of defense: indifference to insults, irony, the recitation of a prayer, "self-exorcism," complete silence, the arranging of statues in triangles of power to oppose any demoniac intrusion. But only too often the evil spirit made short work of these fragile defenses, mocked him, and made him appear ridiculous in his own eyes.

As I was curious to find out more of the origin of this demonopathic delirium, I asked my patient to write out his sad story in detail. I thus obtained the circumstantial account of his sufferings, and, above all, of the devil's plan of attack. It seemed to me very remarkable that this man, who knew nothing of psychiatry, should give me almost exactly the same formulas as those which we owe to the pioneer of the study of mental automatism, G. de Clérambault. Here, then, in our patient's own words, is the way in which the devil acts upon the mind. He works by the introspection of thought, "thought which knows itself to be thinking," which thus produces the illusion of the spirit's duality; but the involuntary recalling of memories, of words once heard—even and perhaps especially the most obscene ones; the remembrance also of past sins, of "sexual depravities"; the automatic language which passes the lips without the participation of the will; the apparent alienation of the will; involuntary exchange of speech with the devil, and the compulsion to entertain thoughts or use expressions quite outside the victim's normal habits; sugges- tions and intrusions into the mind of feelings of inferiority, hatred, anxiety, doubt, uncertainty, which, in their extreme state, bring about confusion; finally, the evil spirit blurs the memory of certain images or scenes, bringing instead before the mind either distorted conceptions (sensory illusions) or conceptions without an object, that is to say, auditive hallucinations, verbal, visual, and coenaesthesic psychomotives.

In a work devoted to the study of the image of our body, I fully analyzed the case of a young girl, Sybil, whose pathological history is all the more remarkable in that it extends over very long periods, and that the origin and material cause of the delirium of possession were clearly traceable. This young girl had been sent to me by an exorcist whom she had consulted. The learned priest decided that this was a pathological case and not one of genuine possession and he therefore asked me to treat her. What was her story? She was convinced that she was bewitched and under the influence of the devil, especially at night. Just as she was about to fall asleep, the devil would come to her bed, strip her of her fleshly body, "double" her, and carry her double to a celestial sphere which she called "astral." There he amused himself with torturing her, wounding her with heavy blows, scourging her, flinging her into thorn bushes, or, worse still, firing revolver shots through her body, and forcing her to endure the most terrible humiliations. The girl would try to defend herself against this appalling power: she attempted to regain possession of the "double" from which she had been torn away. She would beg the devil to give it back to her, and her struggle and entreaties always lasted a long time, until she was quite worn out, when the devil at last consented to give her back the body which he had taken from her. Curiously enough, this "double" was not always given back whole; sometimes it was restored to her bit by bit, with an arm missing, or a leg, and only after a violent struggle did she regain complete possession of her body. Sometimes, worn out with pleading with her tyrant, she would rise from her bed, but as she felt herself to be lacking her body, she would stumble, her legs would give way, and she would fall to the floor. On these occasions Sybil was sometimes capable of observing what was happening around her and was struck by strange phenomena: objects were moving and bending, and she seemed able to understand the alarm clock's rhythmical language.

She was seized by violent compulsions and inhibitions quite opposed to the action of her will; she became the victim of aural and visual hallucinations; but more often even than this, she was able to understand what the devil thought merely by seeing him torture her "double."

Like Père Surin and every other sufferer from the delirium of possession, Sybil used what she thought were the most effectual means of defense against the devil; thus she sprinkled her bed with holy water, always put her rosary round her neck, and following an old superstition, often burned a few lumps of sugar at the foot of her bed. But unfortunately these defenses nearly always proved insufficient or completely ineffectual. Her state grew progressively worse, and any form of life with other people became impossible, so that she had to be placed in a psychiatric hospital, where she fell seriously ill.

Before reaching that stage, however, Sybil had, to all appearances, remained quite reasonable in her daily life; she lived with her father and for many years looked after the house without provoking any serious criticism by her conduct. She was reserved and pious and never fell into any of the sins of the flesh; it was only during her trances that she imagined that the devil defiled her by indulging with great violence in acts whose nature can easily be guessed. In most such cases it is impossible to discover, apart from hereditary defects, the origin of this delirium; but with Sybil the cause of the illness turned out to be quite evident. At the age of twelve she had suffered from epidemic *encephalitis lethargica* and had spent many months in a hospital in Paris. We know today the remote consequences that can follow this illness, and the cause of the demonopathic delirium is in this case clear.

Let us now turn to another case related to the last. Here the patient was a young girl of very good family, who had received a most careful education. She was sent to me by the mother superior of a religious community which she had greatly desired to enter, but her somewhat strange manner was a barrier to her being admitted.

I questioned this young girl, and when I had won her confidence, she told me about her life, her enthusiasms and discouragements, her anxieties and hopes.

"Ever since my childhood," she said, "I have every now and then had the impression of being in another world and of knowing God, the Father of Jesus Christ; while I was still a little girl, I had sublime revelations and even supernatural visions. One day, for instance, I saw the ceiling open and a cloud rend before my eyes; then God spoke to me in my heart."

Here the case is obviously one of "pseudo-hallucination," or psychic hallucinations accompanied by an acute feeling of presence.

Sometimes, also, she felt a soft breath touch her from the left; this, she said, was "like an infusion of God." Later she heard "in her thought" God telling her: "We shall come near you to make our dwelling place." Finally, under the influence of this constant feeling of the divine which seemed to penetrate her, she became convinced that she was soon to receive an order to carry out a spiritual mission on earth, and began to question herself and to seek in external things signs and revelations of this mission.

All the time these strange phenomena were taking place, the girl was going through great physical suffering: at one time it would take the form of overpowering weakness; at another she would feel a pain in the back of the neck which "brought a host of thoughts"; or she would feel various visceral pains, such as characterize what is called *hypochondria dolorosa*. But what troubled her most was the feeling that the devil was incessantly prowling around her; indeed, she felt as if she were being crushed between two opposing forces, one divine and the other diabolical. She was never affected by actual visual hallucinations, but on several occasions it seemed to her that the devil threw himself on her, pressing her on the left side, the side of the heart, and this phenomenon, which took place at night, deeply troubled her. When she was asked to give her interpretation of this strange happening, she replied that the devil wished to mimic the mystical union which she had already been granted.

On the eve of the Feast of the Immaculate Conception the devil visited her as she lay on her bed. "It was," she told us, "like a great dragon swooping down upon me; I did not see him, but I felt him perfectly well"; and "if the devil relentlessly pursues me," she continued, "it is because I have practiced much asceticism, and he wants to make me stumble in the ways of the Lord, for it is written in Ecclesiastes: 'My son, if you will understake to serve the Lord, prepare your soul for trial.'"

I was able to follow this patient's progress for five years and her state never perceptibly improved. Here again, we find in her the feeling of seizure or "exterior action," as Henri Claude put it, increased by tactile and aural coenaesthesic hallucinations, and an unwavering belief in two opposed forces, each attempting to dominate the other: God and the devil.

If we have spent some time on cases of "lucid possession" or demonopathic delirium, it is because, for the psychologist, they contain many instructive features and, moreover, provide the clearest distinguishing marks of false, as against authentic, demoniacal possession.

Do we not find in these patients all the signs of an invasion by a personality alien to their ego—a personality which reveals itself by compulsions, forced actions, inhibitions, by sounds heard perfectly clearly, distinctly, and frequently, by numerous sensory and psychic hallucinations, and by ineffable sensations of an influence present within or around them? The essence of this influence remains a mystery until the day when the patient becomes convinced, during one of these attacks of delirium, that it is indeed an evil spirit who directs his actions, induces his feelings and ideas, in fact who possesses him and holds him at his mercy.

Now this delirium, which is based on the division of the personality, is found in persons who do not pretend to demonopathic possession, but who suffer from the more common kinds of persecution mania so often met with in psychiatric hospitals.

In both categories of sufferer, the most important feature is the feeling of a foreign influence which has entered their personality and dominates it—an influence evil in that it expresses the opposite of the image they have of themselves. They react against this influence by all possible means, including those of the subconscious; and it is precisely by these disguised, roundabout ways that many of our patients unwittingly create a second favorable personality which is opposed to the evil influence and fights against it, keeping the poor patients in a state of painful struggle between an influence which they consider pernicious and an influence easily attributed to the divine or to some other occult power. This rending asunder of the consciousness sometimes leads to the most disastrous consequences, even to self-destruction.

Finally, we must observe that if psychoanalysis frequently brings to light some sexual disorder in patients suffering from demonopathy, it is because in their eyes the greatest sin lies in carnal failings or perversions, the most serious of which is homosexuality.

But this obsession with sin, which rarely leaves the person it has once gripped, also appears as a force invested with a living personality. This is due to a tendency inborn in man, which Napoleon was thinking of when he said: "The greatest power bestowed on man is that of giving to things a soul which they do not possess." The patients we have been considering, following the natural trend of their minds, proceed to identify the devil with the sin from which they feel the most aversion and which they most deeply dread.

So, from the very beginning of the psychopathy, we may find a tendency to a pathological interpretation of things, which can but develop and increase, giving a very significant color to the mental disorder. In some demonopathic subjects I have observed, the interpretative capacity was so active that every single perception became a source of very diverse interpretations or symbolizations, often most unexpected and extravagant. To recall only one example, our retired official, thinking himself to be directly persecuted by the devil, transformed every object of the external world into either a symbol of joy, of resistance to the evil spirit, or on the contrary, into a diabolical manifestation. All his psychological activity, which was great, was thus almost wholly used up in the creation of a symbolic world whose elements he tried to unite into some kind of general harmony, in order to obtain at least temporary spiritual rest.

As we pointed out before, it is as yet impossible to state precisely what are the deepest causes underlying this type of psychosis of influence, or demonopathic persecution. No doubt the patient's original constitution plays a large part, but this is not the whole solution; and if we refuse to admit the thesis of a mental automatism conditioned by some capricious stimulation of the cerebral cortex, then the predictable evolution of the causal process entitles us to believe that a functional psychophysiological disorder is at the source of this psychopathy, and that by countering it we shall, perhaps, be able to deliver our patients from their indescribable sufferings.

What are we to conclude from this account? Surely this: that there exist genuine psychopathic states whose chief symptom is the notion that the moral or physical personality, or perhaps the entire personality, is possessed by the devil. These states may be divided into two quite distinct types: the first is marked by the brutal, catastrophic occurrence of possession, which takes place during trances or severe crises, when the consciousness is in a state of more or less complete dissolution; the second is more complex, and consists of a strictly predetermined psychosis, whose development can be foreseen, and of which a very grave prognosis can be made.

Dream Demons

Jolande Jacobi

In his work *Die Schlaf— und Traumzustände der menschlichen Seele* [The Human Soul in Sleep and in Dream] (1878) Heinrich Spitta, philosopher and psychologist of Tübingen, describes the phenomenon of nightmare as follows: "The apparition of a *Kobold* or a monster, squatting on the chest of the sleeper, moving nearer and nearer to his throat and threatening to strangle him. . . . It is so clear and so evident that it causes great anguish. . . . The sleeper tries in vain to defend himself against this horrible apparition; he tries to cry out, but his voice is strangled in his throat, his limbs seem paralyzed, sweat pours from him, his hands are like ice. Suddenly, he comes to with a cry, to fall back again on his bed, exhausted, but with the relieved feeling that he has just escaped from imminent danger of death." According to Spitta, a moment of functional inhibition, especially in the case of asthmatics, or great disturbances of one's routine, are probably the causes of nightmare.

Dyspnea (an anguished paralysis, oppression, and suffocation), chamade (or wild beating of the heart), with, at times, complete aphonia, rigidity of the limbs, or on the contrary, spasmodic tremblings—all associated with the vision of a monster of hairy, animal appearance, pressing on the chest, have everywhere and always been the characteristics of nightmare.

Those who have studied the matter have inclined to one of two explanations, according to their own general outlook: either the manifestations are due to physical troubles (obstructed respiration or circulation of the blood, caused by the position of the sleeper, the weight of the bedclothes, digestive troubles, feverish delirium, etc.); or they are due to "spirits." Theories characterized as "scientific" hold to the first explanation in attempting to throw light on this widespread phenomenon, which has always been the source of much suffering, as well as of many myths and legends. The first, the purely physical, explanation was also accepted by some of the medical men of antiquity, who based themselves on the conscientious researches undertaken by Soranus of Ephesus at the beginning of the second century A.D. into the nature, origin, and treatment of nightmare. Their successors in modern times have adopted a similar attitude, believing that everything psychic can be reduced to manifestations of purely physical phenomena. The popular notion, however, which found expression in numerous treatises, especially in the sixteenth and seventeenth centuries, derives from the opposite attitude—from belief in "phantoms."

The rigorously medicophysiological theories give little room to the imagination; belief in spirits, on the contrary, nourishes it. It is therefore through belief in spirits that a countless series of myths and legends, of savage and fantastic shadows, has been able to gain general credence. These spirits have various names: *Ephialtes* with the Greeks; *incubi* and *succubi* in the Middle Ages; *Alp, Mahr, Würger,* that is, "strangler," *Gespenst,* or "specter," *Nachtkobold,* or "night gnome," *Auflieger,* or "crusher," *Quälgeist,* or "tormenting spirit," with the Germans; *Kikimara* with the Russians; *Mara* in Nordic idioms, from which is derived the French *cauchemar* (from *caucher,* "to oppress, trample down"

—Latin *calcare*, and *mar*, "demon"); *Schrätelli, chauchevieille*, etc., in Switzerland. This wide choice of names implies many attributes and many legends. The nightmares are presented, now in animal shape, now like humans; sometimes beautiful, sometimes ugly, sometimes masculine, sometimes feminine, and so on. They have been made almost Olympian, for they have been regarded as the avatars of the gods, or again, with very different attributes, as demons. They have been identified with Pan, for example, from whose name we get *panic*; with the fauns, sylvans and satyrs of antiquity. In the Middle Ages, the devil had as courtiers demons and specters, mandrakes, incubi, succubi, sorcerers and phantoms of every kind; sometimes simply obscene, sometimes merely bestial. Skeptics tried to explain away these last, especially when they were conceived as rough and hairy, by saying that they were due to the sleeper's being covered with skins of goats or of sheep, which impeded his breathing. The same reason is given for the belief in "sylvan deities" who attack men. In Montenegro (according to B. Stern, *Medizin, Aberglaube und Geschlechtsleben in der Türkei* [Medicine, Superstition, and Sexual Life in Turkey], 1903), there was a female spirit, winged with flame, called Vjeschitza, who crouched on the chest of the sleeper and either suffocated him or drove him mad with obscene embraces.

The intimate connection between the visions of dream and the hallucinations of the insane gave rise to the old popular belief that the demons of nightmare are also the cause of madness. This was the opinion of the doctors of antiquity, who saw in chronic nightmare the origin of madness, epilepsy, and even apoplexy. The vampire, that night phantom who sucked the blood of the sleeper, was also looked on as one of the nightmare family. Animals, even, and especially horses, were supposed to be subject to the torment of demons, who installed themselves on their rumps. There was also the phenomenon of collective nighmares. Some old accounts worthy of credence—among others, that of M. H. Strahl (1800–60): *Der*

Alp, sein Wesen und seine Heilung [The Nightmare, Its Nature and Cure] (1833)—tell of a whole regiment, of entire villages, of human groups of all categories, having had the same nightmare at the same time. These phenomena arise from the same psychic conditions as those at the root of medieval psychic epidemics, mass flagellation, popular belief in possession and sorcery, and so on.

According to their influence on man and to the forms they assumed, nightmare spirits were divided into good and bad, into provokers of terror and bestowers of erotic delights (those of the *Alpminne,* or "goblin love"). Whatever their character, there was nothing to choose between them as regards their purely diabolical properties, and therefore they were always looked on as dangerous. The incubus, who came at night to tempt women, and the succubus, that nocturnal seducer of men—both being objects of horror to the Middle Ages, but often both feared and desired—had sexual relations with the sleepers. Not popular credulity only, but also the theologians, attributed quite a considerable role to them. No one at that time would have dared to doubt their existence, for did not even St. Augustine believe in them (*De Civitate Dei 15.23*)? Many doctors, especially during the sixteenth and seventeenth centuries, studied them zealously, and often had recourse to very strange speculations to "explain" them. Paracelsus, for instance, who was both a doctor and a brilliant thinker, believed that he had discovered three "bodies" in every individual: the material body, earthly and visible; the "astral" body, etheric, invisible; and the spiritual body, the fire of the Holy Spirit in us. He considered that nocturnal demons were the product of our "imagination," that is, of our "astral" nature. In his *Traité des Maladies invisibles* (ed. Sudhoff, 9, 302), he says: "This imagination comes from our astral body, in virtue of a kind of heroic love; it is an action which is not accomplished in carnal copulation. Isolated and alone, this love is at once the father and the mother of the pneumatic sperm. From these psychic sperms are born the incubi who oppress women, and the succubi who attach themselves to men.'' The great Paracelsus understood clearly, therefore, that succubi and incubi were imaginary visions, or phantoms, and not real persons. His definition corresponds to the findings of modern psychoanalysis, which regards them as products of sexual *phantasia*. Stimulated by credulity, the imagination invented complete *romances* on the misdeeds of these spirits—romances which to this day have been the material for innumerable works of art and poetry. We may mention, among others, the magnificent series of Goya, *Caprices*, and the impressive Succubus in the *Contes Drolatiques* of Balzac.

In the Middle Ages, especially, belief in these demons caused veritable epidemics even in convents. Nightmares, it was believed, tormented women more than men, and widows and virgins more than any others. Many men and women have been burned alive for having had dealings with evil spirits. Every witch was thought to have had sexual relations with an incubus; many innocent women perished at the stake, because one nightmare sufficed as proof of obscene commerce with a diabolical ''rider of women.'' These nightmare demons were supposed to enter through keyholes, through cracks in the wainscoting, or chinks in the window frames, and this proved their kinship with witches and other diabolical creatures. It was thought that they could not beget or conceive, but if by any chance they did give birth to a child, that child was fated to become a witch, a monster, or some other extraordinary creature. The enchanter Merlin, for example, in the Arthurian cycle, was regarded as having had such parentage. In Germany, if a man bore a strong resemblance to an animal, it was attributed to the influence of the demons of nightmare, who themselves were of animal nature; physical malformation, birthmarks, clubbed feet, etc., served as criteria in these matters. To explain their gross, barbarous, and bestial nature, a legend grew up that the Huns had been born of concubinage between women and devils. The people of antiquity had always regarded creatures of the ''fairy'' family as particularly dangerous, because of their seductive, wholly magical power. Some of them were thought to fascinate men by their songs, to render them powerless, and then to tear them apart.

Psychoanalysis has put forward a new "explanation" of dreams, substituting a "psychological" formula for the medieval conception of the "nightmare demon." It hopes thus to establish a therapeutic method which will render this demon harmless and, in some sort, exorcise it. Ernest Jones, one of the foremost of the Freudian school of London, devoted an interesting volume to a specialist treatment of this problem: *Nightmare, Witches, and Devils.* He refutes both the exclusively physiological theories and the folklore theories based on popular belief in "spirits."

In all these cases, he concludes, a phenomenon is involved, based on a violent psychical complex, whose "nucleus is formed by a psychosexual repression, which reacts to peripheral excitations." So far, the problem is clear. But Jones continues: "The latent content of nightmare consists in the representation of the normal sex act, and that in a characteristically feminine manner: oppression of the chest, complete giving of self, expressed by the sensation of paralysis, the eventual genital secretion, etc. The other symptoms—for example, violent beating of the heart, a sensation of suffocation, and so on—are merely exaggerations of the sensations normally experienced during the sex act in the waking state." He holds that "violently repressed desires" can be satisfied in this way; for example, in extreme repression of incestuous desires, sentiments of fear prevail over the sensation of lust. The nightmare, Jones continues, invariably reflects the normal process of coition, and it is distinguished from other forms of bad dream only by its latent content, which is "special and definitely fixed." Thus, the two extremes—attraction and repulsion—can be referred to two forces—desire and inhibition—struggling with each other. Without concerning itself with the precise and detailed content of these nightmares, this interpretation classes the "spirits" in them among those known to the Middle Ages as incubi and succubi, which were always clearly distinguished from other dream devils. The Church, indeed, always defined the incubus as a devil of human appearance, while phantoms of animal appearance belonged to another category of "spirits."

The war with these spirits varied according to the opinion held of them. It is not surprising that a great diversity of means, born of superstition, were in constant use, together with thousands of "serious" medical prescriptions. One of the fundamental ideas of magic is at all times the belief in the influence of incantations on the gods. Hence, the man who believed that the will of the gods was revealed in his premonitory dreams did his utmost to be visited only by favorable dreams. Prevention is better than cure; it is important, therefore, to recognize and promptly follow the warnings of the gods, making them our friends, that they may shelter us from the consequences of bad dreams. It is best to dispel these dreams before they have time to visit us, by means of traditional counterspells, rites, and prescriptions too numerous to list. With certain peoples, for example the Greeks, religious ceremonies were used to prevent dreams of evil augury from being realized; they were liturgically notified, in all sincerity, to the sun god. Exorcised by this "disoccultation," the nocturnal demons had no choice but to vanish. Another propitiatory method was that of sacrifice. It was believed that certain ascetic exercises had power to "rectify" a bad dream. The interminable repetition of a magical formula had the power to avert evil and attract good fortune. Certain Hindus thought to live a hundred years by constantly repeating *Om*—"victory over death"—even if the chanter had already seen himself dead in dream (*La clef des songes de Jaggadeva* [The Key to the Dreams of Jaga Deva], p. 30). Talismans and amulets, always highly valued, were specially chosen according to circumstances, because they were considered very powerful against demoniacal dreams.

The Muhammadans used pieces of paper covered with verses from the Koran and different astrological and magical symbols, which were sewed in the lining of the clothes or the bags worn at night on the breast or around the neck, as a precaution against nightmares. These practices were considered to have excellent results. Other magical formulas, called pentacles, prevented nightmares and induced beneficent dreams. Before one retired to sleep, one rolled them into a little ball and swallowed them with some water.

Superstition has never died; it survives everything and raises its hydra head in the most unexpected places, every time an effort is made to end it. Needless to say, the medicoscientific mind has always rejected its practices, and has attempted, on its own account, to control the birth and growth of dreams by prescribing certain food and drink or, more conformably to modern ideas, by prescribing certain chemical preparations. The doctors of antiquity used bleeding, hellebore, the *Paeonia* (of the family Ranunculaceae) and recommended a suitable diet. The Pythagoreans advised against the eating of beans, which caused flatulence, which in turn caused nightmares. It was fatal to dream as a result of eating beans, for the flatulence due to them was caused by the spirits of the dead, who dwelt in these vegetables and avenged themselves on the sleeper. In his *Treatise on the Incubus or Nightmare* (1816), Dr. A. Waller holds, on the contrary, that nightmares are caused by hyperacidity of the stomach and can be prevented by taking potassium carbonate.

The Middle Ages produced innumerable panaceas, strange and said to be infallible, the fruit of popular experience, individual observation, astrological notions, theories on the "signatures" of plants, etc. In our day, too, wherever superstition thrives, one finds at every step countercharms, with their amulets, talismans, and pentacles, their secret practices and prescriptions.

There were some, notably the psychologists of the last century, who thought nightmare could be explained by purely physiological causes, and that it could be brought on deliberately for experimental purposes, and thus forced out of its hiding place and destroyed. An attempt was therefore made to provoke nightmares, by making the subject lie in a certain position or submit to pressure on a certain part of the body, etc. But these experiments were never successful in provoking a given oneiric result, corresponding to each experiment and repeatable at will. According to psychoanalytical teaching —especially that of Jones, who sees in the different forms of modern psychoneurosis and their various symptoms the "descendants" of the sorcerers, lycanthropes, etc. of other times—one cannot be delivered from nightmare and its horrors unless its cause, discovered by psychoanalysis to be the repression of sexual impulses, is seen in the full light of consciousness.

In spite of its very modern character, the Freudian conception of nightmare is nevertheless to some extent akin to the old concept, which attributed to Pan-Ephialtes the responsibility for *pavor nocturnus* (nocturnal terror), but also the power to liberate from it; the feeling of liberation which succeeds the anguish can be considered, indeed, as equivalent to the realization of a desire. In the second century of our era, Pausonias relates, a sanctuary was erected at Tresena in Argolida to the savior Pan, because he had revealed in a dream to a municipal aedile the effective means of combating a terrible epidemic (Pausonias, 2. 32.6).

Popular belief, also, has always seen in the nightmare devil not only a corrupting action but also a beneficent power, which could reveal certain secrets, as for example the place of some treasure or the formula of a marvelous remedy. Thus the demons of nightmare have gone the way of all the ideas which have issued from the age-old depths of the human soul, and which are at once beneficent and enlightening, maleficent and infernal. One the other hand, while psychoanalysis sees in the nightmare the manifestation and projection of the sexual trend of the unconscious, complex psychology, created by C.G.

Jung, has made of the matrix ideas, or "archetypes" of the collective unconscious, the symbolic messengers of the Kingdom of Dreams, which is the image used to express those instinctive, archaic, and primitive forces of the soul by means of which man is confronted with his "shadow," and profoundly impressed by it. It is in this sense that we can truly say that "the *first nightmare* was the father of all mythology"; without it and its many forms, belief in "spirits" would never have developed to the extent to which it did. Even Kant, for whom scientific explanations certainly took precedence over belief in "spirits," was led to attribute quite a beneficent quality to these spirits, in spite of their terrifying nature: "Without the terrifying apparition of a phantom which crushes us, without the consecutive use of all our muscles in changing our position, the circulation of the blood might be impeded, and death might be the result. It is for this very reason that nature seems to have arranged things in such a way that the majority of dreams bring discomfort with them. For such presentations excite the forces of the soul much more than when everything during sleep is agreeable to us" (*Anthropology*, 1799). In this, Kant is in line with the most modern psychological ideas on the problem of dreams.

Thus it is that the solutions and therapeutics of each age conform to the spirit of that age. It remains to be seen if we today, in spite of all our efforts, have succeeded in discovering all the secrets of this mysterious form of dream.

The Trial of Anne de Chantraine
(1620–25)

The practice of witchcraft and the hatred of its practitioners are to be found in every age and every part of the world. But in sixteenth-century Europe witch-hunting reached a sustained level of ferocity without parallel. We have the bull Summis desiserantes *of Innocent VIII followed by the* Malleus maleficarum *(Hammer of Witches), written by two Dominicans. Calvin was a witch burner. It was under pressure from John Knox that Scotland passed its first law making death the penalty for witchcraft. James IV of Scotland, who was to be James I of England, presided personally at burnings. Most of Europe was involved in the mania; Ireland seems to have been free of it.*

Was it mania? The persecutors were convinced that Satan was in it. Some of the witches were, too. But as the learned English Jesuit Father Herbert Thurston said, "The vast majority of the lives sacrificed were those of innocent victims hunted down in a blind panic of hatred and terror."

The reader may draw his own conclusions from the story of Anne de Chantraine and the Witches of Salem.

At the beginning of March 1620, the *sergent* of the court

of Warêt-la-Chaussée arrested a girl of seventeen, Anne de Chantraine, who had recently come to live in the village with her father and was reputed to be a witch. She was imprisoned and soon brought before the mayor, Thomas Douclet, and the aldermen of the district. She made no bones about relating her deplorable life, and made the most brazen avowals.

The daughter of a traveling merchant of Liege, she scarcely remembered her mother, who had died when Anne was only two years old. Her father placed her in the orphanage of the Soeurs Noires at Liège. The child remained there ten years, and received an education rare for her time and certainly above her station: reading, writing, catechism, needlework. At twelve years old she was placed by the good sisters with a widow of the city, Christiane de la Chéraille, a secondhand clothier by trade. Anne mended old clothes there the whole day long.

One evening she saw her mistress rub grease on her body as far as her girdle and disappear up the chimney. Before leaving, Christiane de la Chéraille recommended her to do the same, which she forthwith did. Passing up the chimney in a gust of strong wind, she found herself in the company of her patron in a huge hall, filled with many people, in which there was a large table covered with white bread, cakes, roast meats, and sausages. There was much joyful feasting and banqueting.

Anne was timidly approaching the table when a young man, "with a look as of fire," accosted her politely and asked if he could "have to do with her." Dismayed by this audacity, Anne was much troubled, and she uttered an ejaculatory prayer, accompanying it with the sign of the cross. Immediately table and food, banqueting room, and revelers all disappeared. She found herself alone in the dark, imprisoned among the empty casks of her patron's cellar, from which she was delivered by that same lady the following morning.

This was Anne de Chantraine's first contact with the infernal powers. The contacts which followed were not so furtive, and the awakening of fleshly desire was first occasioned in her through Christiane de la Chéraille. She then gave herself to the Sabbath with all the violence of her youth. She was present three times a week—on Wednesday, Friday, and Saturday—and took part in all the rites: dances dos-a-dos, copulation with a demon, adoration of the devil in the form of a goat, etc. She received the magic powder and the power of witchcraft.

Laurent de Chamont, brother-in-law and lover of her mistress, king of the sorcerers in that region, very quickly noticed Anne. He was chief of a group who knew how to take a very practical advantage of their Satanic initiation; they entered houses by magic and stole money, vessels, clothes, and food. It was Laurent de Chamont who cut hairs from the sexual organs of his own daughter, Anne, and of the children of Christiane de la Chéraille and, placing them on the palm of his hand, blew them into keyholes; for it was thus, by the help of the devil, that doors of houses and locks of chests were opened.

But the band of nightbirds was soon overtaken. Laurent de Chamont and Christiane de la Chéraille were burned, and their accomplices were dispersed. Six weeks later Anne was also arrested and, after being tried, was sentenced to banishment. Leaving the principality of Liège, she came to her father, who had settled at Warêt, but not daring to remain with him, she hired herself as a milkmaid to a farmer of Erpent, four leagues off—a certain Laurent Streignart, a shady character, who was himself suspected of heresy.

Such were the avowals of Anne de Chantraine, and they sufficed to provoke prosecution. Her trial was immediately put in hand. On March 17 the mayor of Warêt demanded from the Provincial Council a *procureur* for the accused, and the advocate Martin of Namur was named. But because of contemporary troubles, the number of cases under consideration, or the slowness of the judicial machinery, the matter remained for six months in suspense. Anne spent the whole spring of 1620 in the prison of Warêt.

On September 13 the accused was informally examined. That same day the tribunal decided to send one of its members to Liège to obtain more complete information. This step had grievous results for the accused. Together with the report of the interrogation of Laurent de Chamont and of Christiane de la Chéraille, the magistrate returned with the evidence of Gaspard José, who was for a few weeks her employer after the arrest of Christiane, and that of Jean Agnus, her accomplice in flights about the city. All these taxed her with evildoing, with witchcraft and witchflights.

Recalled on October 9, Anne admitted to all the horrors of the accusation, and in particular to having given herself to an unknown man dressed in black, with cloven feet, who appeared to her while she was blaspheming because the heat of the day had dispersed her herd. As a result, she avowed, the cows reassembled of their own accord.

On the fourteenth of the same month two women of the village, and one from Erpent, came forward as witnesses against her. The first said she knew the accused had the reputation of being a witch, and one day when she felt ill, she was convinced she had been bewitched by Anne. Accordingly she complained to the accused, and Anne prepared some pancakes for her. When she had eaten the first, she began to vomit and immediately felt better. The second witness was a friend of the accused and had received certain confidences from her which she made known to the tribunal—commonplaces about the Sabbath and the magic powders. She could give only one definite fact: one of her children had been poisoned and cured by Anne on the same day. The third witness declared on oath that the prisoner had cured two bewitched children by taking away a spell, but that she had also procured the death of a young girl "who lived two leagues south of Warêt."

The accusations having been established, the clerk of the court of Warêt gave her in charge at Namur, where, a few weeks later, the Provincial Council gave an authorization for torture "in order to learn more of the misdemeanors of the accused and of her accomplices."

On December 5 the hangman of Namur, Léonard Balzat, proceeded to torture. It was a short and useless session, because, except for some insignificant details, nothing of importance nor any name of an accomplice was revealed. The following day, this sentence was drawn up by the mayoralty: "In view of the confessions of Anne de Chantraine: to having gone over to the devil and given herself up to him, to having had fleshly intercourse with him several times, to having attended thrice a week dances and conventicles of sorcerers and witches, the court demands that she be condemned to the ordinary punishments of witches, or at least that she be flogged and banished for all time, or suffer any other corporal punishment which the Court may see fit to inflict."

Another questioning took place on February 15, 1621, in the course of which Anne revealed to the judges how Christiane de la Chéraille had taught her to cure the bewitched: "When a poisoned person was brought to her to be cured, she said: 'Devil, do you wish me to remove the poison from this person in whom you have placed it?'—and having said this, she seized him under the arms, turned him one way and then the other, saying the same words and touching the hand of the poisoned person, declaring that he was cured and ending with further curious ritual." She admitted to having received four sous for the cure of a girl.

On April 15 Léonard Balzat returned to Warêt. It was decided that the accused should be submitted to the torture of cold and hot water, and two days later the torture was repeated. This time the torturer poured water which was almost boiling through a funnel placed in her throat, already in a terrible condition. In spite of these two sessions, the judges failed to gain their ends, for Anne de Chantraine did not reveal her accomplices.

Two months passed. On June 14 Léonard Balzat returned

and submitted her to the fearful torture reserved for great criminals and sorcerers. She persisted in her declarations, but nothing more could be found out.

Two days later five witnesses came from Liège to testify on her morals. They were Conrad de Phencenal, from whom she had stolen many tin plates; Anne de Chevron, who had lost linen and jewels; Léonard de Vaulx and his daughter, who brought a theft of 300 florins against her. A young merchant tailor, Wautier Betoren, declared he had been her victim to the extent of a piece of linen, but that a friend of Anne, a certain Perpienne, had given him twenty florins by way of indemnity.

Since she now was established as a thief, avowed under torture as a sorceress, her sentence from the Provincial Council can scarcely astonish us. On July 16 Guillaume Bodart, the deputy commissioner, brought to the *mairie* sentence of death against her, "for the confessed crime of witchcraft, and for having assisted at several larcenies by night, by means of the same witchcraft, in the houses of citizens in the city of Liège." On July 23 the sentence was made known to Anne, and she, overwhelmed with despair, denied all her avowals. In this way she gained time, for only confessions freely admitted counted in law.

The embarrassment occasioned to the judges did not last long. As soon as they were informed, the delegates of the Provincial Council condemned Anne de Chantraine to death anew, on July 26, and this condemnation was immediately read to the girl. She was then asked if all the confessions she had made were true, and she said that they were. The clerk of the court and the jailer then retired, and a religious came to confess her.

Why was the sentence not executed? No document justified such shirking of duty. Had the denials *in extremis* of the condemned moved the magistrates of Warêt? Were motives of law, reasons of *force majeure* added to the documents we now possess? The whole matter is wrapped in mystery. It remains true that the condemned lived on for almost a year in the scabious village prison. It would seem that she was forgotten.

However, during the winter of 1621–22 the mayor made another visit to Namur. On December 9 he received an answer that "in view of the inquiries held by a deputed commission since the sentence pronounced in the court of Warêt on July 21, the aldermen should see to it that the said sentence be carried into execution according to due form and tenor." On the following day this new sentence was read to Anne de Chantraine. She said to her confessor, Père Monceau, who accompanied the clerk of the court, that she was content to die for her sins, but that she persisted in her denials.

Again the judges temporized, and months went by without a solution. In the summer of 1622 the Council decided to reexamine the facts avowed by the accused. Two new councilors were appointed, and in order to facilitate the inquiry, the accused was taken to Namur, where she was imprisoned in the Tour de Bordial, on the bank of the Sambre, at the foot of the citadel.

Proceedings began again. Did torture again play its part, or had the two years of hopeless imprisonment so weakened the accused that she confessed freely; or did the judges simply ignore her denials? We do not know, for this part of the trial is surrounded with mystery. It would seem that the judges were particularly interested in the sanity of the accused. At the beginning of September they asked the jailer if he had remarked anything abnormal about Anne. On September 12 he replied that "in daily conversations, the turnkey, his wife, and others have not noticed that she is in any way troubled in mind or in judgment."

On the same day the jailer, armed with scissors and razor, visited her, cut her hair and shaved every part of her body. He took away her clothes, and left only a rough chemise of jute in their place.

But the councilors began to have scruples. They were not

content with the jailer's report, and they recalled him. When questioned again on the mental state of the accused, he was less sure in his answers than he had been. He said that "the prisoner was stupid, and did not understand what she said, though sometimes she seemed quite right in her mind."

On September 27 the accused was exorcised. Doubts were still felt of her sanity. The judges sent for the jailer's wife and again asked her if "in dealings and daily conversations with the said prisoner, she had not remarked anything abnormal in her mind and judgment." The woman answered that she had not.

On October 17 the definitive sentence was brought in: death by fire with preliminary strangulation. From that day Anne was kept at Warêt-la-Chaussée, the place fixed for the execution.

During the following night Léonard Balzat and his assistant prepared the pyre, a huge heap of a hundred fagots bought in the village itself. In the center, sheaves of straw were placed, and a hollow was made in the straw large enough to contain a stool.

At dawn Anne was awakened by the jailer, the clerk of the court, and a friar minor, who announced the fatal news to her. She was led out. The executioner was waiting with the cart, and the condemned girl climbed into it. When they reached the end of the village where the pyre was prepared, Anne collected all the strength that remained to her. In a loud voice, she acknowledged her sins, denied that she was a witch, and admitted to no accomplice. Léonard Balzat helped her to climb the pyre, seated her on the stool among the straw and abruptly strangled her. His assistant kindled the straw and the fagots. Acrid smoke quickly enveloped her, and the crackling of the flames was like a fearful whisper through the entire village. The pyre burned for two days. At dawn on the third day the ashes were dispersed to the four winds.

The memory of a young, beautiful, and celebrated witch was for many years to haunt the minds of the villagers. Her story was told and retold by the light of a winter's fire. No one, however, knew her name, and no folklorist recounted her trial. Only F. Chavée, in his "Notice sur le village de Leuze" (*Annales de la Société archéolique*, 21 [1895], 481), speaks of "a field situated between Leuze and Warêt-la-Chaussée, made famous by a Liège witch and poisoner whom the justices of the high court of Warêt condemned to death and executed in the year 1623 [*sic*]."

The Devil and Cotton Mather

Marion L. Starkey

1.

What had actually been accomplished on the spiritual plane by the wholesale jail delivery of 1693 was a point which at the time could only be described as moot. In spite of the relief which many communities felt at the lifting of the nightmare, the eagerness with which husbands welcomed back their witches, repenting that they had ever distrusted them, people further removed from the scene could look on the whole process as a monstrous miscarriage of justice, boding no good to the future of Massachusetts. These agreed with Stoughton, "We were in a way to have cleared the land of the witches. . . . Who it is that obstructs the course of justice I know not."

It was true that some of the most obvious symptoms of witchcraft were disappearing. Little was heard from the afflicted girls once the jail delivery got under way. Though logically the return of so many witches to civilian life should have afflicted them even unto death, none of the girls did die; they remained well enough. A few, notably Mary Walcott and Elizabeth Booth, presently settled down and got married.

Some of the others, still manless, and apparently at a loss how to put in their time in these duller, flatter days, turned, it was rumoured, to coarser pleasures; certain of them, never explicitly named in history, went unmistakably bad.

In Salem Village where this development could be watched at close range, there was said to be a general revulsion against them. It was not good to watch a wench at her harlotries and remember that on that harlot's word the good and chaste had been hanged. But at a further remove other interpretations were possible. The girls were being slandered, and the judges with them; would the likes of William Stoughton have been taken in by harlots? Also it was by no means certain that the girls had come out of their fits; it was more probable that these were being callously ignored when they fell into them. Look what had happened in the fall of 1692 when the girls had tried in vain to warn Ipswich of a malefactor. God was punishing an unworthy, half-hearted people by so hardening their hearts that they were incapable of receiving further revelation.

The plain truth was for those who had eyes to see that the devil was by no means bound up, had not lost his battle against New England, but was well on his way to bringing the entire community under his power. Of this there were unmistakable signs.

2.

What was the devil? To the Puritan the question was no less important than the question, what is God. A surprising variety of answers were possible. Some in Massachusetts were still reading an English best-seller two decades old, John Milton's *Paradise Lost,* in which the poet in defeat and blindness had all unconsciously created Satan in his own image, doomed, but not without his grandeur. Such a being could be abhorred but not despised; one might pity, even respect the enemy of mankind. In his contest with

Omnipotence he showed a perverse nobility of spirit; there
was something almost Promethean in the tragic Satan who
from hell defied the lightning of heaven and reached out to
make mankind his own.

Yet how far was such a concept understood in provincial
Massachusetts whose own tastes were represented not by the
organ music of Milton's blank verse but by the jigging and
jingling of Wigglesworth's *Day of Doom*? Certainly Cotton
Mather, who had his own copy of *Paradise Lost*, did not
associate Satan with the grandeur of lost but not ignoble
causes. His Satan had more the spirit of the poltergeist, or of
the comic devil of the early miracle plays. The fellow was
ubiquitous, and as such damnably dangerous and eternally a
nuisance, but as little dignified as the worm that eats up the
garden.

Still a third concept was possible, the strange Adversary
who presented himself before God in the time of Job and was
received with courteous attention. What manner of devil was
this who did not stoop to laying petty ambush for his enemy,
but came openly into God's presence to challenge him; and
what meaning could be read into God's acceptance of a
challenge from such a source? Could it be that such was the
omnipotence of God that the very devil worked for him to
examine the hearts of men and test the limits of their faith?
Was it even possible that God made use of the devil to bring a
new thing on earth, that out of ill good would come?

Yet what good would come out of what the devil had
done in Massachusetts? The phase of the colony's martyrdom
had been not single but multiple. Not the witchcraft only but
the new charter had delivered the faithful into the devil's hand.
Now that people outside the faith could vote and shape the
course of government, the power of theocracy had been for
ever broken. No longer would it be possible to get rid of
perversely creative minds—the Ann Hutchinsons and Roger
Williamses—by exile or death. Demoniac energies had been
loosed now, and God alone could foresee the outcome. Was it

possible that what the devil had promised William Barker of Andover would come to pass under God's providence, that there would be no more sin or shame or judgment, "that all men should be equal and live bravely"?

Well, it was God's will. God had delivered them if not to the devil, at least to an adversary. God save the Commonwealth of Massachusetts.

3.

If symptoms of diabolism had faded at last in Salem Village—so odd a site for God to choose as the battleground between hell and heaven—there was deviltry aplenty in Boston. Even while the judges were dismissing the witches, Cotton Mather's own wife, she who had once had to smother a laugh at the sight of diabolic manifestation as observed in the person of little Martha Goodwin, had been affrighted on her porch by a diabolic vision and had in consequence given birth to a malformed, short-lived child.

And as if that were not enough, Mather himself, because of his charitable interest in certain afflicted maids of Boston, was about to be given to drink of the vinegar of mockery by what he called "the witlings of the coffee-houses." The devil had lately discovered to Boston a new brew which sharpened the wit and incited it to scepticism. Here in the waning days of the witchcraft were wont to sit several of the devil's own who made it their business to keep a derisive eye on the current activities of Cotton Mather and to publish them to the town.

Until lately there had been little occasion to connect the younger Mather with the witchcraft. He who had been so active in the Glover affair, and whose record of the case had helped prepare Massachusetts for the new outbreak, had nevertheless remained surprisingly aloof from the latter. Not that the aloofness had been by intention; it was simply a matter of living far from Salem and having much to detain him in Boston.

Early in the day he had written the Salem authorities offering to receive any six girls into his home for observation and treatment; had the magistrates responded it is probable that they would have exchanged a major calamity for yet another quaint, archaic monograph. The segregation of the girls would have served to localize the psychic infection, and the girls themselves, exposed to the wayward streak of poetry in Mather's composition, would almost certainly have found their fantasies deflected to the more normal preoccupations of adolescence. They would, in short, like a large proportion of the female members of his congregation at any given time, have fallen in love with him. Infatuation is not any guarantee against hysteria; quite the contrary. But in this case such a development might have diverted the antics of the girls to less malignant forms. Young Ann Putnam might, like Martha Goodwin, have ridden an airy horse up and down the stairs and into the pastor's study, to find her catharsis there rather than before the gallows.

It had not been given Mather thus to experiment; he had watched the case from afar and had only thrice taken positive action. One of these occasions had been his drafting of the advice of the ministers to the judges, cautioning them against too great reliance on spectral evidence, though praising their zeal. Even before then Mather had unofficially written in the same vein to Judge John Richards, not only warning him against spectral evidence but against uncritical acceptance of such confessions as might come from a "delirious brain or a discontented heart." He specifically denounced torture as a means of getting confessions.

His only dramatic intervention in the witchcraft had been the speech he had made to the crowd at the hanging of Burroughs. This speech was the only real complaint that his enemies could make against him. There were some who thought that Mather had shown small charity to a fellow minister in his hour of need. Yet not much could be fairly made of the incident. Had not Mather spoken another must, for the crowd before the gallows was fast deteriorating into a mob. Mather who had seen mobs in Boston in 1689 had acted instinctively and without premeditation to do what was necessary to quiet this one. Control of the crowd and not slander of Burroughs had been his purpose.

In any case the incident was now well in the past. It would not have been held a serious count against Mather, nor could his name have been fairly connected with the witchcraft but for what happened after it was all over.

4.

On 22 September 1692, a kind of council of war had been called at Samuel Sewall's house in Boston. Present were Samuel's brother Stephen of Salem, Captain John Higginson, John Hathorne, William Stoughton and Cotton Mather. The subject under discussion was the propriety of making public some of the evidence in the witch trials. Not since Lawson's *Brief and True Narrative* of last spring had there been any authoritative published statement, and the latter had been written months in advance of the sitting of the Court of Oyer and Terminer. Now, with so much irresponsible talk going on, it seemed clear that the time had come for an official report on what the judges had accomplished for Massachusetts. It would be an interim report. At this date the judges expected to go forward with the trials in October. In spite of the rising tide of protest none could know that the seven women and one man who that day hung on the gallows in Salem would be the very last witches to hang in Massachusetts.

Mather stood ready to take on this assignment, and had been anticipating it for some time. To this end he had been accumulating some of his own sermons, notably his "Hortatory and Necessary Address" with its charge upon the conscience of New England. "'Tis our Worldliness, our Formality, our Sensuality and our Iniquity that has helped this letting of the Devils in." In addition he had been after Stephen

Sewall to copy out such of the documents in Salem as could be used in a history of the witchcraft. Some of this material—not quite so much as he had hoped—was now available. If it was the will of his colleagues he would gladly do his best with a subject which had been, he modestly reminded them, "sometimes counted not unworthy the pen, even of a king."

Whatever the faults of the younger Mather, procrastination was not one of them. By early October when [the royal governor, Sir William] Phips returned [from England], the manuscript was not only complete, awaiting the latter's approval, but had already had some circulation among dignitaries of the colony. That he had also done his work well, had achieved what could be regarded as the authoritative version of the affair, was indicated not only by a laudatory preface by Stoughton, but by the fact that Sir William borrowed whole paragraphs for incorporation into his first report to England.

Phips did not, however, encourage publication. Brattle's letter, which denounced the entire premisses of the trials, was circulating as far and as fast as Mather's defense. At a time of such diversity of opinion so hotly expressed the governor found it wise to suppress any publicity whatsoever. It was not until 1693 when the trials had been resumed on a new basis and the "general jail delivery" begun that he judged it wise to let Mather publish his *Wonders of the Invisible World*.

Mather's narrative was the nearest equivalent Massachusetts was to get to a full newspaper report of the mysterious events in court. The public fell on it with avidity and got their money's worth. Mingled in with sermons and philosophizings, Mather had presented a full and accurate account of the examination and trials of five representative witches, George Burroughs, Bridget Bishop, Susanna Martin, Elizabeth How, and Martha Carrier. He had followed the records in painstaking detail, summarizing competently when he did not quote in full. Not even his worst enemies were ever to find fault with his court reporting, and compared with the chapbooks of such cases put out to entertain the English public, it was a journalistic masterpiece.

Yet this document, so well planned and executed, so invaluable to the historian, was to serve the reputation of Mather ill. It had two conspicuous defects: its omissions and its tone. Those who really knew the trials read a significance into the fact that Mather had carefully avoided several of their most embarrassing aspects, Rebecca Nurse's brief acquittal, the powerful reasoning of John Procter and Mary Esty. The avoidance, to be sure, was by no means necessarily Mather's doing; what to include and what to omit had certainly been one of the subjects of discussion at the editorial meeting at Sewall's house. These circumstances could not, however, negate the fact that Mather had lent his hand to fabricating that most dangerous of falsehoods, the half truth.

The tone of the book was another thing again, and wholly Mather's. It suggested that the Dutch divines had spoken against spectral evidence in vain, and that Mather himself in recommending caution in this direction had not meant it. For he had written throughout in a spirit of childlike, marvelling credulity.

Yet how could Mather, given his temperament, have written otherwise of his witches? As well ask Shakespeare to revise *Macbeth* without mentioning the Weird Sisters, or Milton to erase all reference to Satan in *Paradise Lost* as to ask Mather to do other than what he had done. There was in him much of the artist, and artistry in his austere position in theocratic Massachusetts found only such wayward expression as this. To such a temperament—and some of the afflicted girls probably resembled him in this—the details of the witchcraft, of horns that sounded across Essex County at midnight, the airborne excursions to Parris's pasture, the folklore that gaudily embroidered the life of Susanna Martin, were less a horror and an abomination than part of the suppressed color and drama of life. Mather's righteous indignation that such things could be was unconsciously submerged in the thrill of having been present as spectator at a collision between heaven and hell. The witchcraft was one experience that Mather would not willingly have forgone; it was the scarlet thread drawn through the drab of New England homespun.

But men who had been painfully involved in the crisis were little likely to respond to so artless and unconsciously poetic a viewpoint. What impressed them was that in his zeal for discovering witches an eminent Boston divine had stultified his capacity to see human beings and their very real agonies, that in short, to judge by the tone of his record, he had learned nothing at all from experience. So far as he was concerned, the delirium might begin again full force to-morrow.

5.

Indeed the delusion had by no means spent itself. While the afflicted of Andover and Salem were falling one by one into silence, dampened by the lack of a responsive audience, new voices were being heard in Boston. To two of these Mather was giving all the attention he could spare from his parochial duties. He was, in fact, launched on a whole new cycle of psychic research.

The first case to come to his attention was that of Mercy Short, seventeen-year-old servant-maid of Boston, recently back from captivity among the Indians, who, as natural creatures of the devil, had probably had not too wholesome an influence on the girl. It was Mercy who in the course of a call on the Boston Prison in the summer of 1692 had mocked Sarah Good's plea for tobacco and had been afflicted since.

One would have supposed that the hanging of Sarah would have released Mercy, but not at all. Sarah must have delegated the torture of the girl to her surviving confederates, for it went right on through the summer and fall and became a favourite subject of speculation among the frequenters of the coffee-houses. On 4 December Mercy achieved the attention of Cotton Mather by falling into such convulsions during a sermon that she had to be carried out. Naturally Mather looked her up afterwards, both he and a "little company of praying neighbors." He had long been itching to study at close range the type of case responsible for the Salem outbreak; now at last he had one in his own precinct.

From his interviews with this medium he got a first-hand description of the devil, "a short and black man—a Wretch no taller than an ordinary Walking Staff; he was not a Negro but of a Tawney or an Indian colour; he wore a high crowned hat with straight hair; and he had one Cloven Foot." The eyes of this creature flamed unbearably, resembling, according to Mercy, the glass ball of the lantern Mather took with him through the dim streets of Boston on his nocturnal rambles.

Sometimes Mercy's affliction took the form of long fasts, during which she could force herself to take nothing but hard cider. Sometimes she was seared by flames, and her visitors could smell the brimstone and see the burns on Mercy's flesh, though, "as 'tis the strange property of many witch marks," these were "cured in perhaps less than a minute." Sometimes the devil forced white liquid down her throat. Sometimes she had fits of wild frolic when she was deaf to all prayers.

It was not for want of name-calling on Mercy's part that these investigations did not result in arrests. She cried out against all sorts of people, especially some with whom she had recently quarrelled. But Mather, acting with a discretion for which he was not to be thanked, decided that most of these were devil's delusions and charged his "praying company" not to report them. Among Mercy's more oblique accusations was Mather himself; this fact gave him more gratification than otherwise, for he gathered from the context that the devil feared and hated him more than any other minister in New England, a very pretty compliment.

Mercy, responding to fasting, prayer and the invisible ministrations of an angel who sometimes fended the devils off, finally came out of her trance in March 1693, and Mather wrote up his observations under the title of *A Brand Pluck'd out of the Burning*. Somehow he did not publish it. The jail delivery was in progress, and friends and relatives of released witches would not appreciate yet another starry-eyed report of this sort, especially so soon after the *Wonders*, from whose philosophies some of them were cringing. Or perhaps it was the development of Mercy herself which restrained him. The sad truth was that when the devil was cast out of her, seven others took its place, these being devils of the more common and carnal sort. Martyrs are impressive in the long run only when they are also saints; since Mercy was plainly nothing of the sort, Mather's pious account of her sufferings would be oddly received in Boston's coffee-houses, places much more productive of scepticism than the alehouses had ever been. Mather did not risk it.

6.

Mather was, however, by no means done with the devil. In September 1693 he made a trip to Salem to get "furniture" for the completion of the work now nearest to his heart, his *Magnalia Christi Americana*. This was to be his epic in somewhat the same way that *Paradise Lost* was Milton's. His purpose was cognate, though whereas Milton had undertaken to justify the ways of God to man, Mather would seek to justify the ways of man to God, particularly man as represented by the leaders of Puritan theocracy. He would eschew the sonorities of blank verse for the plainer sense of English prose, albeit richly embellished by latinisms, and the sombre glory of such characters as Beelzebub and Lucifer for the more unassuming personnel to be found in New England parsonages; the *Magnalia* was indeed to be primarily a history of the churches in New England. Lucifer, however, would not be ignored in Mather's work; he would again give himself the luxury of describing the Fiend's descent on Salem Village.

To such an end he came to Salem. He delivered two sermons and between them pursued his inquiries. He was much interested in a Mrs. Carver and her viewpoint on late events. This lady was in direct communication with "shining spirits" who told her that "a new storm of witchcraft would fall upon the country and chastise the iniquity that was used in the wilful smothering and covering of the last."

This news Mather received about as a general might receive intelligence that he would soon be called upon to march again. There had indeed been something abrupt, something questionable about the end of the witchcraft. The case had not been so much disposed of as allowed to collapse. It was as if an army of occupation had been called home without awaiting the signing of a peace treaty. It would be little wonder if the devil were to begin a new assault against a people so little capable of sustained effort.

These reflections were reinforced by evidence that the devil was interfering directly in his own affairs. He had prepared two sermons to deliver in Salem and the devil stole them both. Luckily he was able to give them from memory "so the devil got nothing." The story did not end there. When he got home to Boston he found that affliction had started again in his own neighborhood in the person of another seventeen-year-old, one Margaret Rule, From Margaret's lips he learned what had happened in Salem. The eight spectral shapes that tormented her had stolen his sermons and were bragging about it. Yet it was not given to creatures covenanted to the devil to keep a hold on a thing so holy as a sermon by Cotton Mather. In October the spirits relaxed their grip and dropped the missing manuscripts leaf by leaf about the streets of Lynn. Every page was recovered in a perfect state of preservation.

After such portents Mather could not deny his time and prayers to the new victim of the invisible world. Margaret was indeed a pitiful case. Her present physical tortures had been preceded by a spiritual phase in which she was prey to a belief that she was damned. Now she was the victim of witches who desired her to sign the Book. She was resisting heroically and before a cloud of witnesses. For Margaret was yet another who had had to be carried shrieking from meeting; since that had first happened on 10 September, she had become the major theatrical attraction in Boston. If Mather wanted to minister to her privately he must first clear the room of a company—by no means a praying company—of thirty or forty spectators. Frequently he did not take this precaution, with the result that a fraction of the population of Boston was entertained not only by the antics of Margaret but by the measures taken by Mather to exorcize her demons.

Margaret's affliction had begun with an involuntary fast. For nine days her teeth had set against food, though occasionally it was possible to get her mouth open just wide enough to admit a sip of rum. ("That's the devil all over," commented a seaman.) Sometimes it was the devil who forced open her mouth in order to pour scalding brimstone down her throat so that people in the room could hardly bear the smell of the stuff or the sound of the girl's screams.

Marvels happened right under the eyes of the beholders. Some of them saw the woman stuck full of pins. Six men signed affidavits that they had seen her pulled to the ceiling by invisible hands and that it took their concerted might to pull her back to bed again. Mather himself once made a grab for something stirring on her pillow and felt an imp in his hand, tangible and yet invisible, and so startling in that combination that he let it get away.

She dreamed dreams and saw visions. She forecast the drowning of a young man and exactly as she spoke it happened—almost; that is, by God's providence the man wasn't actually drowned but was fished out of the water into which sundry devils had impelled him to leap. She saw the thieving of an old man's will. She saw the faces of her tormenters, or anyway of some of them, particularly that of an evil old woman who had been taken in the recent witchcraft and incontinently released again when the judges lost their heart for proper prosecution. Some witches she could not identify because they, having learned a thing or two, now went about their business veiled. Veiled or no, when Mather got to her, he prevailed on her to "forbear blazing their names lest any good person come to suffer any blast of reputation." He was willing that she name them to him privately and was reassured, for they were "the sort of wretches who for these many years have given over as violent presumption of witchcraft as perhaps any creatures yet living on this earth." Even so he did not report them.

He got small thanks for his self-sacrificing labours on behalf of Margaret Rule. His efforts had been observed by a motley company come off the streets of Boston to see the show, merchants, seamen, scholars, goodwives, everybody. These behaved decorously enough in his presence and on the whole he thought it well that a variety of observers witness the agonies of the girl the better to combat the scepticism of the coffee-houses. What he did not know was that one of these "coffee-house witlings" had not only got in with the rest but was taking copious notes of the séances and preparing to publish.

This observer was Robert Calef, an obscure merchant of Boston. He was a friend of Thomas Brattle and agreed with the sceptical viewpoint expressed in Brattle's letter, and had therefore come to watch Mather in none too reverent a frame of mind. What his cold eye noted in the afflicted Margaret was her craving for the attentions of men. She visibly liked being stroked across face and naked breast and belly by the Mathers, father and son, this being a kind of laying on of hands by which they tried to relieve her, but let a woman touch her and she cried out sharply, "Don't you meddle with me!"

When the ministers withdrew, Margaret told the women to clear out altogether, saying "that the company of men was not offensive to her, and having hold of the hand of a young man said to have been her sweetheart . . . she pulled him again into his seat saying he should not go tonight."

Six days later Calef found her enjoying what Mather had explained to observers as "her laughing time; she must laugh now.'' Mather having already gone for the evening, she was free to make eyes at yet another young man and to fuss with her attendants because they ''did not put her on a clean cap but let her lie so like a beast, saying she would lose her fellows.''

There was talk, to be sure, about her frightful affliction earlier in the day, and there were symptoms of a recurrence when one or two of the women got a whiff of brimstone. Everyone sniffed with them, but Calef and the others couldn't pick up the scent and said so. The women became less sure of themselves; they could smell something, they said; they were not sure what.

Calef, in short, was less than impressed with the martyred Margaret. Even less had he been impressed in the still recent past by what he called a ''Bigoted Zeal stirring up a Blind and most Bloody Rage'' against innocent people by such media as these. He resented the credulous interest of the Mathers, particularly Cotton; this sort of thing had led to public disaster only two years earlier. Calef did not propose to stand by and watch the engineering of a second outbreak. Accordingly he copied out his notes and let them circulate from hand to hand.

Never in his life had Mather been so rudely handled or so affronted as he was by the talk to which these notes gave rise. He was enraged by the description of his stroking the half-naked Margaret so as ''to make people believe a Smutty thing of me.'' His first impulse was to bring suit for ''scandalous libel''; his second not to risk so public an appearance on so delicate an issue. The warrant was issued against Calef, but when the latter appeared before court, none came against him and the case was dismissed.

The larger case was not at all dismissed, however. The controversy between minister and merchant went on for years and culminated at the turn of the century in a book called *More Wonders of the Invisible World*, a work by Calef with the involuntary collaboration of Mather and a probable but disguised contribution by Brattle. Its core was the later witch writings of Mather, including his unpublished account of

Margaret Rule. To this Calef added his own appendix to
Mather's *Wonders*, furnishing full details on cases which
Mather had neglected, notably that of Rebecca Nurse, and
adding reports by such survivors as the Carys and John Alden.

Its publication was one of the most afflicting things that
had ever happened to Mather, his sorrow's crown of sorrow.
And indeed, though Calef's work was a valuable addition to
the history of witchcraft, it did inflict an injustice on Mather in
connecting his name inseparably with a tragedy with which he
actually had had little to do.

Increase Mather, who himself had drawn Calef's fire,
owing to his proposal to New England ministers in 1695 that
they continue to collect "Remarkables," among them
evidence of the agency of the invisible world, stood loyally by
his son and made a spectacle of the infamy of the book—or so
the story goes—by having it burned in the Harvard Yard. This
fine symbolic gesture had oddly little effect in preventing its
circulation.

7.

Margaret Rule had in the meantime come out of her fits
long since. It was well that Calef never heard of her last séance
with Mather, for during it she dreamily named the wizard
whose Shape was currently afflicting her, and it was none other
than Cotton's.

Mather was terrified. Superstition played little part in his
fright, nor did he anticipate taking a place by Burroughs on the
gallows. What unmanned him was the derision of the
coffee-houses if this accusation ever got around.

Heroic measures were necessary, heights of prayer to
which he had never won before. He won them now. Finally,
after Mather had spent several hours in the dust before his
God, the "shining spirit" that had intermittently appeared to
Margaret came again and informed her that Mather was now
her father in Christ and that through God's providence he had

saved her. The angel also opened her eyes to the actual demons crowded around her. They were rather pitiful; the devil himself stood over them lashing them to further effort, for all the world like an overseer whipping his slaves. Indeed the demons were fainting under the punishment and under the strain of their hopeless endeavour. At last they cried out to Margaret, "Go and the devil go with you. We can do no more." Then they fled the place. Nor did they come again, at least in that guise. Margaret's affliction and Boston's best show were both a thing of the past; hereafter Margaret had no more difficulty in getting privacy for her interviews with her "fellows."

Mather for his part learned to keep strictly away from her. His "spiritual daughter" did not turn out to be a very nice girl.

Exorcism

F.X. Maquart

The office of exorcist is one of the four minor orders conferred in the Catholic Church on the future priest. The exorcist has a twofold power directed against the twofold action of the devil on men: temptation and possession. Against the first he uses the *ordinary* exorcism, which is exemplified in the exorcisms of the rite of baptism. Against the second, which is preternatural, the Church uses the *solemn* exorcism which she does not allow her priests to practice at will. For them, as a general rule, the power is restricted, and the only persons authorized to exorcise the possessed are priests specially deputed to this office by the Church.

Various considerations have led to this strict reservation of the practice of solemn exorcism. The struggle of the exorcist against the demon is not free from moral or even physical dangers, and the Church neither will nor can lightly expose her ministers to these. From the standpoint of the patient, moreover, it would be gravely imprudent to rush into an exorcism in a case of merely apparent possession, when the trouble was really due to some mental disease. This might very well aggravate the ill instead of curing it. In spite of all the severity of the Church in this matter there is still room to regret the ill-considered and imprudent action of certain priests devoted to this dangerous ministry.

"Exorcism is an impressive ceremony, capable of acting effectively on a sick man's subconsciousness. The adjurations addressed to the demon, the sprinklings with holy water, the stole passed around the patient's neck, the repeated signs of the cross, and so forth, can easily call up a diabolical mythomania in word and deed in a psyche already weak. Call the devil and you'll see him; or rather not him, but a portrait made up of the sick man's ideas of him," wrote Père Joseph de Tonquédec. It is only to priests whose high moral worth protects them from all danger, and whose knowledge and judgment enable them to make a sure estimate of the case put before them, that the Church entrusts the dangerous task of pitting themselves against the devil.

For what is it that the exorcist has to do? Like a physician called in to an illness he has first to arrive at a diagnosis and then judiciously apply the remedy. He is asked to formulate a practical judgment, a judgment directed to action; not one that announces a speculative truth, like the narrator of historical fact or the man of science, but a practical truth: "In this case all the indications, not indeed certainly but with high probability, point to an actual diabolical possession, and call for an exorcism."

The Roman ritual provides the exorcist with precise instructions, which, if strictly and judiciously carried out, should enable him to pronounce on the case with an easy conscience. The first is this: that "he should not at the outset allow himself to believe in possession too easily." Far from leaving him to jump to the conclusion that he has to do with a possessed person, it expressly warns him to examine critically all he has been told and everything he sees that might, at first sight, suggest possession.

We find in the Acts of the National Synod of Rheims, held in 1583, the following warning: "Before the priest undertakes an exorcism, he ought diligently to inquire into the life of the possessed, into his condition, reputation, health, and other circumstances, and should talk them over with wise, prudent, and instructed people, since the too credulous are often deceived, and melancholics, lunatics, and persons bewitched often declare themselves to be possessed and tormented by the devil, and these people nevertheless are more in need of a doctor than of an exorcist.''

A wise recommendation certainly, and one that is only too clearly called for. The ecclesiastical world is prone to a naive credulity in this matter. When it encounters those who fall a prey to obsessions, to impulses or inhibitions violently opposed to their usual temper, and who labor, as they often do, under the impression that they are victims of some alien and evil power, then at once it begins to think of the action of the devil and to recognize a true possession. "Here is a man who normally hates sin, blasphemy, impurity, cruelty, and every kind of gross behavior; and suddenly he finds himself strongly prompted to indulge in all he hates. Do these promptings come from himself? Is he not the passive victim of some alien power? Here is a lady, intelligent, educated, of high moral character, whose habitual speech is faultlessly polite, and suddenly she finds her head ringing with a phrase of brutal obscenity which she goes on repeating to herself mentally without ceasing. Surely it is not she who has conjured it up; she merely submits to the infliction with pain and disgust. Again, well-brought-up and pious persons find their minds filled with vulgar jests, with contemptuous and ironic phrases, abusive of persons and things entitled to the highest respect. That may be relatively harmless but worse follows. We meet with unhappy people who are harassed by sexual impulses, by masturbation, by the desire for amorous assignations, and so forth, who sometimes struggle against them but also sometimes yield, with responsibility in some sort diminished as if they were driven on by an evil fate. Others finally—and this puts the last and boldest stroke to the diabolic picture—are haunted by the notion of giving themselves over to the devil or calling him up from the abyss. They do so sometimes, often also simply believe they have done so; or ask themselves again, in anguish of spirit, whether perhaps they have not done it. . . .

"Conversely, there are those who find themselves pulled up short before some action in which they are anxious to acquit themselves well. They are paralyzed when they try to pray, their lips stick together and refuse to utter the words. A man in this condition may want to receive Holy Communion, but as soon as he kneels at the altar rails, his throat contracts, and he cannot swallow the Host. Others, again, cannot even enter the church without a strange sinking; their legs seem to give way beneath them and they feel ill. Hence perhaps eventually they come to suffer a revulsion from all religious things—a revulsion which in persons fundamentally Christian and pious causes great astonishment and consternation, so that they begin to think themselves under the dominion of the devil.

"Worse still: there are some unfortunate people who when they want to do this or that find themselves doing the very opposite. For example, they have only to try to recollect themselves and at once they are assailed by obscene thoughts about God, or Christ, or the Blessed Virgin; or else they are swept into a denial of various dogmas, into revolt, blasphemy, and so on. Call to mind those priests who feel themselves invincibly drawn to invalidate the most important acts of their ministry. Here we might very easily be led to recognize the hand of 'the spirit that denies,' of the spirit who everywhere sets himself in opposition to the work of God" (Père de Tonquédec, on whose studies I have gratefully relied throughout).

Why is it that the priest, faced with this kind of thing, is so ready to conclude to the presence of the devil? His theological formation and the daily exercise of his ministry dispose him beforehand and quasi-instinctively to the passing of moral judgments; and, finding it impossible to impute moral responsibility for acts so evidently discordant with the characters of their authors, he tends to assume the presence of a preternatural cause even when there is only question of the patient's "unconscious" or of acts devoid of liberty. The question he asks is: Virtuous or vicious? whereas he ought to ask: Normal or abnormal?

"We give the name 'marvelous' to verifiable exterior phenomena, which may suggest the idea that they are due to the extraordinary intervention of an intelligent cause other than man."

A marvelous phenomenon is thus an observable phenomenon. Consequently it can be submitted to scientific examination. A sweat of blood, stigmata, diabolic manifestations, all belong to the category of the marvelous. They can be observed. A conversion, on the contrary, an interior work of grace, cannot in itself be a marvelous phenomenon.

The marvelous, furthermore, calls up the idea of an extraordinary intervention, an intervention by an intelligence that is other than that of man.

"The wonted aspect of the world, the order it displays, the marks of design it bears upon it, may already suggest the idea of the action of a higher intelligence. But this constant, common, expected action, having nothing exceptional about it, lies by that very fact outside the scope of our subject."

The phenomena of nature are subject to the laws of nature, and subject also to human activity. The genuinely marvelous, therefore, will be something that neither nature nor human action can explain. It is essentially a natural phenomenon; but instead of being effected in conformity with the laws of nature, it comes about in an extraordinary way. Thus the sudden healing of a wound, or the knitting up of a bone, which nature normally brings about gradually, is to be explained only by the extraordinary intervention of a higher cause. The cure effected is not, in itself, beyond the powers of nature, but nature will not reconstitute the tissues instantaneously. There we have the extraordinary, the modal supernatural, the marvelous. It is, as its definition indicates, open to

observation, being a phenomenon similar in nature to all other
sensible phenomena. Whether slow or instantaneous, the
reconstruction of tissue can be observed and can be registered
by radiography. Thus the mode of production of the marvelous
is itself also observable. It is equally easy to ascertain that a
lesion which cannot naturally be healed in less than several
weeks or months has, in fact, closed up suddenly. Thus the
marvelous occurrence is observable, not simply as an
occurrence, but also as marvelous, that is to say, as having
been produced in opposition to, or outside the scope of, the
laws of nature. We see, then, that the supernatural mode itself
can be negatively established by science.

We say "negatively" because science, which is confined
to the observable, can ascertain only that the phenomenon is
produced in a way which, as far as our present knowledge
goes, is naturally inexplicable. The mission of science is to
explain observed phenomena, and it either succeeds or does
not succeed.

It belongs to the discernment of spirits to fix the
character, whether miraculous or simply marvelous, of a
phenomenon that science has declared inexplicable *in the
actual state of our knowledge*. The difficulty raised by this last
phrase must be dealt with by metaphysics. "It is useless to
insist on the hidden virtualities of physical or psychological
nature and on our ignorance of their possible scope: there are
limits here which no sane mind will obstinately refuse to
respect. We do not know the whole positive efficiency of
natural forces, but we know some of their negative limitations.
We do not know how far they will go, but we believe
ourselves able to say that they won't go as far as this point or
as far as that. By combining oxygen and hydrogen you will
never get chlorine; by sowing wheat you will *never* get roses;
and a human word will never of itself suffice to calm storms or
raise the dead. There is no kind of possibility, even negative,
that you can set against that; no 'perhaps,' however much in
the air it may be, is permissible here. If anyone, sowing

wheat, should believe that 'perhaps' he might get roses, he is in an abnormal state of mind.''

If the exorcist is to bring his examination to a successful issue, he will need a special scientific competence which neither his theological training nor the practice of this ministry can give him. In particular, he will have to be careful to avoid any false application of his theological science. Being habituated to theological reasoning, he will tend to explain the facts by remote, universal, abstract, or unobservable causes; his diagnoses will take on a moral complexion: when he has no reason to doubt the moral character of the witness, he will be too ready to take his word for it that he has no wish to deceive. Something else is wanted here, and first of all the facts, not taken for granted but established with historical accuracy. For that he will need not merely a critical examination of the witness, but an objective criticism of his testimony itself. After that he will have to eliminate every concrete, immediate, or observable natural cause of the manifestations presumed to be diabolic.

He ought also to disregard the judgments, which never fail to make an impression, of the patient's entourage. Père de Tonquédec cites the case of a young man unanimously pronounced by the clergy of his parish to be possessed, when in fact he was simply ill.

To carry out this examination the exorcist has to be a good observer; he must have eyes to see. Some people are naturally more observant than others; it is a matter of temperament. But ordinary, cursory, empirical observation is one thing, and scientific observation is another. The first takes place at random, without method; significant details are often overlooked, and a mass of others retained which are wholly without interest to the scientist. The second, on the contrary, is methodical, strict, and aimed at an explanation of the facts. It calls for the observance of rules, for the use of instruments. It would be well if the exorcist carried it out with a psychiatrist or a neurologist at his side, and then he should note the signs that the latter tends to pass over as not concerned with his specialty. Since, in this matter, history, medicine, neurology, psychology, psychiatry, all converge on the same point and have each their word to say, some competent knowledge of all these subjects will have to be available. Whatever the medical knowledge of the exorcist—and it ought to be extensive—he cannot dispense with specialists without running the risk of mistaking illness for possession.

The fact is that certain symptoms are common to neuroses, particularly to neurasthenia, hysteria, and some forms of epilepsy, and also to genuine possession: for example, dual personality, at least partial, accompanied by vicious manifestations out of keeping with the character of the subject. Other neuroses will lead the patient himself, or his neighbors, to suspect possession. "An emotional person for example, who has been subjected to a threat of vengeance or a curse, may find himself morally and physically deranged. His social standing suffers from the shock. He loses his position, and then one position after another, because he can no longer fill them efficiently. Henceforth, as it seems to him, misfortune dogs his footsteps. . . . Similarly, the restless neurasthenic dreamer gives himself up to brooding over the dark designs of fate, over the mystery of the world; he feels the attraction, the fascination of these depths, and believes himself able at last to discern in their shadows the hand of a sinister power uplifted against him."

Symptoms of this sort invariably make an impression, and the exorcist has to fortify himself against it. In no case are they specific indications of possession. The theologian Thyraus, who before the end of the sixteenth century wrote a treatise dealing with this matter, a treatise cited with approval by Benedict XIV, rejects twelve of the accepted signs of possession as unreliable, in spite of all opinions to the contrary. They are mostly to be found in neuroses. The first—"the avowals of those who are intimately persuaded that they themselves are possessed"—is referable to mental obsession or to hysteria. "The abnormal mental and physical plasticity and malleability of the hysterical subject lays open his mind, attitude, actions, even his very physical organism, to receive the stamp of any dominant idea or vivid image. Let this be the idea of the devil, of his power, of his possible invasion of a human personality, and the subject at once begins to 'ape the devil,' just as under other suggestions he might have aped any other personage, and to start behaving like a 'limb of Satan.' A persuasion of this sort is sometimes due to psychasthenia, and is very often communicated to the patient's neighbors. It may even suffice to remove him from his usual haunts to get rid of his devil as well." "The uncalled-for assumption of gross and savage manners" is similarly and rightly considered by the same author as having no diabolical significance. "The hysterical person who takes himself for an instrument of Satan shows a horror for all religious things, an inclination to evil, to gross speech, licentious attitudes, violent agitation, and so on." In certain states bordering on epilepsy we occasionally meet with a need, an itch, to do evil, to plunge into it and wallow in it. "This bad behavior consists precisely in what is most repugnant to the explicit feelings of the subject: gross blasphemies, revolt against God, insults hurled at priests, at religious persons, senseless brutalities, impurities committed even under the eyes of witnesses, sacrileges carried out with every kind of sadistic refinement." "I have met with young girls," goes on Père de Tonquédec, from whom we quote these details, "who would spit out the sacred Host after having received it, or keep it back in order to profane it in unworthy ways; and people who befouled the crucifix, trod the rosary underfoot, etc."

Thyraus also rightly discards the sign of deep and prolonged sleep. It might perhaps be one of the tricks of the devil, but it might also be a symptom of epilepsy. Similarly, diseases that prove incurable by medical art have nothing in common with possession. In spite of all its recent immense progress, we are too well aware of the limitations of medicine, especially in the field of mental troubles, to have any need to resort to the devil in order to explain the incurability of certain ills. Intestinal pains which give the patient the impression of a physical possession are easy to diagnose; they are due to a delusion similar to that which mental pathology calls zoopathy, or belief in the presence of an animal in the viscera. There is also the case of the imagined incubus, originating in abnormal sensations or hallucinations localized in the genital organs. "In every case that has come to our notice," says de Tonquédec, "these pathological causes were amply sufficient to explain the patient's assertions." The same can be said of the other signs that Thyraus rejects. To attribute to a demon the bad habits of certain people who always have the devil on their lips, to take straightway as possessed all those who renounce God or give themselves over body and soul to the devil, "all those who are nowhere at ease because they believe themselves everywhere molested by spirits, or those who, being tired of life, attempt to put an end to it"—all this would be incredibly naïve. One need not even be ill to get into the habit of dragging the devil into one's talk at every opportunity. As to those who give themselves over to Satan, there is nothing to be gathered from that in favor of possession; it is a sign that conveys nothing unless some preternatural signs be added. The case of "Rosalie," reported by Père de Tonquédec, in which no truly preternatural sign appeared, can be explained in the most natural manner. "This dramatic piece of stagecraft, this tragedy in which the role of the demon was played to such perfection, did not," concludes the author very justly, "surpass the powers of hysteria."

The Roman ritual indicates three specific signs of possession: "use or understanding of an unknown tongue; knowledge of distant or hidden facts; and exhibitions of physical powers exceeding the age or condition of the subject." The ritual does not consider the list as exhaustive, but adds: "and other phenomena of the same sort."

Let us consider the three signs enumerated; they are worthy of close attention. The facts revealed by metapsychical science present us with problems that considerably complicate the matter. The modern application of scientific psychical methods to apparently marvelous facts will not allow us to use the criteria of possession so easily now as in days gone by. The scientific world, and not only it but the theological world as well, is more and more inclined to admit today the reality and purely natural character of telepathy. As M.R. Dalbiez very rightly emphasizes (*Etudes Carmélitaines,* October 1938), this attitude is no longer defended only by advanced authors, it is to be found in the manuals in use in seminaries, as for example, in the excellent *Cursus philosophiae* by Père Boyer, S.J. This author considers the reality and natural character of telepathy as very probable. It is the same with radiesthesia. Nobody will be tempted to have recourse to the devil to explain discoveries made at a distance by radiesthesia with the help of a divining rod or pendulum, or even without any instruments at all. We therefore stand in need of a thorough critique of the psychic criterion "knowledge of distant or hidden facts."

So also, we shall find the formula " 'physical powers exceeding the age or condition of the subject' very vague. Our forefathers would certainly have considered action at a distance, the displacement of objects without apparent contact, as a fact of the preternatural order, requiring the intervention of spirits. Nowadays we have to be more cautious." Yet have we really enough evidence to make us think, as M. Dalbiez does, that this curious phenomenon is perfectly natural? Without going so far as to consider, with him, that the physical criteria are worth very little, it is certain that this question of the "criteria of possession" needs a little restatement.

Consider, to start with, the criterion of "xenoglossolaly," of speech in an unknown tongue. If it is strictly understood, it retains its probative force.

"We should first consider the possibility of a cryptomnesia, a reappearance of buried linguistic recollections. In true xenoglossolaly there is an elaboration, in a tongue unknown to the subject, of an intelligent and unprompted reply to the question put." Under what conditions is this to be recognized with certainty? According to M. Dalbiez, "if, as is most commonly the case, a member of the audience, or the interrogator himself, knows the language in question, no xenoglossolaly is demonstrable; for we can suppose that he formulates the answer unconsciously and that the subject absorbs it by thought reading. For the same reason, the fact that the subject understands a command or a question put in a language unknown to him but known to the experimenter is not proof; he can still have recourse to thought reading. The sole case of real probative force is that in which the subject propounds, in a language unknown to himself and to those present, a series of intelligent and well-adapted answers to be translated later on by an expert. In such a case, all idea of the subject's knowledge of physical or psychical objects at a distance is excluded, since the answers could not have been read in any book or in any mind, for the simple reason that they did not exist. The last-ditch partisans of a natural explanation have a choice here between only two hypotheses. Either one of the subject's ancestors must have spoken the language, and the subject must have inherited this knowledge in his unconscious mind—which appears highly unlikely; or else the subject absorbed the elements of the language from some grammar or from somebody's brain—which appears equally unlikely, the structure of a language being an abstraction."

We readily admit the demonstrative force of this last case cited by M. Dalbiez. But is he not rather too severe in rejecting that in which the interrogator or one of the audience knows the language unknown to the subject? We should hesitate to differ from so eminent a scholar if he had not himself put out his remarks as simple and very incomplete suggestions, laying claim to no finality. We submit for the judgment of readers a few complementary reflections which may throw some light on the problem of the cogency of the criteria of possession.

A critique of these criteria must hold firmly to the principle of economy; that is to say, it must not appeal to a preternatural explanation of any alleged marvel if a natural one would suffice. But the scientific principle is not properly used if it is given a metaphysical sense that it does not bear. We are not entitled to reject the marvelous character of an occurrence in the name of the principle of economy just because there is a metaphysical possibility of a natural explanation. We have to establish that in fact that natural explanation is credible.

In the cases rejected by M. Dalbiez on the ground of the possibility of thought reading, it seems that we can reason thus. Thought reading is a rare occurrence and supposes some special gift. If the patient possesses this gift, he has either had it from birth or has acquired it in later life. In either case it should be possible to establish the fact. If he has had it from birth, it is unlikely that he has never yet turned it to account. It is therefore almost out of the question—and purely gratuitous —to think that he has it, if he has never made use of it till now. If, on the other hand, he developed it, then his acquaintances could not be ignorant of certain attempts, at least, by dint of which he came to have it. If it be established that the patient has never displayed any gift of thought reading, then this gift is not to be relied on to explain his knowledge of foreign languages he has never learned. If the inquiry remains without decisive result, no conclusion of a scientific character can be drawn. But is it not evident, in that case, that the exorcist could prudently consider himself in the presence of one possessed?

Can we not argue in the same way on the subject of action at a distance, or displacement of objects without apparent contact? Even if one supposes that all human beings emanate a fluid, a certain technique would be needed for its effective use, as indeed is the case with radiesthesia. But such a technique is not to be acquired all at once. We can therefore appeal to this cause only if we can establish its existence. Let us suppose a case of levitation. Even if we grant that a natural explanation is possible, it must still be established that this explanation of the particular case under review is forced upon us. Here is one in which, if the facts are set out with complete accuracy, such an explanation would be impossible. (We do not vouch for the factual authenticity of the story, but if everything took place as reported, we should not hesitate to ascribe it to preternatural causes.) It is a case in which the patient was transported to the ceiling at the command of an exorcist, in defiance of all the laws of gravity. But let us leave the missionary who witnessed the occurrence to speak for himself.

Msgr. Waffelaert cites a letter from a missionary on a case of possession at which he was present. "I took it upon myself, during an exorcism, to command the demon, in Latin, to carry [the possessed] to the ceiling of the church, feet first and head downward. His whole body at once became rigid, and as if all his limbs had lost their power, he was dragged from the middle of the church to a pillar; there, with feet joined and his back against the pillar, and without using his hands, he was carried in the twinkling of an eye to the ceiling, like a weight drawn violently upward but without apparent means. Suspended from the ceiling, feet up, head downward . . . I left him there in the air for more than half an hour, and not having resolution enough to keep him there any longer, and not a little frightened myself at what I saw, I commanded [the spirit] to bring him back to my feet without doing him any hurt. . . . He was returned to me at once, like a bag of dirty linen, unharmed" ("Possession diabolique," *Dictionnaire apostolique de d'Alès*). If this story is true—and a historical criticism will have to settle that—no natural cause could explain it. Even supposing that levitation is naturally possible, no natural explanation will meet this case. Neither the missionary whose command the patient obeyed, nor the patient who obeyed it—the sole possible natural causes—can be invoked here. No man, unless invested with a power surpassing the ordinary powers of human nature, could perform this prodigy. The presence of extraordinary power must not merely be supposed, but taken as proved.

To recognize the hand of the demon in such a case is not to suppose the presence of the preternatural gratuitously. Let us run over our logic, starting from the definite establishment of the facts. If these facts are naturally inexplicable, even by appeal to extraordinary powers (such as telepathy or thought reading), then, since they must have a cause, we must turn perforce to a preternatural cause. The existence and possible causality of the preternatural is not assumed, but rigorously proved. It is not for the man of science to prove it—or even reject it, since science knows nothing about it—but for the metaphysician and the theologian. The metaphysician knows, in the light of his proper science, that above man there exists a Being, namely God, whose power surpasses all the powers of every created or creatable nature. The theologian, furthermore, thanks to revelation, knows that above man, but below God, there exist purely spiritual creatures, the angels and the devils. They have power over bodies; they have a more penetrating intelligence than ours; not being bound by space, they can transport themselves instantaneously from one distant locality to another. The sole limitations on their knowledge are to be found in the knowledge of future free and so unforeseeable events, and in the knowledge of the secrets of the human heart—in so far at least as these are not manifested exteriorly. But being more sagacious than we, they know how to interpret the slightest exterior signs of our thoughts.

In view of the powerlessness of science to give a natural explanation of the facts established, the theologian is therefore entitled to conclude, in the light of theology, that a case of knowledge of the future has God alone for its author; and that a case of knowledge at a distance, of xenoglossolaly, or of levitation, is to be attributed either to an angel or a devil. If the facts already recognized as naturally inexplicable tend to an evil end, the theologian will legitimately conclude to the intervention of the devil. If this critique is strictly applied, the three criteria of the ritual still retain all their force today.

We think that M. Dalbiez is too severe when he declares that in his eyes the physical criteria, taken as a whole, are weak. He is right in holding that we have to be more cautious about them today than was the case in the past; but if some of these phenomena, once regarded as preternatural, are now to be taken as natural, that is by no means so with all of them. There will have to be established in each particular case the existence of an extraordinary natural power.

The psychic phenomena call for a very important remark: all conversations held with the patient must be carefully analyzed. If they present the same system of association of ideas and of logicogrammatical habits that he exhibits in his normal state, then the possession must be held suspect. It is difficult to admit with certain theologians that the demon, cramped in his action by the native disposition and habits of his victim—as the cleverest artist depends on his instruments—borrows, as if in spite of himself, the habitual expressions of the possessed, and speaks more easily and willingly the language known to the possessed than that used by the exorcist.

In genuine possession the action of the demon doubtless dominates the body, seizes on its organs and uses them as if they were his own, actuates the nervous system and produces movements and gesticulations in the limbs, speaking, for example, through the patient's mouth—that is precisely the thing that characterizes possession—but, as Père de Tonqué-dec rightly insists, "this corporeal ascendency presupposes a more or less deeply seated and dense substructure of the corresponding psychological processes. The postures of the possessed are not imposed on him in any mechanical fashion; they proceed from a subjacent mental state but one which remains in a way exterior to his own personality."

We shall have fully achieved our purpose if the preceding pages have sufficiently brought out the difference between the critical attitude of the Church when faced with demonic marvels, and the naïve attitude of uncivilized tribes—a difference which superficial or ill-disposed minds are bent on ignoring. We know that primitive peoples are fond of appealing to hidden forces, foreign to nature, whenever a surprising event comes along to disconcert their ignorance. This attitude has been supposed to be typical of a prelogical mentality, but unduly. However questionable in other ways, it is simply an expression of the natural need of the human mind to seek an explanation for everything: appeal is made, without knowing it, to the principle of causality. But an erroneous application is made of the principle when these people straightway place the cause beyond nature; not knowing, in their ignorance of the exigencies of science, how to find it within nature itself.

Postscript

Joseph de Tonquédec

In the matter of the sign indicated by the ritual of exorcism "use or understanding of an unknown tongue," we may ask: Can this be put down to "thought transmission" when either the exorcist or one of his assistants knows the language employed?

To answer this question we must know what we are talking about; above all, we must know precisely what we mean by "thought transmission."

It seems clear, to start with, that there can be no question here of a personal act of thought that is seized on by another. That would be wholly meaningless. Thought is a vital act belonging inalienably to a particular subject. It is not absurd to credit it with certain effects which could make themselves felt outside the thinking mind; but taken in itself it remains private. We can appropriate the results of an action, but we cannot possess ourselves of the action itself.

Most of those, therefore, who talk about thought transmission conceive it in the following way. A thought, an image, a phrase is formed in a mind, and thence it radiates to another mind in which it is reproduced like an echo or a reflection. This second mind has therefore nothing to do with the work of its elaboration; its part is confined to receiving it as it is. It need not even understand the meaning of the message but may simply repeat it mechanically like a parrot. This, it is considered, is what happens in the case of a person possessed who speaks in a language he does not know, or answers a question put to him in such a language.

Let us leave this last application aside for the moment, since it is precisely the point under discussion. And let us frankly admit that many phenomena characterized as "thought transmission" conform to this type. Here is an example, taken from a very interesting brochure by M. H. de France, *Intuition provoquée et Radiesthésie* (p. 48):

In Martinique a Creole proprietor asked M. de France to prospect a domain where he thought that a treasure was buried. The latter agreed. "Suddenly," he says, "my divining rod stirred, and I indicated a certain direction with my left arm. The Creole, much disturbed, approached me and said that he had dreamed the whole scene that had just taken place. In his dream he had seen a white man accompanied by several other people. This man, just as I had done myself, had left the group and made some sweeping gestures with his left arm, indicating the same spot. . . . Unfortunately nothing was found! I had been the victim of a transmission of thought. Stories of buried treasure are common in the Antilles, and it was therefore natural that a native should have such a dream. When I had come near his house, he had believed that his dream was about to be realized. So strong was his eagerness for this that he had influenced me unconsciously."

Many phenomena called "clairvoyance"—which, however, does not necessarily imply thought transmission —belong to the same category. What in this case is given to the seer is not an abstract affirmation or negation such as is exchanged in ordinary conversation; it is not a piece of precise information that is intelligible in itself. It is a picture, a fragment or some more or less coherent fragments of a picture, a number of visual or audible images whose meaning remains to be determined, and which the seer interprets afterward by the use of his natural faculties and according to his own ideas. Hence the possibility of numberless errors. The matter transmitted is chiefly in the sensible order. Is it so exclusively? When, for example, it is a question of somebody's character, of his profession, and so on, can it all be given in purely sensible signs? We should not like to say so.

Transmissions of this species, moreover, are far from being clear and easily explicable phenomena. They remain profoundly mysterious, and it is not our purpose here to venture on any kind of explanation. But we must remark that the receptive subject plays no active part in the matter. He can prepare himself for it, create a void in his mind, put himself into a state of receptivity, and so forth; but what he receives comes from elsewhere, and he receives it in a passive fashion.

Now the sign of the presence of the devil indicated by the ritual is something very different. There is no question here of the automatic transmission of a ready-made answer, all written out in advance in one brain, and reproduced as it stands like an echo, without needing to be understood in another brain. The ritual uses the word *intelligere.* It speaks of an intelligent conversation between two interlocutors. The conversational use of a language is a whole of conscious and voluntary psychological acts consisting in the combination of a number of vocables to express a determinate thought. Now it is just the same in an exorcism as it is in an ordinary conversation: the answer made by a person questioned to his questioner does not exist in one sole ready-made formula in the mind of the latter. To a given interrogation there is no sole and single answer, but dozens of them, with possible nuances that run out to infinity. One can refuse to answer, one can disallow the question, one can respond by insults, rudeness, evasions; one can answer haughtily or slyly, indulge in irony or jesting, invoke the remoter principle that governs the matter, and so on endlessly. The ritual prescribes that we demand to know the name of the possessing spirit; now there are some hundreds of them, and the exorcist cannot divine in advance which one will be employed. He is more likely to be nonplused by the one that he hears.

If the questions are put in an idiom unknown to the patient, then whatever the language in which he makes a pertinent reply, but with all the more reason if he replies in the unknown tongue, it will have to be confessed that to explain it by automatic thought transmission is to go a little too quickly. There is no doubt about one thing. A conversation is going on between two equally conscious minds who understand what they say themselves and understand each other.

This would be the place to make similar discriminations between different cases of telepathy. Telepathy is not necessarily a kind of "long-distance photography" of persons, objects, or material scenes. Much more often it is the symbol—not in the least the reproduction—of a reality that is distant in time and space. For example: a dying man lies on his bed undressed; and he appears standing up and fully clothed. Only the expression on his face, a few gestures perhaps, or some words, indicate the melancholy character of the event. Now the construction of this symbol is the work of intelligence; it presupposes the lucid activity of a mind. The problem is simply to discover to whom this mind belongs. And we should be very wide of the mark if we tried to explain such a thing by "radiations" like those of wireless telegraphy.

Satanism Today

Richard Woods, O.P.

Baudelaire's frequently quoted dictum "The devil's cleverest wile is persuading us that he does not exist" seems at first sight strangely belied as the last quarter of the twentieth century begins. The Church of Satan, founded in 1966 by Anton Szandor La Vey, Exarch of Hell, now numbers more than seven thousand members—grouped into twenty-five "daughter grottoes"—throughout the United States. Complete with newsletter, creed, and ceremonies, this contemporary Satanist movement is a religion in the popular and technical sense. Hell's Angels, frequently in the public eye when La Vey founded his church, are still playing Hun across the nation, their recent exploits including murder at the Altamont Festival in California. A few years before, another church was founded in London, the Process Church of the Final Judgment, a community of black-cloaked youngsters who reverence Satan, Lucifer, and Jehovah, the "three gods of the universe." Theologically reminiscent of the Marcionites of the second century, the cult has migrated to America, where chapters are located in major cities.

More familiar reminders of Satan's presence to mind are found in popular films, from the most recent to televised revivals, and the ever-constant rumors of Black Masses celebrated in chic living rooms or abandoned basements. Two best-selling novels of the early seventies, William Peter Blatty's *The Exorcist* and Thomas Tryon's *The Other,* dwelled on incarnate evil in more and less explicit terms. Even the two-finger peace sign, a revitalization of the Churchill victory emblem, has its origin in the ancient hand sign against the evil eye and bears a homologous relationship to the devil sign, which employs the index and little fingers to represent horns. (Forked symbols generally, such as the up-ended pentangle star, signify the devil.)

While popular thought seems to be as attuned to the devil as ever, theological thought, especially since the Vatican Council that ended in 1965, has tended to relegate Satan to an ever-greater distance from the center of speculation and preaching. Perhaps the most strenuous objections to the devil come not from atheists and psychiatrists, as might be expected, but from the clergy. (An increasing number of religiously inclined persons, including Anton La Vey, have begun to wonder whether contemporary theologians believe even in God.) It may well be that there has also been a shift in popular thought, but no one has bothered to research it; many liberal Catholics upon inquiry actually seem embarrassed about believing in Satan. Even Hell's Angels treat him more as a mascot than a divinity, a sort of totemic symbol. But if there is a general movement in religious thought away from belief in the devil, why the recent upsurge of fashionable and pathological diabolism? The Manson Family slayings and the ritual suicide at Vineland, New Jersey, during the summer of 1971 might well stand as proof of Baudelaire's saying if the participants, like La Vey, did *not* believe in Satan, but that seems not to be the case.

Clues for an understanding of the present impasse among theologians, diabolists, and "ordinary" Christians must be sought in the history of dogma, the cultural evolution of the West, and the psychological origins, characteristics, and values of the belief in the existence of a superhuman, unalterably evil intelligence bent on the destruction of the human race. For the history of Satan is found in primitive and archaic religions as well as Hebrew-Christian scriptures, profane literature, and folklore. Oddly enough, as the British demonologist Eric Maple has remarked, from an examination of these sources one is left with a striking impression that the Satanic element manifests a steady *increase* in mankind's religious consciousness despite both popular belief and disbelief in his existence and activity in this world, Baudelaire notwithstanding.

1. A Rumor of Demons

Malicious spirits of one or another kind have figured in human beliefs about the world since the beginning of recorded history, perhaps in their earliest form as malevolent forces animating storms, floods, scorching winds, and other disasters. The ghosts of wicked men might also return to wreak havoc on the living, and both types of "demon" needed placating lest they ultimately destroy the people. Belief in such man-hating spirits is as near a universal anthropological axiom as one could want, and we can conclude that it must bear some corresponding value for archaic and primitive peoples. (The word *demon* comes directly from the Greek *daimon*, a tutelary spirit, intelligence, or *genius*—in Latin—that inspired men to good *or* evil, being beyond both itself.)

Contemporary and historical religious experience, no matter how mythopoeically, consistently reaffirms the importance of the role of the demonic in mankind's spiritual evolution. Despite the recent decision by the Catholic hierarchy to omit the ordination of exorcists from the preliminary steps to the priesthood, and notwithstanding the dearth of "official" exorcisms in most dioceses, unofficial religious exorcisms are possibly increasing in America, England, and Europe; certainly in Latin America, the West

Indies, and Africa they are still common. Among the
pentecostal sects and especially within the Jesus movement,
driving out evil spirits by the laying on of hands has become
almost common. And although attempts to exorcise the Justice
Department and the Pentagon may imply a redefinition of
demonic possession in the minds of younger Americans, it
obviously indicates their easy acceptance of the fact of
incarnate evil.

Pagan and Judeo-Christian attempts to retrench demonic
power in the world have sometimes resulted in tragedy,
however. Vicious persecutions of reputed witches and
sorcerers, such as that which convulsed Nigeria in 1951, are
but one consequence of an exaggerated emphasis on the power
of evil.

2. THE BLACK MASS

In addition to a truly demonic persecution of suspected
diabolists by rope and stake, the medieval belief in Satan's
influence produced a monumental work of horror: the Black
Mass. Among the early accounts of witches' Sabbaths, there
are only vague allusions to sacrilegious rites, although the
Waldensians and Luciferians had indeed mocked the Catholic
sacraments. But the logical conclusion stemming from the
belief that devotees of the devil parodied Christian ritual was
that witches and wizards would eventually be accused of doing
so as well. By the sixteenth century, ritual sacrilege had in fact
become one of the prime accusations against them; by the
curious dialectic of the self-fulfilling prophecy, what had
started as a suspicion in the minds of the Inquisitors became a
fact not only in popular fancy but, in rare cases, in actual
practice.

Accounts of Satanic masses are numerous, most of them
spurious. (A contemporary manifestation of the perennial
interest in such practices can be found in the form of a
semiauthentic, melodramatic re-creation of a Black Mass on

the album *Witchcraft*, recorded by a Chicago rock group who call themselves The Coven. The European and American success of Britain's Black Sabbath rock group provides similar evidence.) Although these versions were literary inventions to begin with, they may have been practiced at times, and there is reason to believe that they are still enacted. Basically a ritual inversion of the Catholic Mass, the Black Mass employs black candles, reversed symbols and gestures, and conscious profanation of the Host, which, in former times, was to have been consecrated by a defrocked priest or stolen from a Catholic church. Such perverted rites, when actually employed for magical purposes, blossomed into truly hideous proportions, including ritual murder and varieties of sexual pathology. Two apparently actual cases involving Satanic masses both originated in France, hundreds of years apart.

Gilles de Rais, a marshal of France, a baron, and prototype of the Bluebeard stories, was burned alive at Nantes in 1440 for the alleged murder of two hundred children from the district of Tiffauges who had been sacrificed at demonic masses. By the seventeenth century, sacrilegious masses were common enough to warrant the establishment of the notorious "burning court" of Louis XIV, which uncovered a most unusual situation implicating in ritual magic and murder the flower of France's nobility. One of Louis's mistresses, Madame de Montespan, rose to that envied position by the adroit use of magic, including amatory masses, by which she believed she could win and maintain the king's favor. For this purpose she had enlisted the aid of several clergymen and a remarkable fortuneteller, Catherine Deshayes, who also dabbled in extortion and abortion. La Voisin, as Catherine Deshayes was called, was investigated and arrested by the Paris police and on her conviction was burned alive in 1680. Hundreds of others were implicated in La Voisin's tawdry circle, of whom thirty-six were executed, five condemned to the galleys, and one hundred forty-seven imprisoned. It was only later that the role of Madame de Montespan was uncovered, but the lady was not for burning. Louis grew distant (not unnaturally), and eventually Madame retired from court, and her part in the grim business was not made public until after her death. In this case, too, the ritual magical perversion of the mass was the central act of the cult.

By the nineteenth century, the Black Mass had become, in popular thought, the chief stock in trade of Satanists and magicians. It was mentioned in the writings of Eliphas Levi and later in the extensive works of those marvelously wicked magicians MacGregor Mathers and Aleister Crowley, who waged a sort of unholy war for control of the occult Order of the Golden Dawn. Crowley, who prided himself on flamboyant anti-Christian antics, calling himself "The Great Beast," "666" and "The Wickedest Man Alive," is (erroneously) believed to have composed and celebrated Black Masses—an idea he probably nurtured. An international scoundrel, heroin addict, satyr, adventurer, novelist, and student of the occult, Crowley was expelled from France and Sicily and was merely tolerated in his native England. Victorian diabolism was not an exclusively British foible, however, whether in fancy or fact: in 1895, three years before the young Crowley joined the Order of the Golden Dawn, a Satanic chapel was discovered in Rome's Borghese Palace, a hidden room sumptuously decorated with infernal emblems and icons.

Throughout the present century, supported by half-fictitious tales from the pen of romantics such as the late "Rev." Montague Summers, newspaper accounts from practically every European and American nation report on occasion that a Black Mass or similar festival has been performed in a deserted church or cemetery, brownstone flat or garage. However, today's version of the Black Mass is a mild echo of the infanticidal orgies of Gilles de Rais and Madame de Montespan, and constitutes more a collegiate prank performed by curious amateurs.

3. FOR THE HELL OF IT

Satanic rites have never been restricted to Black Masses, of course, and to discount contemporary diabolism as a lot of harmless fun-and-sex games would be as fatuous as to hear in their reports the death knell of Christian civilization. Nevertheless, some sects have taken to animal sacrifice to express their "ancient" lineage, and human sacrifice is not out of the question. Several recent deaths reflect an undeniably morbid aspect of the occult revolution. Drugs, too, figure prominently in some cults, while sexual "abandon" may or may not be a feature. Some evidence indicates that sadomasochistic rites leading to serious injury are not rare among California cultists.

Voodoo is becoming increasingly noticeable in many southern and southwestern states, as well as in New York City, Los Angeles, Chicago, and of course, New Orleans, where the tradition is centuries old. Not long ago the Chicago *Daily News* featured a story about a Houston housewife who was driven to near hysteria when she discovered on her front porch a large jar containing a dog fetus and a frog, a charm that was to have made her sterile. Black magic is not uncommon in major cities or country hamlets in the waning of the twentieth century, and perhaps the most bizarre contemporary incidents of cultic Satanism occurred in Hollywood and a small New Jersey town.

As the court proceedings in the Tate–LaBianca murder cases continued for more than a year in 1970 and 1971, many Americans were shocked and frightened by the extent of the diabolical influences characteristic of the Manson Family. The grim combination of sex, drugs, witchcraft, and Satanism that led to the horrible slaughter of seven persons in a ritual sacrifice seems indeed to belong in some sleazy film. The mood of revulsion and terror following the Manson slayings was not diminished, to say the least, when Dr. Victor Ohta and his family were murdered less than a year later by a young occultist with ecological paranoia.

That Hollywood was the scene of the Manson slayings may have mitigated the horror many Americans felt as news of the event burst from their television sets and newspapers, for Southern California is accepted by many as a new Gomorrah. But the tragic ritual slaying of a teen-age Vineland, New Jersey, Satanist had no such cushion to muffle its fearful report. Believing that he would return at the head of a legion of devils, Patrick Newell was pushed to his death by two friends after performing a Satanic ritual. The cult of Satan had spread to as many as seventy young Vinelanders before the killing, according to one report. A month later, an elderly man was stabbed to death in Miami by a twenty-two-year-old Satanist who believed that she had seen the devil in person. Further episodes of grim diabolism can be found in newspapers and magazines, a possible factor in the faddish popularity of pathological occultism. Such reports have, as well, bolstered the ranks of fundamentalist preachers inveighing against the rise in Satanism throughout the land.

In May of 1972, the upper-middle-class surburban community of Waukegan, a few miles north of Chicago, was shaken by lurid accounts of diabolical rites being performed by groups of drug-drenched teen-agers and adults. These nighttime revels, often reported to be enacted in local cemeteries, included Satanic invocations, animal torture, and even human sacrifice. The sacrificial victims were said by frightened teen-agers to be babies born out of wedlock, offered by their mothers to the Satanic cult.

The local police were incredulous at first, but as reports in the Waukegan *News-Sun* continued, an official investigation was launched. Other than the stories told by the teen-agers, who wanted out of the cult but were fearful of reprisals, little evidence turned up. The bodies were either carefully buried or burned, and no incriminating clues were left by the cautious Satanists. Despite the lack of material evidence, and even given the fact that the participants were admittedly heavy drug users, many citizens of the area fully believed every detail. As in the case of the Vineland, New Jersey, Satanists, the story seems to have culminated primarily in the increasing efforts of several ministers intent on exorcising the demons from the teen-agers and inveighing against the godlessness of modern society, which lies at the bottom of the episode.

Odd though such tales sound to the liberal, sophisticated citizens of America, there is enough circumstantial evidence, and occasionally the discovery of mass graves of animal bones, to suggest that the Manson Family was not a singular phenomenon. Apparently, well-organized Satanic sects do exist throughout America, and some, at least, are vicious and even homicidal. How typical such examples are is perhaps impossible to determine; it is nonetheless true that the devil is getting attention formerly given only to movie stars and Mafia chieftains. The significance of contemporary diabolism has another side, however, and a far different one in its antecedents and consequences for contemporary society.

4. SATAN TODAY: THE DEVIL IS DEAD

Compared to the exotic misdeeds of the criminal and the deranged, Anton La Vey's Church of Satan, despite the rhetorical flourishes behind the success of *The Satanic Bible*, La Vey's magnum opus, seems somewhat tame. Despite the Black Mass and other scary mumbo jumbo in the "missal" section of his *Bible*, the La Veyan liturgy is comparatively innocuous. Nevertheless, the "Church" is a real religion; La Vey and his wife, Diana, spend a good part of their time directing Satanic weddings, funerals, and Black Masses, surrounded by enough archaic symbols, vestments, and artifacts to satisfy the longings of the most *outré* antiquarian Catholic—aspergilla, bells, candles, incense, chants, and even swords. Although La Vey admits to practicing magic and despite his wholesale borrowings from witchcraft ceremonial, most contemporary witches stay well away from the Church of

Satan. To them La Vey's magic is more a gimmick, a device to stimulate the release of sexual energy and whatever else wants releasing in the La Veyan way—anger, lust, revenge, greed, pride, etc.—than a form of worship. In all Dr. Anton La Vey seems a bit more reminiscent of John Wellington Wells, Gilbert and Sullivan's sorcerer, than of Cagliostro or Crowley. And for good reason; as Howard Levy of Chicago, La Vey, before he became the Exarch of Hell, had a career that included lion taming, palm reading, and calliope playing for the Clyde Beatty circus. He was also a police photographer and nightclub entertainer. It is not without significance that among those to whom *The Satanic Bible* is dedicated appears the name of Phineas Taylor Barnum.

Far removed from La Vey's exotically devilish parlor games is the Satanic Process Church of the Final Judgment. Its members' black cloaks, long hair, beards, and especially their inclusion of Satan and Lucifer along with Jehovah as the "three gods of the universe" can easily give the impression that this youthful religious community enrolls hippie Satanists in the grand tradition of Crowley and La Vey. On the contrary, the Processeans are thoroughly countercultural in their religious and communitarian life style, but they can be called occult in only a very technical sense: like contemporary witches, and quite unlike La Vey, they actively shun the public limelight. There is no trace of witchcraft among them, however, and their ritual bears no resemblance to a Black Mass (or any other known ritual). In fact, behind the liturgical expression of their world view there is a strong psychological interpretation of the forces at work in the universe rather than a reliance on demons or the mythical anthropomorphism typical of La Vey's explanations of the role of Satan. Yet, like La Vey, they do not seem to believe in hell or a personal, individual devil. Any link with the sadistic satanism of Charles Manson, as was alleged in Ed Sanders's *The Family*, has been shown in court to be nonexistent. The Process Church has nothing in common with "typical" diabolism.

One of the more fascinating aspects of the Process creed merits a brief comment: the assertion that the end of the world is near. While not original among religiously oriented countercultures, Process eschatology is rather unlike the preachments of fundamentalists of the variety of Seventh-Day Adventists as well as the Children of God. Processeans maintain that the world has been geared for self-destruction by human engineering. To be sure, there is a good chance that someone may push the ultimate button one day soon, whether by conscious design, madness, or stupidity—the possibility of a nuclear "accident" has been well elaborated by novelists and film-makers. Too, contemporary man has recently learned that Armageddon is in the very air he breathes and the chemicals accumulating in his body tissues and perhaps especially in the overpopulating of the planet, with its near-inevitable consequences of famine and epidemic. A sense of doom is not, therefore, novel today, but it is refreshing to find it so honestly recognized among religious persons rather than cloaked in pre-Christian mythologies and Pauline metaphors. In their attitude toward the end, however, the Processeans resemble the pentecostal-fundamentalist Jesus sects: they anticipate it with glad hearts, believing that in the coming transformation of human consciousness there will occur the destruction of inner and outer repression and the triumphant liberation of love.

Organizationally, the Process Church is an international movement. Beginning in London in 1963, the original Processeans migrated to Mexico, then to the United States. The leaders are still British, but the composition of the chapters is ethnically eclectic. There is little fluidity in the structure of the church, however; a definite hierarchical order exists, and discipline is manifest. Still, the spirit of the group is anything but rigid and authoritarian. The obvious charisma of the leadership is perhaps the reason; they stand out as gifted, articulate, and self-confident exponents of a new way of life increasingly attractive to many young people.

Strongly evangelistic, and in principle opposed to the established churches—a rejection that finds expression in the clothes, liturgy, theology, and publications of the group—the Process Church is not antagonistic to Christianity. Antivivisectionist, antinarcotic, apparently pacifist, the church is based on a belief in one God, the supreme, incomprehensible Universal Being. His three "avatars"—Satan, Lucifer, and Jehovah—represent ways in which mankind has experienced His presence both historically and personally; these three are personality factors in each of us, as well as forces in the cosmos. In Christ the three are united again, and love is the binding force overpowering the hate, retribution, and punishment also at work in the world. In their complicated theology, rich in symbol and psychological insights, the Processeans take us again to the Gnostic Marcionites of the apostolic era, much as pentecostalism has sought to recapture the pristine fervor of the infant church.

5. The Devil's Advocates Today

Anthropological and mythological approaches, such as Eric Maple's *The Domain of Devils*, Paul Carus's classic *The History of the Devil and the Idea of Evil*, Dennis Wheatley's unreliable *The Devil and All His Works*, are even less inclined to grant extramental reality to the demons of popular belief and folklore. Traditional views of a semiincarnate evil spirit of surpassing intellect and power are not absent from the contemporary situation, however. The recent neoprimitive movement among the young—the Jesus freaks, the Children of God, pentecostalists, and other fundamentalists—seems content with the familiar concept, albeit less folksy and more terrifying. J.R.R. Tolkien's *Lord of the Rings* thoroughly remythologized Lucifer for perhaps millions of new readers, while Satan rules malevolent and fierce in popular horror fiction and fantasy novels from the pens of Ray Bradbury, H.P. Lovecraft, August Derleth, and others. Dr. Arthur C.

Clarke gleefully recast Satan as a misunderstood extraterrestrial of benevolent disposition in his superb fable *Childhood's End*. As in the case of Ira Levin's morbid *Rosemary's Baby*, William Peter Blatty's exciting detective-horror-religious novel *The Exorcist*, which unblinkingly accepts the view of diabolic possession and demonic siege that characterized Catholic thought in the first half of this century, remained for months at the top of the best-seller list in 1971. If Blatty's theological and psychological assessment is passé, he nevertheless has been able to exploit the still-viable popular idea of personified evil in creating a highly readable and salable melodrama. The widespread enthusiasm for *The Exorcist* testifies to the fact that despite liberal theologians' attempts to purge Christianity of the presence of the devil, they have at best been only partially successful. Today's surprisingly resistant notion of Satan is an important facet of contemporary religious consciousness, which demands a fuller investigation.

Myths of eternal progress notwithstanding, the twentieth century is morally not superior to the Dark Ages and Renaissance and perhaps inferior to the medieval ideal. It is not surprising that as early as 1968 Theodore Roszak had sniffed the drift toward occultism among the young, oppressed and weary of the barbarism of politics, the autocracy of technology, and the debility of organized religion. In a year of assassinations and riots, the American melting pot must have indeed resembled a witches' caldron, a weird brew of flowers, incense, pot, tear gas, rhetoric, bayonets, and blood. Enter: Hell's Angels, Anton La Vey, the Process Church, and the occult revolution.

Satan in the Old Testament

Auguste Valensin, S.J.

It is hard to believe in Christ the Redeemer without at the same time believing in his antagonist, the devil. We try to get around the difficulty, nonetheless. Cannot this inconvenient character be relegated to the category of the theatrical mask? Semitic poetry and the popular imagination have a way of personifying the forces of nature, psychic forces included—the whole thing is simply a dramatic conceit. . . . What, we ask, is the truth behind the images? Jesus and the apostles borrowed these literary properties from the Old Testament, possibly even from the Apocrypha or the Gnosis. They had to speak the language their compatriots were used to. We must translate it into the terms of today; it would be treachery to our Master to present his thought to the modern mind in language that has fallen into disuse.

The aim of this essay is to throw some light on the character of this language. Jesus used the religious vocabulary of his people, which has come down to us in the Bible: a quick survey of the Old Testament will make it easier for us to understand the words and images in which he spoke.

THE BEAST

The Beasts in the Desert

The proud citadel of sin is reduced to waste land:

"And that Babylon, glorious among kingdoms, the famous pride of the Chaldeans, shall be even as the Lord destroyed Sodom and Gomorrah. It shall no more be inhabited for ever, and it shall not be founded unto generation and generation: neither shall the Arabian pitch his tents there, nor shall shepherds rest there. But wild beasts shall rest there, and their houses shall be filled with serpents, and ostriches shall dwell there, and the hairy ones shall dance there: And owls shall answer one another there, in the houses thereof, and sirens in the temples of pleasures" (Isa. 13:19–22).

We come on this kind of description everywhere in the Prophets. Isaias (34:11) and Sophonias (2:14) both saw similar beasts prowling in the ruins of Nineveh. Desolate Babylon is the home of more of them (Isa. 13:21, 22.; Jer. 50:39). Later on in Edom—type of the nations banded against Israel—we find dozens of them. Dogs and wildcats, screech owls and crows and other creatures harder to identify, hold a demonic Sabbath in the land of Edom, which, deserted and burned down, has gone back to the primeval chaos (Isa. 34).

How are we to interpret this horde of horrors? Crows and vultures are in place on a field of carnage. The jackal and the ostrich, renowned for the mournfulness of their cries, give the idea of keening (Mic. 1:8; Job 30:29). Many of the animals are picked from the list of impure or forbidden beasts, those that are loathsome to Yahweh (Lev. 11:14–18; Deut. 14:13–17). The picture is one of sadness and desolation, filth and sin.

It is more surprising to find Lilith and the satyrs. Lilith was the name of a famous Babylonian female demon. The satyrs (*seïrîm,* "hairy ones," goats) are well translated *devils* in the Vulgate; we know, besides, that people offered them idolatrous sacrifices (Lev. 17:7). This repulsive, death-dealing crew—to which popular imagination adds yet more and viler monsters—suggests a saraband of devils, dancing in the ruins, filling the night with weeping and gnashing of teeth.

The reason is that the desert is the home of sin. Assisting at the purification of Jerusalem restored, Zacharias saw Impiety being carried off to Babylon, where a throne was built for it. In the ritual of the Levites, it is to the desert that they chase the scapegoat and the sparrow covered with the lepers' filth (Lev. 16:10–21; 14:7). The animals of the desert, both real and fabulous, are in the Bible the symbols of sin, dismal and deformed.

The Ravages of Disease

Another class of demons attacks the flesh of man. These beasts are invisible, but the damage they do is tangible. They are in need of bodies to infect.

The Babylonian magic figurines show us what the ancient East supposed diseases to look like. An example is Pazuzu, the southwest wind, which carries malaria: on top of a naked, exaggeratedly thin body is a monstrous head with goat's horns on the forehead. Four wings and the claws of a beast of prey indicate the speed with which it dives down on its victim, plunging sharp nails into his flesh. "I am Pazuzu, son of Hanpa," says the inscription, "king of the evil spirits of the air. I swoop with violence from the mountains, spreading fever as I go." The elements of the demon fauna seen on the talisman plaques are crabs and scorpions, lions and panthers, reptiles and beasts of prey.

The Bible uses analogous language. The author of the ninetieth psalm urges the Israelite to trust in the protection of the Most High; if he does he will survive the most horrifying epidemics: "thou shalt not be afraid of the terror of the night.

Of the arrow that flieth in the day, of the business [plague] that walketh about in the dark: of invasion, or of the noon-day devil [disease]'' (Ps. 90:5-6).

The old Latin version said "the noon-day devil." In this connection Father Calès says: "One might regard the plague *(débér)* that walks by night and the contagion *(qétéb)* that kills at midday as two demons, one of the night, the other of the day, who according to the popular beliefs of the ancient East, were responsible for epidemic diseases." The believer has nothing to fear from these maleficent beings. With angels to guard him he can spurn the asp and the basilisk, the lion and the dragon. These are the same beasts that were represented on the amulets of Babylon.

In Israel magic is forbidden. All scourges come from the hand of God. We see them in his bodyguard when he comes to judge the earth (Hab. 3:5). They are tools for the carrying out of his tremendous plans: "They shall be consumed with famine and birds shall devour them with a most bitter bite: I will send the teeth of beasts upon them, with the fury of creatures that trail upon the ground, and of serpents. I will heap evils upon them and will spend my arrows among them" (Deut. 32:23-24).

Later theology sings the praises of these instruments of divine justice: "Fire, hail, famine and death, all these were created for vengeance. The teeth of beasts, the scorpions, and serpents, and the sword taking vengeance upon the ungodly unto destruction. In his commandments they shall feast, and they shall be ready upon earth when need is, and when their time is come they shall not transgress his word" (Sirach 39:35-37).

Are these terrifying creatures mere personifications or are they really evil demons? That is a question we must come back to later, only pausing here to point out that in the psalter the distressed man pleading for justice denounces his all-too-concrete persecutors under the form of diabolical beasts: "Their madness is according to the likeness of a serpent: like the deaf asp that stoppeth her ears. . . . God shall break in pieces their teeth in their mouth: the Lord shall break the grinders of the lions'' (Ps. 57:5, 7).

The Phantom of Death

More fearful even than these poison-toothed diseases is their father, Death, the king of all horrors. The author of the Book of Job gives a picture of the agony of the ungodly man: "Fears shall terrify him on every side, and shall entangle his feet. Let his strength be wasted with famine, and let hunger invade his ribs. Let it devour the beauty of his skin, let the first-born death consume his arms. Let his confidence be rooted out of his tabernacle and let destruction tread upon him like a king" (Job 18:11–14).

"This personage," says Msgr. Weber, "calls to mind the god of the mythological underworld. . . . The poet can indulge in these allusions without endangering the reader's faith.'' This is no more than a personification as in the lament of the weeping women: "death is come up through our windows, it is entered into our houses . . ." (Jer. 9:21).

Sheol (Hades, hell), the kingdom of Death, the haunt of the dead, is also spoken of as a person. All we see of him is an insatiable gullet: "Therefore hath hell enlarged her soul, and opened her mouth without any bounds" (Isa. 5:14). He swallows people up, he engulfs them. He it was who ate Dathan, Core, and Abiron alive; he swallowed the army of Pharaoh when the earth opened beneath it (Num. 16:30–4; Exod. 15:12).

The Abyss *(tehom)*, the liquid element underneath and all around the earth, is as greedy a monster as Sheol and has a lot in common with him. He, too, is one of the Powers of Death—the victim cries to God in his distress: "Draw me out of the mire, that I may not stick fast: deliver me from them that hate me, and out of the deep waters. Let not the tempest of waters drown me, nor the deep swallow me up: and let not the pit shut her mouth upon me" (Ps. 68:15–16).

The gulf and the gaping well are symbols of Sheol. Often Sheol and the Abyss turn up side by side: "The sorrows of death surrounded me: and the torments of iniquity [Calès: Belial] troubled me. The sorrows of hell [Calès: Sheol] encompassed me and the snares of death prevented me" (Ps. 17:15-16).

Sheol under the ground is like the belly of a vast octopus with waterfalls for tentacles: "they sunk as lead in the mighty waters. . . . Thou stretchedst forth thy hand, and the earth swallowed them" (Exod. 15:10, 12).

These tentacles are so strong that they can snatch down a boat from the high rim of the rock of Tyre: "I . . . shall bring the deep upon thee, and many waters shall cover thee. . . . I shall bring thee down with those that descend into the pit" (Ezech. 26:19–20).

Worse still, there was so much water in the Abyss that it spread all over the earth and the darkness gathered round it like a cloak (Gen. 1:2; Ps. 103:6).

Whatever name we give this greedy monster—Death, Sheol, the Abyss, Abaddon (perdition), Belial (nothing, nirvana) or anything else—the point is, what, if any, is his connection with the demonic beings we have been speaking about?

The diseases, naturally enough, are the servants of Death; the text from Job cited earlier showed the King of Horrors cheering on his pack. In Osee plague *(débêr)* and contagious fever *(qétéb)* are called Death's weapons. Death is the hub of the evil powers, uniting them to make an organized empire. One can treat with it as with a person; the impious make bargains with Death and hell (Isa. 28:15, 18; Wisd. 1:16)—who are as greedy as any person could be to batten on the unfortunate (Hab. 1:13; 2:5; Prov. 1:12).

Thus the power of the nether regions takes on a moral and religious character: it stands out against God. Creative activity struggles with the Abyss. One word is enough to rout it—one utterance from Yahweh reduces the adversary to silence. The verb *gaar* (like its Greek equivalent—*epitimân*) has the special meaning of a shout of battle, of triumph over the powers of evil. This shout puts to flight the Abyss and the towering waters, as well as the enemy hordes (Isa. 17:13; 50:2). It repels Satan himself: "The Lord rebuke you" (Zach. 3:2). (In the New Testament, Jesus uses this word to command the sea, the demons, and St. Peter when He calls him Satan [Mark 1:25; 4:39; 8:33; 9:24].) Elsewhere we find the battle described in greater detail:

"There went up a smoke in his wrath: and a fire flamed from his face: coals were kindled by it. He bowed the heavens, and came down: and darkness was under his feet. And he ascended upon the cherubim, and he flew upon the wings of the winds. And he made darkness his cover, his pavilion round about him: dark waters in the clouds of the air. At the brightness that was before him the clouds passed, hail and coals of fire. And he sent forth his arrows, and he scattered them: he multiplied lightning, and troubled them. Then the fountains of waters appeared, and the foundations of the world were discovered: At thy rebuke, O Lord, at the spirit of thy wrath" (Ps. 17:9–16).

One is reminded at once of the war between Marduk and Tiamat. In point of fact there is no mention of Tiamat in the Bible, and the philological connection with *tehom* is not strong enough to make a literary link with the Babylonian myth. Other monsters of the liquid element have the names Rahab and Leviathan—these names, also found at Ras-Shamra, suggest a Canaanite or Phoenician origin.

These fabulous dragons represented the great empires. Speaking of the exodus from Egypt, Isaias (51) recalls the old victory of Yahweh over Rahab. The allusion may be to the sea that divided to let the Israelites through, but Lower Egypt itself, with all its marshes and canals, is a power of the sea: the crocodiles on the Nile were to furnish Job with a portrait of the Leviathan, and in poetry Rahab is a name for Egypt (Ps. 86). In other places we find the dragon of Bel, which swallowed up the people of Israel, symbolizing Nabuchodonosor himself (Jer. 51:34, 44; cf. Jon. 2).

These images go back a long way. Isaias (28:15, 18) called the alliance which the counselors of Ezechias brought about with Egypt a league with Death, a covenant with hell. He described the Assyrian invasion as a vast flood of water (8:7; 28:15, 18; cf. Ps. 45).

Death, the Abyss, Nothingness: these are the enemies of God and His people. Yet they, too, are in the Creator's hands. It was God Himself who enveloped the earth in the Abyss, who swaddled the sea in darkness on the day of its birth (Job 38:8ff.; Ps. 103:6). He created the Leviathan as a toy for his children (Ps. 103:26; Job 40:24). God sends those whom he wishes down into the belly of Sheol and takes them back when he chooses (Jon. 2; Ps. 87; I Kings 2:6), just as he sent his people down into Egypt and took them out again on the day of salvation.

The Demoniacal Beasts

What order of reality do these beasts belong to? The dolefully howling jackal, the scorpion that strikes in the dark, the sea with its perils and monsters, are very real creatures indeed. Are their repulsive faces masks that hide invisible beings, demons of impurity, disease, and death? What light do the sacred writings throw on this?

Toward the second century, when the Jews were translating their sacred books into Greek, they used the word *daimonia*, demonic beings, for idols and pagan gods and also for several of the fantastic animals named above.

Ought we to conclude from this that Death and Pestilence and Sin had a kind of separate existence in the eyes of the Jews? Even if not actual personalities endowed with a will for evil, are they maleficent energies, comparable with animals whose movements are dictated by instinct? A man in the clutches of these beasts of prey falls ill or dead or into sin, but it is possible to chase the vile things far from the homes of men, out into the desert, down into Sheol.

To the modern mind, sin and sickness and death have no

existence apart from the sinner, the sick man, the corpse. The ancient East had a different way of looking at things. There is no doubt, for example, that for Babylon, Pazuzu, Labartu, the Seven Evil Ones, and the other deathly monsters were real—the magic texts can be interpreted no other way. Was it the same in Jerusalem?

Superstitious practices were mixed in with the religion of the people; the Law and the Prophets witness to that. The Israelites were prone to share the popular belief in the forces of evil, but they cannot have had very clear ideas as to their nature. But what of the pure religion which the Biblical texts reflect, the religion that is the only mouthpiece of revelation—did it contrive to find a place for them in its pattern? Magic and idolatry alike were forbidden. Monotheism precluded the existence of anything not created by God, and all the works of God are good. The Book of Wisdom says explicitly: "God made not death, neither hath he pleasure in the destruction of the living. For he created all things that they might be: and he made the nations of the world for health: and there is no poison of destruction in them, nor kingdom of hell upon the earth" (1:13–14). It is a faithful echo of the first chapter of Genesis.

Then are Death and his offspring the diseases to be relegated to the dream world of symbolic language? The texts forbid us to come to any such definite conclusion. Death is only a personification; the Bible, anxious to avoid dualism, refrains from making the power of evil into the antithesis of God. When we come to the mythical monsters Rahab and Leviathan, hesitation has already begun to set in. Fr. Lagrange thought that "these were certainly both real and terrible in the sacred writers' eyes. They struggled with God in the beginning—a prefiguring of the fallen angels' battle." As for fever and the other maleficent beings, the official religion did not have to combat them with the same energy. They were no great danger, as long as men did not fight them with magic but prayed to God instead, beating their breasts and crying for mercy. Yet under the animal hides, one increasingly tends to discover no blind instinctive power but a will, good or evil, a spirit, an angel.

THE ANGEL

The Powers of Heaven

Passing now to the world of angels, we meet again vast natural forces, but instead of chthonian and abysmal powers we find the powers of heaven.

On the day of creation "The morning stars praised me to gether, and all the sons of God made a joyful meolody" (Job 38:7).

The heavenly army fought for Israel against Jericho (Josue 5:14) and against Sisara: "War from heaven was made against them, the stars remaining in their order and courses fought against Sisara" (Judges 5:20).

When Yahweh appears as a warrior to confound his enemies or save his loyal subjects, he has around him all the armies of heaven (Ps. 17, quoted earlier). So he appeared on Sinai (Exod. 19:16–20) and at the going out of Egypt (Ps. 76:17ff.)—even earlier, at the Creation, we read: "Who makest the clouds thy chariot: who walkest upon the wings of the winds. Who makest thy angels spirits: and thy ministers a burning fire" (Ps. 103:3–4).

Cherubim and whirling flame stand guard at the entrance of the garden of God (Gen. 3:24) and in his palaces the heavenly powers chorus his praises (Ps. 148).

These powers are essentially good, even when God uses them for the destruction of his enemies. Are they capable of becoming evil? There are several allusions in Job to the defects that God finds even in the stars, even in his angels (Job 4:18; 15:15; 25:5). These do not necessarily refer to the fall of the angels: the formula is a general one—there is imperfection inherent in every created thing, even creatures who dwell in heaven. In the Book of Isaias (14:12–14) the fall of the king of Babylon is pictured as the fall of a star (Lucifer); there are signs of literary poaching here, from the fall of Enlil. Similarly the destruction of the city is described as being like the collapse of Bel (Marduk) and Nabo (Isa. 46:1). Nowhere in the Old Testament do we find any clear revelation about the fall of an angel.

The heavenly powers are capable of bringing about the fall of men. Spellbound by their beauty, men take these creatures for gods (Wisd. 13:3). This is an age-old temptation. Babylon and Canaan worshiped the stars. Even when they are hard masters for men, there is no perversion, strictly speaking, of the celestial beings themselves (Deut. 4:9; Jer. 16:11–12). The fault is entirely with the men who make them into idols and it is they who must take the consequences.

The Spirits

When God wished Achab to be deceived, a spirit broke from the ranks of the army of heaven and offered to turn into a lying spirit in the mouth of the prophets (3 Kings 22:22): the angels of God are instruments that carry out His will.

He sent angels of destruction against Sodom (Gen. 19:13), against the Egyptians (Exod. 12:23; Ps. 57:49), against Sennacherib (Isa. 37:36) and even against His own people (2 Kings 24:16ff.). Later the Book of Wisdom gives the name Destroyer to the plague that attacked the disobedient Jews in the desert (18:25). Possibly the name Asmodeus comes from the Aramaic *achmed*, to exterminate. But a mission of revenge does not necessarily suppose an evil agent—the Word of God Himself might take it over (Wisd. 18:15).

The spirits of temptation are more surprising: the spirit of jealousy (Num. 5:14), of ill will (1 Kings 18:10), of discord (Judges 9:23), of lying (3 Kings 22:22), of fornication (Osee 4:12; 5:4).

Yet it is as envoys of God that they attack Saul, Abimelech and the Sichemites, as well as the prophets of Achab. All this was fully accepted in ancient times—we must remember that David was not startled when the ill will of Saul was stirred up against him by Yahweh himself (1 Kings 26:19): he, too, after all, was urged on by the anger of God to commit sin, in ordering the census of the people (2 Kings 24:1).

Satan

When, a long time later, in the fourth century, the chronicler again took up the history of David's reign, he substituted Satan for the anger of God as the force that impelled the king to make a census of his people (1 Par. 21:1). Was this just a theological scruple, or was he being more accurate?

What do we know of this personage Satan? His name is full of meaning. The etymology of the Hebrew word *satan* (and of its synonym *satam*) is doubtful, but its sense is unmistakable. The verb means "to obstruct," like the angel of Yahweh that stood in Balaam's way and foiled his wicked intentions (Num. 22:22–32). This hostility may show itself in warfare; we find it more often in the tribunal, where the *satan* is the accuser, the calumniator, the *diabolos* (Ps. 108; cf. Apoc. 12:10–12).

There are human Satans, like the princes, one Edomite, the other Aramaic, whom God raised up against Solomon after he had let himself be seduced by foreign women (3 Kings 11).

The Bible has two other references to Satans who are angels. The text of Zacharias gives the precise date. On the 24th chevat, in the second year of Darius—the middle of February 520 B.C.—Zacharias had a vision in the night. Jesus (the high priest) appeared, standing before the angel of Yahweh like a man on trial in mourning garments; on his right, Satan is counsel for the prosecution. The Lord rebuke you!—the shout of Yahweh rings out against Satan. Jesus is vindicated, and the angel makes him take back the insignia of his priesthood (Zach. 3:1-5). Here Satan is the accuser, trying to bring about the damnation of the man God wants to save.

Most people are familiar with the other passage, the prologue to the Book of Job (1ff.). The date is disputed—it was probably some time in the fifth century. Yahweh's consultation with the children of God is like the council he held with the army of heaven in the days of Achab. Satan is the accuser. His evil intent is obvious from the outset. His job is to find out the truth. This, no doubt, he has been told to do by God, but the idea of goodness vexes him; he does not believe in it; he does not want to believe in it. If Job remains loyal, it will be from motives of self-interest: Satan throws God the challenge. He wants to put Job—and therefore God—in the wrong.

Yahweh gives him a free hand and we know the result for poor Job. From being the malevolent accuser, Satan turns tempter. All the desert demons and the diseases are at his beck and call; he makes use even of Job's wife, but he cannot manage to extract the blasphemy that would put Job at his mercy and deliver him up to death.

Satan's purposes are revolt against God and the perdition of men. But his power has its limits. He needs God's permission to unleash the scourges of the desert and a further permission to set on the pack of diseases. There is no mention of a divine permit to make Job's wife obey him—that is the mystery of human liberty and its weakness. This mystery has its strong side, too. Satan cannot overcome a freedom that submits itself to God not through self-interest but because God is God.

THE ANGEL AND THE BEAST

The Satan of the Old Testament is an enigmatic character. He is the black sheep in the family of God, always contrary—one might say Judas among the twelve. He has not yet revealed himself as the head of the powers of evil, the god of this world standing up to the King of Heaven. But already he is hand in glove with all the evil forces; he seeks them in the depths of the desert, he knows how to find them in a woman's heart. He is not the king of horrors, the personification of death, but he is allied to death and spreads it on every side.

He it is that brought death into the world, says Wisdom, and the idea goes back to Genesis. The name Satan was not used then, but a serpent, a creature of God, the symbol of skill and prudence, slithered between the trees of Paradise, put its spell on the woman and insinuated its poison into her—and sent humanity hurtling down to death. God never cursed sinful man but the serpent is under a curse that can never be repealed.

All through the Old Testament the image of the serpent goes on being associated with temptation—and woman and the fruit of the vine are his willing tools: "Look not upon the wine when it is yellow, when the color thereof shineth in the glass: it goeth in pleasantly. But in the end it will bite like a snake, and will spread abroad poison like a basilisk. Thy eyes shall behold strange women, and thy heart shall utter perverse things. And thou shalt be as one sleeping in the midst of the sea, and as a pilot fast asleep, when the stern is lost" (Prov. 23:31–34).

What a contrast with the golden age of messianic peace, when the Son of Jesse will inaugurate the reign of a justice and wisdom, relying not on the judgment of the senses but on the spirit of Yahweh alone; when the lion and bear will graze next to the sheep and the cow, when the woman's child can put its hand in an asp hole and the baby at the breast play safely with the serpent's young (Isa. 11:1–8).

The serpent is an image used by prophets and wise men. Satan is real. A poisonous and shifty serpent, he works for the reign of death upon earth. For this end he mobilizes the forces of nature and the men who betray themselves to him. God lets him go as far as His wisdom thinks fit. He uses the wickedness of Satan in the same way as He uses the wickedness of men:

"You thought evil against me: but God turned it into good, that he might exalt me, as at present you see, and might save many people" (Gen. 50:20).

THE POWER OF EVIL

The outward forms given to the powers of evil in the Old Testament are not unlike the spontaneous products of the human imagination. The nightmares of sleepless nights, the wanderings of delirium, and the fear of death all give animal shape to the occult forces over which man knows himself to have no control. Psychology and comparative folklore also have something to say on the matter.

The Word of God uses human terms to reveal to man the language that is His own. The forces of death are foul beasts, the phantoms of fevered dreams. The Creator Himself battles with these monsters—what does this mean?

Theology says that God created *out of* nothing—then immediately this *out of* is corrected. The Old Testament says rather that God created *against* nothing, though here again we must not be tied down to the limitations of a phrase. The formula is rich in teaching. Sin thrusts the earth back into the depths of the Abyss, reduces it to the condition of wilderness, of chaos (Isa. 6:11; Jer. 4:22–26), from which the act of creation had rescued it.

That is because every creature is willed by God: *Dixit et facta sunt*—but the free creature has been given the power to attain the fullness of its own reality by cooperating with the action on itself of the will of God: "God made man from the beginning, and left him in the hand of his own counsel. He added his commandments and precepts. If thou wilt keep the commandments and perform acceptable fidelity for ever, they shall preserve thee. He hath set water and fire before thee: stretch forth thy hand to which thou wilt. Before man is life and death, good and evil, that which he shall choose shall be given him" (Ecclus. 15:14–18).

The divine will always fulfills its aim; a created will can fall short if it is out of line with the design of the Creator. It is sin that prevents the development of man and stops him from achieving his end—part of him is still immersed in nothingness and he falls into the toils of death. Nothingness and death have no positive value; what exists is an incomplete creature, a broken vase, a withered trunk, a building in ruins. God created the world in opposition to nothingness; the free creature must create himself in opposition to sin.

The demonic animals are only images. But there are men ensnared by sin, possessed by malice, poisoned by envy against the brothers who have done better than they have. There are mobs more monstrous than Rahab, human tides hurled against the people of God by dragons as rabid as Nabuchodonosor and Pharaoh. There are even spirits never encumbered with our clay, who were created for the light and have refused it, and who long to drag us into their own darkness. These are the real diabolical powers.

In the face of these powers of evil the Old Testament leaves us to the strength of our free will, with the example of Job and the prayer of the Psalms to aid us. In the Old Testament, indeed, Satan is of very little importance; his empire has not yet been revealed. It is in the New Testament that he is shown up as the chief of the coalition of evil forces—and when he is unmasked he is seen to be defeated.

Demoniacs in the Gospel

F. M. Catherinet

A remarkable episode in Christ's struggle against Satan is set before us in the synoptic Gospels: the deliverance of individuals possessed by the devil. We shall consider in turn (1) the facts, (2) the problems they raise, and (3) the principles proposed by theology for their solution.

1. THE FACTS

A preliminary series of texts affirms, in a general way, that the possessed were restored to normal health by Jesus. These possessed are distinguished from the merely sick, but first texts give us no detailed description either of the trouble afflicting the patients or of the means employed to free them from it.

Jesus "was preaching in Galilee and casting out devils" (Mark 1:39). Before the Sermon on the Mount "a very great multitude of people . . . came to hear him and to be healed of their diseases. And they that were troubled with unclean spirits were cured" (Luke 6:18); for "they presented to him all sick people that were taken with divers diseases and torments, and such as were possessed by devils, and lunatics, and those that had the palsy, and he cured them" (Matt. 4:24).

When the emissaries of John the Baptist came to ask Jesus whether he was really the Messiah, before replying, "he cured many of their diseases and hurts and evil spirits, and to many that were blind he gave sight" (Luke 7:21).

During his public life Jesus was commonly accompanied by the Twelve and by "certain women who had been healed of evil spirits and infirmities," among whom were "Mary who is called Magdalen, out of whom seven devils were gone forth" (Luke 8:2; cf. Mark 16:9).

When Jesus sent the Twelve to preach the Kingdom of God in Galilee, he charged them to "heal the sick, raise the dead, cleanse the lepers, cast out devils" (Matt. 10:8), thus giving them "power and authority over all devils and to cure diseases" (Luke 9:1; cf. Mark 6:7). In the course of this or another such mission John "saw a certain man casting out devils in thy name" (i.e., in Jesus's name) and, taking offense at this, forbade him "because he followeth not with us." The Master disapproved of this rather narrow-minded zeal, but did not deny the fact of the expulsion of the devils: "Forbid him not; for there is no man that doth a miracle in my name and can soon speak ill of me" (Luke 9:49 and Mark 9:38).

The seventy-two disciples received a mission similar to that of the Twelve, to preach the coming of the Kingdom of God in Galilee and Judea. They "returned with joy, saying: Lord, the devils also are subject to us in thy name." And He approved of them, saying: "I saw Satan like lightning falling from heaven. Behold I have given you power to tread upon serpents and scorpions, and upon all the power of the enemy, and nothing shall hurt you. But yet rejoice not in this that spirits are subject unto you: but rejoice in this, that your names are written in heaven" (Luke 10:17–20).

When the Pharisees let Him know of Herod's threats, he replied: "Go and tell that fox, Behold I cast out devils, and do cures today and tomorrow, and the third day I am consummated'' (Luke 13:32).

The power thus exercised by Jesus was to become the prerogative of the apostles after his death. ''And these signs shall follow them that believe: in my name they shall cast out devils: they shall speak with new tongues . . . they shall lay their hands upon the sick, and they shall recover'' (Mark 16:17–18). And so indeed it came about, as is testified in the Acts of the Apostles (8:7; 16:16–18; 19:12–17).

Let us note before we go further that it is not simply the Evangelists who here speak of casting out devils, but Jesus himself who (1) claims the power to cast them out and distinguishes it from that of healing diseases, (2) appeals precisely to this power to vindicate his Messiahship, and (3) hands it on expressly to his disciples as having a special place among the miracles they are to work in his name. We shall have occasion to return to these remarks.

Now let us turn to the more detailed descriptions of the expulsions of devils.

The first occasion on which Jesus met a demoniac is highly dramatic. It took place in the synagogue at Capharnaum, at the beginning of His public life. ''And in the synagogue there was a man who had an unclean devil, and he cried out with a loud voice, saying: Let us alone, what have we to do with thee, Jesus of Nazareth? Art thou come to destroy us? I know thee who thou art, the Holy One of God. And Jesus rebuked him, saying: Hold thy peace and go out of him. And when the devil [having ''torn'' or convulsed him—Mark 1:26] had thrown him into the midst he went out of him, and hurt him not at all'' (Luke 4:33–35; Mark 1:23–26).

Similar scenes are mentioned in the gospel record of a day spent by the Savior at Capharnaum. He healed the sick. ''And devils went out from many, crying out and saying: Thou are the Son of God! And rebuking them he suffered them not to speak [and to say who he was] for they knew that he was Christ'' (Luke 4:41; cf. Mark 1:34; Matt. 8:16). St. Mark, speaking of like happenings, tells us (3:11–12): "And the unclean spirits when they saw him, fell down before him, and they cried, saying: Thou art the Son of God. And he strictly charged them that they should not make him known."

It was by action from a distance that the devil was cast out of the daughter of the Syro-Phoenician woman. The mother, a Syro-Phoenician Gentile, came to Jesus and fell at his feet and besought him, without allowing herself to be put off by two rebuffs; and Jesus said to her at last: "For this thy saying [that the whelps may eat of the fallen crumbs of the children] go thy way: the devil is gone out of thy daughter. And when she was come into her house she found the girl lying upon the bed and that the devil was gone out" (Mark 7:25–30; cf. Matt. 15:21–28).

In the case of the deformed woman cured in the synagogue on the sabbath, we must attend carefully both to the description of the infirmity and to its attribution to the devil by the Evangelist St. Luke and by Jesus himself:

> And he was teaching in the synagogue on their sabbath. And behold there was a woman who had a spirit of infirmity eighteen years: and she was bowed together, neither could she look upwards at all. Whom when Jesus saw, he called her unto him and said to her: Woman thou are delivered from thine infirmity. And he laid his hands upon her, and immediately she was made straight, and glorified God. And the ruler of the synagogue (being angry that Jesus had healed on the sabbath), answering said . . . And the Lord answering him said: Ye hypocrites, doth not every one of you on the sabbath day loose his ox or his ass from the manger and lead them to water? And ought not this daughter of Abraham whom Satan hath bound, lo, these eighteen years, be loosed from the bond on the sabbath day? (Luke 13:10–17.)

To this case of possession, whose effects, as described, are strikingly similar to the symptoms of a local paralysis, we must add two others in which the descriptive analysis is more picturesque and more complete. Both are reported by the three synoptic Gospels, by St. Matthew with sobriety, by St. Luke with precision, and by St. Mark with a wealth of vivid detail that seems to come straight from life. We shall reproduce St. Mark's accounts, completing them here and there when necessary with the bracketed matter from the other Evangelists.

Here first is the case of the possessed of Gerasa.

Jesus lands on the eastern side of the Lake of Genesareth, in the country of the Gerasenes.

And as he went out of the ship, immediately there met him out of the monuments a man with an unclean spirit, who had his dwelling in the tombs, and no man could bind him, not even with chains. For having been often bound with fetters and chains, he had burst the chains, and broken the fetters in pieces: and no one could tame him. And he was always day and night in the monuments and in the mountains, crying and cutting himself with stones. [He had gone unclothed for a long time—Luke.]

And seeing Jesus afar off, he ran and adored him. And crying with a loud voice he said: What have I to do with thee, Jesus the Son of the most high God? I adjure thee by God that thou torment me not. For he said unto him: Go out of the man thou unclean spirit. And he asked him: What is thy name? And he saith to him: My name is Legion, for we are many. And he besought him much, that he would not drive him away [into the Abyss—Luke] out of the country.

And there were there near the mountain a great herd of swine feeding. And the spirits besought him saying: Send us into the swine, that we may enter into them. And Jesus immediately gave them leave. And the unclean spirits, going out, entered into the swine: and the herd with great violence was carried headlong into the sea, being about two thousand, and were stifled in the sea.

And they that fed them fled and told it in the city and in the fields. And they went out to see what was done: and they come to Jesus, and they see him that was troubled with the devil, sitting, clothed, and well in his wits: and they were afraid. . . . And they began to pray him that he would depart from their coasts. And when he went up into the ship, he that had been troubled with the devil began to beseech him that he might be with him. And he admitted him not, but saith to him: Go into thy house to thy friends, and tell them how great things the Lord hath done for thee, and hath had mercy on thee.

And this he did not only in "the whole city" (Luke), but "in Decapolis" (Mark 5: 1–20).

Of all the gospel narratives this is the one that gives us the clearest characterization of the devils in possession of a human organism. There they create and maintain certain morbid disturbances not far removed from madness. They possess a penetrating intelligence, and know who Jesus is. They prostrate themselves before Him unblushingly, beseeching, adjuring him by God not to send them back to the Abyss, but rather to allow them to go into the swine and take up their abode there. Hardly have they entered into the swine than, with a display of power not less surprising than their versatility, they bring about the cruel and wicked destruction of the poor beasts in which they had begged refuge. Craven, obsequious, powerful, malicious, versatile, and even grotesque—all these traits, here strongly marked, reappear in varying degrees in the other gospel narratives of the expulsion of devils.

The ridiculous, vulgar, and malicious side of diabolical possessions appears also in the narratives of the Acts, notably in 19: 13–17, where at Ephesus we meet with "some also of the Jewish exorcists who went about [and] attempted to invoke over them that had evil spirits the name of the Lord Jesus. . . . And there were certain men, seven sons of Sceva, a Jew, a chief priest, that did this." They had cause enough to rue it, for one fine day one of those possessed replied: "Jesus I know, and Paul I know; but who are you? And the man in whom the wicked spirit was, leaping upon them and mastering them both, prevailed against them, so that they fled out of that house naked and wounded."

The demoniac whom Jesus found at the foot of the

Mountain of the Transfiguration, and whose malady baffled the apostles, displays, along with deaf-mutism, all the clinical indications of epilepsy. Here once more we shall have to turn to St. Mark's account (9:14–28):

> And coming to his disciples he saw a great multitude about them, and the Scribes disputing with them. . . . And he asked them: What do you question about among you? And one of the multitude answering said: Master, I have brought my son to thee, having a dumb spirit; who, wheresoever he taketh him, dasheth him, and he foameth and gnasheth with the teeth, and pineth away: and I spoke to thy disciples to cast him out, and they could not. Who answering them said: O incredulous generation, how long shall I be with you? How long shall I suffer you! Bring him unto me. And they brought him.
>
> And when he had seen him, immediately the spirit troubled him; and being thrown down upon the ground, he rolled about foaming. And he asked his father: How long time is it since this hath happened unto him? But he said: From his infancy; and oftentimes hath he cast him into the fire and into waters to destroy him. But if thou canst do anything, help us, having compassion on us. And Jesus saith to him: If thou canst believe, all things are possible to him that believeth. And immediately the father of the boy crying out, with tears said: I do believe, Lord; help my unbelief.
>
> And when Jesus saw the multitude running together, he threatened the unclean spirit, saying to him: Deaf and dumb spirit, I command thee go out of him, and enter not any more into him. And crying out and greatly tearing him, he went out of him, and he became as dead, so that many said: He is dead. But Jesus, taking him by the hand, lifted him up; and he arose [and Jesus restored him to his father—Luke].
>
> And when he was come into the house, his disciples secretly asked him: Why could we not cast him out? And he said to them: This kind can go out by nothing but by prayer and fasting.

2. THE PROBLEMS
How find the correct interpretation of these data?

(1) Although the Evangelists sometimes use the word "heal" or "cure" in connection with the deliverance of the possessed by Jesus, the contexts themselves suggest that this "healing" has to be taken in a special sense. Thus the woman with the bent back is represented as "delivered from her infirmity" in Luke 13:12, after having been "bound by Satan these eighteen years," and now she is to be "loosed from this bond" (verse 16). So also the epileptic is "cured," but precisely because the "unclean spirit" has been "cast out" (Luke 9 and parallels). The fact is that the deliverance of possessed persons, in all cases where it is related in any detail, is presented under conditions that clearly differentiate it from the cure of mere disease.

To be precise, the plight of the possessed is attributed to "the devil," a hidden, malicious being, capable of tempting even Jesus; a being who is "the power of darkness" and has "his hour" during the events of the Passion; who acts with as much deceit and wickedness as intelligence. He "enters" the possessed, he "dwells" there, and "comes back"; he "enters" into the swine. The possessed "has a devil," an "unclean devil" (Luke 4:33); he is an "unclean spirit" (Mark 1:23). The devil "goes out" of the possessed, and into another place, into the desert, into the swine, into the Abyss; and that precisely because he is "driven"—that is the word most commonly used. When Jesus approaches he shows "terror," he "falls down," "beseeches," declares that he "knows" the supernatural status of Jesus. The latter "speaks" to him, "questions" him, gives him "commands" and "permissions," and imposes silence. *Not one* of these traits can be found in the behavior of the merely sick toward Jesus, nor in the way in which Jesus sets out to cure them.

(2) The attitude of Jesus in the presence of the possessed does not allow us to think that in acting and speaking as he did he was merely accommodating himself to the ignorances and prejudices of his contemporaries.

What is in question here is no mere current mode of

speech (as when we describe the sun as "rising" from the horizon, and "going up" toward the zenith), but a doctrine that expresses an essential aspect of the mission of the God-man in this world: "In hoc apparuit Filius Dei ut dissolvat opera diaboli" (John 3:8). On points of such importance touching the supernatural world, Jesus could by no means indulge in tolerant equivocations. He never used them. Look at the ninth chapter of the Gospel of St. John. There we have the case of the man born blind. The disciples, either personally mistaken or possibly sharing the views of the Essenes or some other Jewish sect, asked the Master: "Who has sinned, this man or his parents, that he should be born blind?" They were not alone in putting down his blindness to sin. When the man, now cured, was standing up bravely to the interrogation of the Sanhedrin, they cut him short with: "Thou wast wholly born in sins, and dost thou teach us?" Here then we are certainly in the presence of a prejudice or error common among the contemporaries of Jesus. But since this error touched the supernatural order, Jesus allowed himself no conformism; he would entertain nothing but the simple truth, and put it without compromise: "Neither hath this man sinned nor his parents; but that the works of God should be made manifest in him."

Now Jesus, who would not so much as once let pass a mistaken word dropped on matters of religion, *never* corrected his disciples' expressions on the subject of demonic possessions. And He spoke of them Himself in identical terms, strictly squaring his action in the matter with the ideas and language of his countrymen. It is plain that he simply adopted them.

What is more, he took up a position of his own on the point and defended it. The controversy is set out in all three synoptic Gospels (Luke 11:14–26; Mark 3:22–30; Matt. 12:22–45). Jesus had cast out a devil who had made his victim blind and dumb. The Pharisees accused Him of driving out lesser devils by the power of Beelzebub, "Prince of the devils.'' The occasion was a good one to let them know that there was here no question of demonic possession but only of disease. Jesus did not seize it. The devils, he said, do not cast each other out; if they did, they would long ago have put an end to their own "kingdom." No, they are driven out because they have now come up against someone "stronger than themselves," and their defeat is the sign that "the kingdom of God is come upon you." This defeat will not prevent Satan from launching a counteroffensive, and it may even have a striking success in some cases, since the devil driven out will come back "with seven other spirits more wicked than himself." That is because human bad faith, such as had just been shown in the Pharisees' accusation of Jesus, constitutes that voluntary and obstinate blindness called "blasphemy against the Holy Ghost" and opens the way to the definitive return of the reinforced enemy. Here then, as elsewhere, and even more clearly than elsewhere, it is evident that Jesus speaks of the devil and of possession by the devil as realities, and that on this point he finds no errors to dispel either among his disciples or his adversaries.

The true problem raised by these possessions does not lie there. We must now try to formulate it in precise terms and see whether this may suggest some line of thought on which its solution may be found.

(3) Let us abstract for the moment from the method that Jesus adopts in delivering the possessed and consider only the symptoms of their state as given in the more or less detailed descriptions preserved in the Gospels. It can hardly be doubted that a study of the morbid symptoms, and of these *alone*, would lead every doctor to see in the deformed woman a paralytic, in the energumen of Gerasa a furious madman, in the child healed on the morrow of the Transfiguration an epileptic—and so on. Moreover, each possession that is individually set before us is accompanied by an infirmity: the devil strikes his victim dumb (Matt. 9:32; 12:22; Mark 9:16; Luke 11:14); deaf and dumb (Mark 7:32; 11:24); dumb and

blind (Matt. 12:22); "lunatic" (Matt. 17:14); he provokes convulsive crises (Mark 1:26; Luke 4:35; and especially Mark 9:18-20 and parallels above cited). From a purely medical standpoint all these morbid phenomena are closely connected with a diseased state of the nervous system. We can readily appreciate how a psychiatrist might be tempted to isolate these phenomena, to base his whole judgment on nothing else, and to conclude that under the name of "possession" the Gospels present us simply with cases of neurosis. Now at last we face the problem of demonic possession in all its force.

(4) But to set out to solve this problem from a purely medical standpoint is to follow a false trail. Only a part of the facts could be thus explained. How do these neurotics recognize and proclaim the Messiah? How could their disorders be instantaneously transferred to a herd of swine and bring about its destruction? How comes it that the Thaumaturge here acts by threats not directed against the patient himself, but against another? How is it that he always effects by one brief word a cure that is instantaneous, complete, and final? Think of the time a modern psychiatrist needs, the slow and laborious methods of persuasion he employs, in order to "cure"—when he does cure—or even to ameliorate the disorders of his pitiable clientele.

These questions become still more pressing when we remember that all the ills enumerated above—dumbness, deafness, blindness, paralysis, apparently due to the same neuropathic cause—are often met with in the Gospel unaccompanied by any mention of the devil, and are cured by means that have absolutely nothing in common with these imperious and threatening exorcisms, or with conversations with an interlocutor who is other than the patient. We must cite some examples of this.

Here is the case of the deaf-mute of Mark 7:32-35 (the Greek text makes him a "deaf-stammerer," which still more clearly indicates the nervous character of the trouble).

And taking him from the multitude apart he put his fingers into his ears, and spitting he touched his tongue. And looking up to heaven he groaned and said to him: Ephpheta, which is: Be thou opened. And immediately his ears were opened, and the string of his tongue was loosed, and he spoke right.

No mention of the devil, no threats, only a few symbolical gestures with a word expressing their meaning. It is simply a miraculous cure of a nervous malady. It is not the expulsion of a devil.

Everybody remembers the cure from a distance of the paralyzed servant of the centurion of Capharnaum who declared himself unworthy to receive Jesus under his roof (Matt. 8:5–13; Luke 7:1–10); also that of the paralytic whose zealous friends uncovered the roof of the house where Jesus was teaching, and let down the bed with the patient at Jesus's feet; and whom the Master cured with a word affirming that "the Son of Man hath power on earth to forgive sins" (Mark 2:1–12 and parallels). Once more, no threats, no exorcisms, but words full of kindness for both centurion and paralytic, with no attribution of the illness to the malice of the devil.

And here is the cure of the blind man as related by St. Mark (8:22–26):

And they came to Bethsaida; and they bring to him a blind man, and they besought him that he would touch him. And taking the blind man by the hand, he led him out of the town: and spitting upon his eyes, laying his hands on him, he asked him if he saw anything. And looking up, he said: I see men as it were trees, walking. After that again he laid his hands upon his eyes and he began to see and was restored, so that he saw all things clearly. And he sent him into his house.

It is not certain whether this particular case of blindness can be put down to nervous causes, unlike the case of the deaf and blind demoniac (Matt. 12:22) noted above. The comparison shows at least that blindness, whatever its immediate cause, whether nervous or other, was sometimes taken by Jesus for a *disease* to be cured without exorcism, and sometimes for the result of *possession*, to be put an end to by expelling the devil.

Here, if we do not mistake, is the sole case in the Gospels of a "progressive" miraculous cure, effected, however, in a few moments and without any of the long and complicated methods of modern psychiatry. But here again are no devils, no threats, no commands to "go out of him," and no exorcism.

It will be seen from these texts that the two notions of "nervous malady" and "diabolic possession" do not always coincide exactly. The Gospel presents possessions accompanied by neuroses, and neuroses pure and simple. The means used to restore the patients to their normal state also differ according to which of these two categories the subjects belong to. Any simple identification of possession with a nervous malady is incompatible with the Gospel. After all these explanations and detours we can now at last condense the enunciation of the real problem raised by these gospel narratives into the following formula:

Whence comes it that diabolical possession is always accompanied in these descriptions by the characteristic clinical signs of an abnormal state of the nervous system? Can we furnish an explanation, or indicate the cause, of this strange but nonetheless regular concomitance?

3. PRINCIPLES OF THE SOLUTION

To the question thus precisely put, mystical theology (falling back on dogmatic theology and on scholastic philosophy) provides important elements of the answer. We must now bring these elements together into some kind of synthesis.

Scholastic philosophy distinguishes two groups of faculties within the one indivisible human soul. One group belongs to the sensible order—imagination and sensibility;

and the other to the intellectual—intelligence and will. When all is duly ordered in a human soul, its activity is directed by the will, which commands both the imagination and the sensibility, according to the lights it receives from a reason informed by the truth. But reason, in its turn, under the normal conditions of its exercise here below, is only capable of attaining to the truth if the sense faculties provide it with a suitable aliment that they themselves have prepared. This interaction between the faculties affects also the will, whose decisions may be influenced, even very strongly, by the attractions brought to bear on it from the side of the sensibility. However, the hierarchy of the faculties remains, and the will *alone* sovereignly decides the *free* act, which it can carry out, postpone, or omit as it chooses.

But—still following the teaching of scholastic philosophy—it is the above-mentioned spiritual soul that gives life to the body, animates or "informs" it. There are not two souls in man, one spiritual and the other corporeal, but one only. Now it is precisely by its lower powers, by the sensibility, that the immaterial soul puts out its hold on the body. In the one unique but composite being of the human individual, it is here that we find the point of junction. If we approach this indivisible point from the side of the spiritual soul, we shall call it the sensibility; if we approach it from the side of the life of the body, we shall present it as the vital movement proper to the nervous system. This very close union between the nervous system, which pertains to the body, and the sensibility, which is a faculty of the soul, permits the transmission of the commands of the will to the body and its movements. It is this union that is dissolved by death. It is this union that is weakened by mental disorders; for these are definable as disorders of the nervous system, carrying ipso facto a disorder of the same importance into the sensibility, and resulting at the limit in madness. Then the will finds all the machinery of command put out of action and no longer controls either the sensibility or the nervous system, which are both abandoned to their only two alternatives of dazed depression or of furious excitement.

Now it is precisely at this point of intersection and liaison between soul and body that theologians locate the action of the devil. He cannot, any more than other creatures, act directly on the intelligence or the will; that domain is strictly reserved to the human person himself and to God his Creator. All that the devil can do is to influence the higher faculties indirectly, by provoking tendentious representations in the imagination, and disordered movements in the sensitive appetite, with corresponding perturbations in the nervous system, synchronized as it is with the sensibility. Thereby he hopes to deceive the intelligence, especially in its practical judgments, and still more especially to weigh in on the will and induce its consent to bad acts. As long as things stop there we have "tempation."

But—with God's permission, accorded for the greater supernatural good of souls, or to put no constraint on the freedom of their malice—things need not stop there. The devil can profit from a disorder introduced into the human composite by a mental malady. He can even provoke and amplify the functional disequilibrium, and take advantage of it to insinuate and install himself at the point of least resistance. There he gets control of the mechanism of command, manipulates it at his pleasure, and so indirectly reduces to impotence both the intelligence and, above all, the will; which for their proper exercise require that the sensible data shall be correctly presented and that the means of transmission shall be in good working order. Such are the main lines of the theory of diabolic possession worked out by Catholic theology. And this theory is strengthened by other considerations which support and reinforce the explanations given above. Let us merely note that if death, and so also the ills that prepare it, came into the world, this was "by the envy of the devil" turned against our first parents (Wisd. 2:24), a thing that justifies the title by which he was stigmatized by Jesus: "homicida ab initio"

(John 8 : 44). By fastening, in possession, on the precise point at which body and soul are knit together but can be disassociated, he maintains the line of operations that he chose from the start in order to wage his war against humanity.

If all this is correct, we shall have to infer with the theologians that all true diabolic possession is accompanied, in fact and by a quasi-necessity, by mental and nervous troubles produced or amplified by the demon, and yet having manifestations and symptoms that are practically and medically identical with those produced by neuroses. The psychiatrist, therefore, is free to study these symptoms, to describe these mental troubles, and to indicate their immediate causes. There he stands on his own ground. But if, in the name of his science, he pretends to exclude a priori, and in all cases, any transcendent cause of the anomalies in question, then he trespasses beyond the bounds of his special competence. Precisely by confining himself to his own methods he automatically forgoes any inquiry of this kind. Never will he find the devil at the term of his purely medical analysis, any more than the surgeon will find the soul at the point of his scalpel, or any more than the dog, seeing his master in anger, can estimate the moral or immoral character of these strange gesticulations; all that belongs to another order. But the doctor who wants to remain a complete man, above all if he enjoys the light of the faith, will never exclude a priori, and in some cases may well suspect, the presence and action of some occult power behind the malady.

We return to the Gospel and to its diabolical possessions. It is precisely to account for it all that Catholic theologians have elaborated the theory sketched above. It is the business of the psychologists and the doctors to complete the sketch by providing it with all the precise analyses and formulas that the progress of modern science permits and requires. It is also for them to say whether it would not be very advantageous, for the medical profession and theologians alike, to drop the attitude of suspicious isolation in which they stand to each other, and to unite their efforts and methods with a view to obtaining a truly adequate interpretation of facts relating to several complementary branches of human knowledge—facts such as the diabolic possessions of the Gospel and their healing by Jesus.

The Devil in Dante

Auguste Valensin, S.J.

In spite of the title the *Divine Comedy*—a title Dante himself did not give his poem—the characters he portrayed were not divine but human beings. To all intents and purposes his epic is a human comedy, even though its scene is the other world. That did not prevent Dante from giving a part to angels in heaven and demons in hell, as befitted his chosen scenario.

What was his conception of these demons, and in particular, how did he portray Lucifer, the prince of demons?

1.

Dante's ideas on demons follow those supplied by the traditional Christian interpretation of the Apocalypse. The demons, according to him, are "intelligences exiled from their celestial home country," "outcasts of heaven" who fell from it like falling rain. As soon as they were created, they had to go through a test to ensure their free entry into the friendship of God. In the theology lesson Beatrice gives Dante in Canto 29 of the *Paradiso* she tells him that the test only lasted a few seconds. The fall of Lucifer and the other angels who joined in his revolt was the result of pride. These fallen angels

—"black" angels—are the demons properly so-called.

The guardians of hell are not demons in the sense in which the word is interchangeable with devil. Dante uses the word *devil* six times in the *Divine Comedy* and each time applies it to fallen angels. The term *demon* is more general and less exact. Socrates used it for the kind spirit that, he thought, used to warn him of evil. In the Middle Ages they called the pagan gods demons. One of the bad popes was accused of invoking—when throwing dice—the help of Jupiter, Venus, "and other demons." In classical mythology the word demon was applied to the beings halfway between gods and men. In the *chansons de geste* people such as Nero and Pilate are included among the demons. In Giacomo da Verona's *De Babilonia civitate infernali* Muhammad is a demon.

Dante, who normally applies the word demon to devils, uses it on one occasion for a damned soul (*Inf.* 30. 117). Twice he gives it to guardians of hell, once to Charon and once to Cerberus (ibid. 3. 109 and 6. 32), but this does not mean that we are to regard these guardians as genuine devils. Besides, if Dante had meant to conceal devils under the appearance of these mythical characters, he would not, as he did, have recalled the deeds of their past lives—precisely such deeds as put them in a different category from fallen angels.

We have even more grounds for thinking this of the *assistant* guardians. These are not even legendary figures but animals, monsters, harpies, and centaurs (ibid. 12 and 13). Admittedly Dante gives us one rapid vision of the devil in the form of a serpent, but this is a definite reference to the passage in the Bible about original sin (*Purg.* 8. 97ff.).

Before Dante there stretches a whole tradition with an established idea of what the devils were like and an accepted picture of hell. The demons—fierce, grotesque executioners —are charged with the torture of the damned. As the fancy takes them, they boil them in caldrons, roast them on spits, fry them, or slice them up across and lengthwise. The hell of

Dante's forebears is a torture chamber in which childish imagination has been let loose, with no rules, no principles, no scheme behind its choice of details. Coarse popular imagery, this, designed to terrify but to provoke laughter, too. The two aspects go together, explained by a sort of rudimentary theology: everything that degrades the devils is good, so it is right to make them ridiculous. At the same time they must be frightening, so that Christians may beware of them. How at the same time mock and fear them, gibe and tremble? The explanation is that the mocker and the trembler are not the same person. Fear of the devil is a help for the hesitating—every man sometimes has within him a fainthearted Christian whom pure love is not enough to sway. But when a man's soul is united to the power of God, what has he to fear? For him this ontological mockery of the demons is a very proper nourishment for what might be termed mystic hilarity.

This point of view was taken up by Dante—but with modifications. In the *Divine Comedy* the proportion of diabolical slapstick is greatly reduced. It comes only into the scenes of quarreling devils at Malebolge (*Inf.* 21 and 22)—the one episode in which the devils are protagonists and our interest is permitted to dwell on them; the poet-theologian grants us a moment's distraction, the virtuoso introduces a variation, we come on a pencil sketch on the edge of a deep and austere work of art. Apart from that, the demons do not especially engage our attention, which Dante wishes to turn exclusively to the damned.

In hell itself the demons carry out their tasks like anonymous officials; they are the arm of divine justice. Thus we meet them in the second chasm of the eighth circle, scourging the panders, who were condemned to walk around and around it.

On this side, on that, along the hideous stone, I saw horned demons with large scourges, who smote them fiercely from behind.

Ah! how they made them lift their legs at the first strokes! truly none waited for the second or the third.

(*Inf.* 18. 34ff.)

Similarly, in the ninth chasm their job is to split down the middle, as they go by, those who have divided Christianity.

Even a cask, through loss of middle-piece or cant, yawns not so wide as one I saw, ripped from the chin down to the part that utters vilest sound;

between his legs the entrails hung; the pluck appeared, and the wretched sack that makes excrement of what it swallowed.

Whilst I stood all occupied in seeing him, he looked at me, and with his hands opened his breast saying: "Now see how I dilacerate myself, see how Mahomet is mangled! Before me Ali weeping goes, cleft in the face from chin to forelock;

"and all the others, whom thou seest here, were in their lifetime' sowers of scandal and of schism; and therefore are they thus cleft.

"A devil is here behind, who splits us thus cruelly, reapplying each of this class to his sword's edge, when we have wandered round the doleful road; for the wounds heal up ere any goes again before him."

(*Inf.* 28. 22ff.)

In each case Dante barely indicates the action and is far from taking the opportunity to wallow in details. The demons have no personality: they are robot demons, supers who do their job almost without appearing on the stage.

Also—and here Dante is making a break with the existing literary tradition—most of the damned are not tormented by demons. Instead of being given up to the whims of torturers, they undergo a punishment marked out with precision, corresponding to their crime, and its execution is usually confined to themselves, or else to animals or natural forces.

Dante gives us no information as to the dispositions, knowledge, or sufferings of the demons in hell. He may have deliberately refrained from painting the devils in detail so as not to take away from his main subject.

As for the demons *outside* hell, we are told quite a lot

about their character and the part they play. They are endowed with a will that always seeks evil; they are each other's enemies; they are liars; they try to catch souls with the bait of false pleasures. They attack the good everywhere. When a preacher instead of teaching the Gospel tries to exalt himself or to be funny, it is because there is a devil lurking in the peak of his hood.

The *Divine Comedy* gives us three typical examples of the devil's intervention at the hour of death. The first anecdote is about Guido di Montefeltro (*Inf.* 27). This warrior, whose activities had been foxy rather than leonine, became a monk to expiate his sins and thus piously would he have ended his life had he not been led back to his perfidious ways. According to what he is supposed to have told Dante, Boniface VIII appealed to Guido to help him confound the Colonnas. At first he refused. Then, on the assurance that the pope could absolve him in advance from the sin he was about to commit, he finally gave the successful advice to make but not keep a certain promise. When he died, Francis of Assisi came to fetch his soul, but in vain. Guido was easily proved guilty by a black cherub, on the ground that a man cannot be absolved from a sin he does not repent and therefore cannot at the same time will sin and absolution, "per la contradizzion che nol consente." The devil ended up, to Guido: "Ah! you never knew I was a logician!"

The second example concerns his son, Buonconte di Montefeltro (*Purg.* 5). Buonconte was killed at the battle of Campaldino in 1289, and his body was never found. This was because as he was dying, the sinner was inspired to call on our Lady. That saved him: when the devil came to take possession of his soul, an angel snatched it away from him. The devil, enraged, cried, "O you from heaven, why are you doing me out of my right? Was one small tear enough to rob me of my prey? Very well, so be it! At all events I can do what I like with his body"—and using the strength that belongs to his nature, the devil stirred up a violent storm and swept Buonconte's unburied body down the Arno.

The third example is outstandingly odd. Given that in a state of grace God lives supernaturally within us, working in and through us, the idea easily follows that in a state of sin it is the devil who lives in us. The next stage is possession and by going a bit further one reaches Dante's fabulous notion—why should not the devil continue to use a man after he is dead? No one would suspect that he was dealing with a corpse. This was the fate of Branca d'Oria and his father-in-law, Michel Zanche. "They are here with us in hell," says one of the damned to Dante. "What's that? What are you saying? Don't be absurd—d'Oria is still alive, eating, drinking, sleeping, wearing clothes. . . ." "No, d'Oria's body is animated by a devil, who makes him talk and move just as if it were his soul" (*Inf.* 33).

What more striking way could there be of demonstrating what it means to be given up to the devil by sin? This flight of fancy was not Dante's own. We find it in a number of earlier authors, just as we find the theme of angel and devil fighting over a corpse. So far, then, there is nothing to show that Dante had any original views on matters diabolical. Up to this point his demonology is a summary, an outline. Not only has he made no effort to produce anything new about the psychology of demons, but as if to avoid the rocks on which the imagination of his predecessors foundered, he seems to have done his best to get out of describing demons altogether He replaces them, where he can, by animals and monsters or by mythological characters who are already fitted out with both history and physiognomy.

Only when Lucifer himself comes on the scene does Dante begin to show interest in the devil and give us a new conception of his character.

2.

Lucifer is the name of the demon prince. It is Dante's favorite name for him, but he also calls him Satan, Beelzebub, and Dis.

Dante agrees with orthodox theology that Lucifer fell from heaven and takes from the Apocalypse the fact that this fall brought him down to earth. It was his own idea that there was such a close link between the drama in Paradise and the present condition of the earth.

Let us imagine this globe fixed at the center of creation, with its austral hemisphere (as we will call it here, for convenience' sake) facing the point of the Empyrean, the throne of God. This hemisphere used to be the solid one, the other being completely covered in water. When Lucifer landed on the earth, it was so frightened by the approach of such a monstrosity that it fled of its own accord under the waters, leaving an ocean in its place. More land came out on the other hemisphere, to compensate. In a moment the face of the globe was changed and the part farthest from God, the boreal hemisphere, became habitable—as far as Dante was aware, in fact, it was the only inhabited part of the earth.

Falling headfirst onto our world, Lucifer went in as far as the center and there stopped, unable to fall farther. At once a mass of earth shrank back all around the reprobate and, retreating along the path by which Lucifer's fall had brought him, formed a vast bulge in the waters of the austral hemisphere—the mountain of purgatory. This was Dante's own idea. Up to then purgatory was thought to be somewhere near hell, in the middle of the earth, or in one of the planets.

Lucifer is suspended in space, equidistant from the four corners of creation, with the upper half of his body hemmed in by ice and the lower half surrounded by rocks. His head and torso are in the northern hemisphere, the rest of his body in the southern hemisphere. So placed, he has Asia on his right, Africa on his left. Jerusalem, where the crime was committed, is on his head, and under his feet is purgatory, the place of expiation. Heaven and earth are linked in history: the shape of this world is the outcome of the drama on high, and Satan himself is the maker of his own hell.

As with so many of Dante's fables, we are free to deem this fantasy childish or magnificent. It depends on our opinion of its author. We may look on him as an irresponsible imagemonger, the first to be taken in by his own myths, or we may see in him a Platonic idealist for whom material realities are pictures of those that are spiritual and more truly real: his task being the poetical re-creation of the Cosmos, he constructs its "objective correlative"—that is to say, an analogy of intelligibles. Thus he must use the pattern of the stars, the relationship of numbers and the geographical symmetries as an iconography both for synthesized truths of another and higher order and for subtle ideological correspondences.

Lucifer's vast material bulk gives an indication of what his spiritual size must have been. The perfection of him who was once the greatest of angels is expressed inside-out by the vacuous hugeness of mere quantity—it is the inverted reflection of it that we see in his present delusive immensity.

As usual, Dante cleverly fills out his fantasy with careful detail and gives us the data for working out Lucifer's dimensions. Three unusually tall men put end to end would not equal in length even the torso of the giant Nimrod, yet the average man's arm is nearer Nimrod's in size than the giant's is to Lucifer's. Those are the data, slightly simplified. To provide material for calculation is one thing; to calculate is another. Dante was wise to leave the working out to us—and we should be foolish if we accepted his invitation to do so without a pinch of salt. The data of the problem hint vaguely at colossal proportions. Working out the sum and finding the exact measurements would merely be deceptive. In cases like this, details are like imitation pillars, painted in perspective—it is better not to look at them too closely. An approximate calculation, in fact (it was made by Galileo and later by others with slightly varying results), gives Lucifer's height as roughly 1⅓ miles—puny compared with what the unaided imagination suggests.

Lucifer has three heads of different colors, red, off-yellow, and black. He has six wings, two around each head. We need not go into the fanciful interpretations that have been put on the meaning of these heads—they were not the work of Dante; long before his time Satan was so represented, in sculpture, paintings on glass, and miniatures in manuscripts. In these images the purpose of the three heads is to make Satan a symmetrical antagonist to the Trinity. Probably Dante meant them the same way. One of the faces, opposed to the Person of the Father, symbolizes jealous impotence and is fittingly colored a liverish yellow. The second, balancing the Person of the Word, symbolizes ignorance and stupidity, which have in a manner of speaking become the substance of Satan—this head is black. Finally the third, being the opposite of the Paraclete, who is love, must suggest Satan's essential hatred and is therefore red.

All Lucifer's activity is confined to these three heads and their wings. His wings fan up the wind that freezes Cocytus. His jaws munch unceasingly at the three greatest criminals in the world, Brutus and Cassius, traitors to the supreme political authority, and Judas, traitor to God. The rest of his body is condemned to immobility.

This ugly creature is Lucifer, once the most beautiful of all the angels.

The poets go down the body of Lucifer to get to the center of the earth and climb up to the surface on the other side. It is an odd picture. Vergil takes Dante on his back and slides down Lucifer's chest, using the hairs as steps. When he reaches the hips, readjustment is needed. Before he reached the center of the earth, he was going down; now, to get away from it, he must climb up. Still carrying his burden, Vergil has to make a half turn on his own feet. He points his head downward, to have it on top and, having come down Lucifer's torso, proceeds up his legs. The poet on his back is startled—it feels as if he were going back again (*Inf.* 34).

An amusing description, which the author of the *Divine Comedy*, who was making use of ideas as yet little known, undoubtedly thought the reader would find both startling and instructive. I think it is worth pointing out a scientific howler: we are told that when Vergil gets to the center, it is a tremendous effort to change his position—he does so "con fatica e con angoscia" (*Inf.* 34. 78) because it is the place where all the weight of the world is concentrated. The contrary is true. One of Newton's theorems proves that the nearer a thing is to the center of the earth, the less it weighs. Dante, who was small and probably weighed about a hundred and forty pounds on the earth's surface, would at just over a mile from the center have weighed no more than five ounces, at one yard a hundred-and-twentieth of an ounce and at the center nothing. This could scarcely have been tiring for Vergil!

Dante's originality does not lie in his portrait of Lucifer's appearance but in his philosophical conception of his personality. It is here that he begins to make innovations; it is in this that the figure he created is unique. Milton, Goethe, Byron, Victor Hugo, Carducci, Vigny, Baudelaire, and nearest to our time, Paul Valéry imagined the devil as the quintessence of the spirit of evil, a microcosm of hell, an active Satan, intelligent and mischievous, with something of his magnificence still clinging to him—something at times even attractive: a power struggling against a power, ground down but retaining strength enough to keep from yielding. A figure of this mold, who defies God even under torture, is indeed to be found in Dante, but his name is not Lucifer but Capaneo (*Inf.* 14. 46–61). Dante's Lucifer is an exhausted creature whose energy is spent, whose history is over. He is forced to spend eternity as the lowest link in the chain of living things. He who was once among the most vital of created spirits has turned into a kind of dull brute. At no point is he referred to as *thinking*—he has no inner life, no rebelliousness, no passions. He just goes on munching and munching and automatically opening and shutting his wings. All we perceive in him is infinite misery—an abject misery in which there is nothing touching. This being, whose likeness to God is as nearly rubbed out as it can be, does nothing apart from his mechanical movements but keep silence and weep. His silence is empty like a lonely desert, and the tears that, if they streamed from two eyes, might have roused compassion, are productive only of repugnance, since they gush from six eyes at a time, pour down three chins, and mix with the blood and froth of three sets of jaws. This is the vanquished of God, more like a machine (a sort of bellows-cum-mincing-machine) than an intelligent being. If he is the King of Hell, "Emperor of the Dolorous Realm," he is so only in the sense that he is its most perfect expression, that is, the lowest thing in it.

Lucifer's torments might seem relatively gentle in comparison with those of the other damned souls. This is true in terms of feeling but not to the eyes of thought. Dante purposely sacrifices the impression to the idea. When he thinks of the worst of all criminals, the range of sensible punishment seems to hold no torture parallel to the sin. He denies Satan a spectacular torment which might have appalled the imagination, and chooses a punishment whose unequaled horror is apparent only to the mind: icebergs and rocks, which surround without touching him, darkness and loneliness, immobility, silence—the point of the description is its symbolism of a punishment that is essentially metaphysical. The interpretation is that the enemy of God, while still existing, is thrust as far away from being as he can be, held by force, against his nature, on the confines of nothingness. Pain might draw pity—Lucifer's ontological degradation witnesses far more effectively to his defeat.

Thus conceived, Lucifer is the antithesis, the antipodes of God. At one extreme we see supreme immobility, the fruit of plenitude, of the fact that God is the one Being who lacks nothing and is therefore in search of nothing. At the other extreme is forced immobility, that of a being, so to speak, exiled from himself, whose destitution is so complete that he lacks even the means of turning back into himself. At one extreme is God, "materially (metaphorically) outside the universe but spiritually (really) at its hub"; at the other Lucifer, "materially at the hub of the universe but spiritually (really) outside it" (Guido Monacorda, *Poesia e contemplazione*). At one extreme God, toward whom in obedience to a sort of spiritual law of gravity all his true lovers are drawn by the weight of their love (the more one loves, the nearer one gets to him—it is like falling upward); at the other extreme Lucifer, toward whom souls laden with concupiscence are drawn lower and lower.

Dante's Satan has nothing of the Titan about him. He is not even a Nietzschean figure and we must admit—in defiance of the ideas of the romantics, which cannot but involve a reckless tolerance of evil—that this may be for the best. Stripped of the elements of a potential epic hero, Lucifer is no higher than a *bestial thing* (the two words necessarily go together here). Within the spiritual scheme, he is still alive enough to be repellent and still has just enough being to demonstrate, like an obscene mutilation, the being he lacks. Less striking at first sight, less pitiable, less theatrical than the conceptions of others, Dante's Lucifer is a typical Dantesque character, evolved by reason and full of theological sense.

The Devil in Art

Germain Bazin

The devil, perhaps even more than God, of whom he is simply a worthless imitation, is beyond our imagining. God is One; and, however incommensurable he may be, the human soul, being grounded in unity, tends toward him, in its aspiration toward Being, as toward its First Principle. But the devil is legion; he cannot reach to such a total unity, and the essence of his condition as the Accursed One, the King of Hell, consists, of necessity, in the infinite distance that separates him from the First Principle of his being. This was the anathema that hurled his blank, disjointed soul into the abyss of Chaos, making him Lord of Hell and sovereign over discord. For this prince of all deformity and heterogeneity feeds insatiably wherever contradiction reigns.

No other sacred book has expressed this characteristic of the devil more powerfully than the Lalita Vistara describing the assault of Mara, the devil of tantric Buddhism, on the redeemer Bodhisattva:

The devil Papiyan [Mara] . . . prepared his mighty army, four legion strong and valiant in combat, a fearful army that struck terror into the hearts of all who beheld it, an army such as had never been seen or heard of before, by men or gods. This army had the power to take on all manner of different appearances, transforming itself endlessly in a hundred million ways. Its body and hands and feet were wrapped in the coils of a hundred thousand serpents, and in its hands were swords, bows, arrows, pikes, axes, mallets, rockets, pestles, sticks, chains, clubs, discuses, and all other instruments of war. Its body was protected by excellent breast plates. Its heads and hands and feet turned in all directions. Its eyes and faces were flaming; its stomachs, feet, and hands of all shapes. Its faces glittered in terrible splendor; its faces and teeth were of all shapes, its dog teeth enormous, fearful to behold. Its tongues were as rough as mats of hair, its eyes red and glittering, like those of the black serpent full of venom. Some were spitting the venom of serpents, and some, having taken the venom in their hands, were eating it. Some, like the Garudas, having drawn out of the sea human flesh and blood, feet, hands, heads, livers, entrails, and bones, were eating them. Some had bodies of flame, livid, black, bluish, red, yellow; some had misshapen eyes, as hollow as empty wells, inflamed, gouged or squinting; some had eyes that were contorted, glittering, out of shape; some were carrying burning mountains, approaching majestically, mounted on other burning mountains. Some, having torn up trees by their roots, were rushing toward the Bodhisattva. Some had the ears of stags, pigs, elephants—hanging ears or boars' ears. Some had no ears at all. Some, with stomachs like mountains and withered bodies made from a mass of skeleton bones, had broken noses; others had stomachs like rounded jars, feet like the feet of cranes, with skin and flesh and blood all dried up, and their ears and noses, their hands and feet, their eyes and heads all lopped off. . . .

Some with the skin of oxen, asses, boars, ichneumons, stags, rams, beetles, cats, apes, wolves, and jackals, were spitting snake venom, and—swallowing balls of fire, breathing flame, sending down a rain of brass and molten iron, calling up black clouds, bringing black night, and making a great noise—were running toward the Bodhisattva. . . .

This lengthy extract from a text illustrated with so much color and brilliance by the painters of Turkestan is worth quoting, by way of preface, as a remarkable example of the "demonic style." This fantastic accumulation of ever-changing monstrosities never manages to be more than a sum of so many parts, a mass of fragments that can never be resolved into a unity. Ugliness, plurality, chaos—throughout civilizations most remote from each other in time and in space, these are the characteristics of diabolic art. Being himself unable to create, the lord of all impurity, who fell from grace because, for the space of a single instant, he imagined himself the equal of the demiurge, he tries to practice his delusions by turning himself into the ape of God. Artists have no difficulty in portraying this Prince of Darkness, for he is more easily represented than God, living on what he can borrow from the faces of God's creatures, and combining, in his impotent rage, the various features in the most absurd manner. Satan creates his monsters from shattered remnants of creatures.

We must not expect to discover the most powerful manifestations of demonic art in the art of the West. In any case, if we spent much time on this branch of our subject we should probably be simply repeating what has already been so pungently stated by René Huyghe in his section of *Amour et Violence* (Etudes Carmélitaines, 1946). In the irregular, disjointed, chaotic style that he reveals as typical of German art, we can see a clear example of the demonic, even though this is simply the reverse side of the angelic style to which this art aspired—a point that, perhaps, it would be a mistake to underestimate. This oscillation between two extremes, without ever being able to find a proper balancing point, lies at the very heart of the German soul.

The destiny of Western man has centered upon the search for unity, and hence for the divine, both within man and outside him; so it is not surprising that he should have achieved so little of an outstanding nature in his representations of the devil. If we restricted ourselves to the figure of the fiend himself, we should find that only Romanesque art, which in any case is steeped in Orientalism, has produced pictures of any value in this respect. The meekness of the Gospel, spread abroad by St. Bernard and St. Francis, dealt Satan a mortal blow; Gothic art was too profoundly humanized to give adequate representation to him; while the mystery plays helped to transform him into a comic character with childish properties borrowed from the kitchen—his fork and melting pot, gridiron and long spoon. It is not until the Renaissance that we come across the gloomy monarch in truly demonic guise—for a man like Hieronymus Bosch (in spite of what others may have said about him) is more typical of modern times than of the Middle Ages. In a psychoanalytical study of civilization, the sudden uprush of Satanism in Bosch's paintings would be quoted as a symbol of the first onslaughts made on the faith. Catholic apologists would probably discover in it a premonition of the heresy that was to descend upon the succeeding century. For the historian of ideas, Bosch is symptomatic of the crisis of unrealism that afflicted the fifteenth century, caught between the faith of medieval times and the first beginnings of modern rationalism. In an essay that has since become famous, Huizinga has shown how the later Middle Ages degenerated into a vapid unreality, how all the medieval ideals of courtesy and chivalry and the divine became simply shadows of themselves. The same thing happened to the figure who stands in everlasting opposition to these ideals—Satan; and Bosch became the portrayer of this dream of darkness, as Fra Angelico had been the artist of the dream of light. In the pictures of this Dutch artist one finds the genuinely fantastic creations of the ape of God, the forms that the legions of the lower world assume to bring humanity to destruction. To produce these pictures, the devil, the Prince of Anomaly, seems to have plunged both hands into the created universe of dead and living forms, including even things created by men, and then hurled the absurd results of his infernal industry in all directions. The monsters thus created, being born of disorder, necessarily carry within themselves malevolent powers: they are the anticreation, with a frantic desire to degrade the divine workmanship; but the mere name of the one God, uttered by St. Anthony, is sufficient to bring to nought these triumphs of the devil's wiles, these evanescent negations of the divine creation.

The Accursed One makes a melancholy appearance in the middle distance of an engraving by Dürer. As is usual in the German tradition, he is here represented in the form of a pig. There are few pictures of the spirit of evil more striking than this hideous snout skulking behind Death, following a man on horseback, ready to pounce on his victim the moment he shows the slightest sign of weakness. One wonders whether it was thus that the Lord of Hell used to appear to haunt Luther in his nightmares. According to the Faustian tradition, the devil has another incarnation as a dog; in Goethe's work a sinister spaniel goes up and down under Doctor Faust's windows, and it may be the same creature lying at the feet of Dürer's *Melancholy.* Then, as a result of the Counterreformation, which restored a balance in art, and also under the idealizing influence of Raphael and his successors, the devil disappears for several centuries. With *The Miseries of War* he comes to life again in Goya's imagination, and here again it is an animal that stamps the currency of man's terror of the demonic; but this time it is a goat, the creature that figures in the *Witches' Sabbath.* Delacroix, who was a great reader of *Faust,* also determined to try his hand at the devil, but his imagination was far too literary, and he could do no more than re-create the puppet of the Middle Ages and produce a figure to frighten the children—Mephistopheles, whom Gounod, with that ludicrous incarnation of his, finally reduced to the level of the ridiculous.

Of all the forms of art, the one most free from diabolic influence was the Greek. The Greek genius salvaged the divine element from the demonic animalism that still surrounds it in the idols of Egypt and Babylon and found the most perfect form in creation to embody it, the only form in which a spark of the divine intelligence shines—Man. Passionately devoted to the task of bringing the multiplicity of the universe, by a great effort of reason, into a unity, and thus reaching beyond the chaos of phenomena to the hidden harmony of the world, the Greek imagination, following the very principles of the structure of creation, operated in a manner that was genuinely divine. The very definition of harmony, given by Archelaus as "the unification of all that is discordant," provides a welcome antithesis to the spirit of diabolism, with its frantic desire to spread discord in the universe.

This result was not, however, achieved without patient effort. The real miracle that the Greeks accomplished lay in their triumph over the slavish state of mind that for centuries had kept man in terrified subjection to the pressure of cosmic forces. The only way man had hoped to give his life some sort of fixed basis in what was no more than a blind play of chance had been by inventing magic rites to create a system of equilibrium by which the beneficent forces in the universe could be attracted down to earth and the forces of evil repulsed, and in early Greek times the image still has its full magical significance as a prophylactic. The vase drawings, with their black figures, have a kind of frenzied rhythm that comes from the vitality breathed into them by the devil; while on the pediments of their temples there are monsters jeering at the demons in an endeavor to drive them away. But when the luminous figure of Apollo appears on the west front of Olympia, it is a sign that the powers of darkness have been overcome; and from that time onward the human countenance supplants the monsters and shines out, encircled with divine brightness, in its full beauty. Goya used to say that when reason sleeps, the monsters are born. For thousands of years reason had been in a hypnotic trance and allowed the monsters to go on frightening mankind, but in the fifth century reason came to glorious life and put the monsters to flight. Thanks to the intellectual power of the Word, the Greeks succeeded in exorcising the devil; to chain up the bloodthirsty Erinyes, they only had to summon the benevolent Eumenides. Most important of all, they were so enamored of beauty of form that they were able to use this as their strongest weapon to drive the devil back; for he is the antithesis of everything beautiful. The sixth century had had its Satanic aspect. On the ornaments of the temples, acting as a sort of lightning conductor to keep away the evil spirit she represented, appeared the horrible face of the Gorgon; her ugly grin leers out at you from the pediment of the temple to Artemis Gorgo, at Corfu. Often, on the sides of the black-figured vases, she can be seen in flight, like a locust out of Hades, with Perseus—a very different figure from the proud hero of the classical age—in flight before her. Perseus himself is a figure as frightening as a Tibetan devil, with his flat nose, staring eyes, wide-open mouth, boar tusks and lolling tongue. But with the revelation of the fifth century, the death-dealing face of the Gorgon retreats into the background, her demonic face transformed into a beautiful countenance smiling at Perseus and trying to capture him, no longer by its horror but by its charm.

The devil's real home is the East. There, for the first time, the spirit of evil is personified as a mighty opponent of the spirit of good in the dualistic systems of Mazda and the Jews and Islam, who imagined him as a dark "double" of God, either, like him, uncreated, or a creature who had fallen from grace. However, as these philosophic religions were opposed to the making of images, the person of the devil was given no artistic representation. It needed Christianity, with the plastic imagination it had inherited from the Greeks, before any attempt could be made to embody him out of his abstraction. But the Christian artists borrowed his features from Assyrio-Babylonian demonology. The bronze statuette of the demon Pazuzu, who appears even in the seventh century B.C. symbolized as the southwest wind bringing fever and delirium, has all the characteristics of the devil of the Judeo-Christian tradition as he is to be seen on the wooden panels of our cathedrals and in our illuminated manuscripts. The Mesopotamians, more haunted by the problem of evil than their neighbors the Egyptians, felt their destiny threatened by malevolent spirits that they tried to conjure away by means of magic rites. The presence of a demonic spirit can be felt deep down in the minds of the Assyrian despots who for centuries spread terror in Asia, feeding on hecatombs and tortures. For the taste for blood is one of the most undeniable signs of the presence of the Evil One. It is worth noticing that these old representations of the face of the devil already bear all the characteristic signs of the diabolic art whose principles we are trying to establish, for it is composed of heterogeneous elements taken from the animal kingdom, which, compared with the gods (whose faces are human), are no better than abortions. The Egyptians, who were profoundly humanized —they seem to have been the first civilization to conceive of a myth of redemption—paid practically no attention to the devil world. Though they were more inclined than the Chaldeans and the Assyrio-Babylonians to see God in terms of naturalistic animal powers, they nevertheless rose far above mere bestiality by the serenity which they engrafted upon it. In contrast with Mesopotamian art, which was harsh and tragic, the art of Egypt, with its profound tendency toward unity, is the first pointer toward the harmony of the Greeks.

But it is to civilizations far beyond those that were the source of our own, the vast countries of the Far East, that we have to look if we want to see man measuring himself in a titanic struggle with the devil. In those endless stretches of country, where the human soul seems crushed under the exuberance of nature and the immensity of its surroundings, the concepts of God and of the devil remained for a long time undifferentiated. Through the mists of the ancient Chinese religion, of which we still know practically nothing, we can glimpse a humanity bent under the burden imposed by infernal powers. In the ritual bronzes of the Chow period, we find a conception of the monstrous reaching a metaphysical height such as no other civilization has ever known. On the sides of the *li*, the *lien*, the *touei*, the mask of *tao-tieh* juts out, a hybrid combination of tiger, dragon, bear, ram, and owl; "diffused in matter and only to be perceived in flashes," the monster symbolizes "the omnipresence of a mystery always on the point of dissolving into terror." "Two generations, convulsed by bloody tyranny (let us remember, behind the purifying influence of Confucius, the history of the warrior kingdoms and the opening years of Ts'in), can see nothing, when they attempt to fathom their destiny, except the threatening mask of *tao-tieh* in the bosom of a cloud." Under the hegemony of "the wild beast of Ts'in" the history of China can be summarized in a list of executions: in 331 B.C.—80,000; in 318—82,000; in 312—80,000; in 307—60,000; in 293—240,000; in 275—40,000; in 274—150,000; finally, in 260, the record—400,000 (and yet their lives were supposed to be safe, unless they were enemies). In those days, "when soldiers only received their pay if they produced the heads," the leaders, to raise their prestige, "did not hesitate to throw the vanquished enemy into boiling caldrons and then drink the dreadful mixture—or, better still, force the victims' parents to drink it" (René Grousset, *Histoire de la Chine*, pp. 31, 36, 48). Here, just as in Dürer's engraving, Death walks hand in hand with his accomplice, the devil.

Chinese art, at the time of these sanguinary events, was animated by a rhythm genuinely diabolic. On the sides of their vases geometrical elements are juxtaposed like the fragments of a broken labyrinth or the folded coils of a truncated reptile, and yet this arabesque never creates a unity out of these scattered remnants. It is a cosmos in dissolution, even though its primordial order can be perceived behind the centripetal force that shatters its separate forms.

To this land drenched with blood the Buddhist missionaries brought the gentleness of Kwan Yin and the smiling benevolence of the Bodhisattvas. The demonic style, and the brutal force that goes with it, passed on to another section of Asia, which had more recently emerged from the limbo of prehistory: it conquered Japan. Though at the time of Nara, serenity may shine out in the countenance of the divine Maitreya, nevertheless, the "celestial emperors," whose mission is to guard the Buddhist paradise against the attacks of earth and hell, reflect the demonic cruelty of the Samurai. So strong is the diabolic tendency that this benevolent spirit has all the facial characteristics of the devil. The Shitenno of Nara shows a very strange iconographic relationship with a devil of Vézelay, who might be his younger brother; they have the same flaming hair, the same dilated eyes, and the same jaws open in a cry of terror. This is a very puzzling meeting to find between demonic inspiration from two extremes of the civilized world. But the terrifying power of the Japanese masterpiece leaves the little Romanesque puppet far behind—it could frighten only simple souls like children, on a Punch and Judy stage.

India, which gave birth to the gospel of Buddhism, investigated the problem of evil more profoundly and more intensely than any other civilization. In the iconography of India there are very few figures that, properly speaking, can be described as demonic, even though the return to barbarism, signified by Hinduism (which was a degenerate form of Buddhism), often brings the demonic smell to our nostrils. And there is certainly some sort of demonic influence in the inorganic chaos that proliferates all over the temples of later times. For this proliferation is the very image of that endless variety of form found in the material universe, to which all beings, even the gods, are condemned, and in which the thinkers of India saw the very principle of evil. More than any other people, they emphasized the beneficent power of the one and the curse inherent in multiplicity. By what was perhaps the boldest metaphysical effort that human thought has ever made, Brahmanism tried to resolve the eternal dualism in one grandiose myth—the myth of the terrible Siva, both god and devil, mystic lover and seeker after blood, obsessed by the will to destroy and yet frantic to create: a cosmic myth that raises evil from the level of appearance to a level of transcendental reality at which it becomes transformed into the highest good.

Though China seems originally to have been at the mercy

of demonic forces, nevertheless under the influence of the later philosophers a humanism developed that had the effect of tempering these violent instincts—at least as much as was possible in a land as fierce as Asia. There was another part of the world where demonism flourished—a strange continent that followed a lonely destiny on this globe of ours, peopled by races who were brought into sudden prominence, for a moment of prehistorical time, by a brutal conquest, and then hurled back into nothingness. Here God was always portrayed in exactly the same way as the devil; and in no other country has the sign of blood, which is the sign of Satan, shone out so clearly. It is the land of America. In no other part of the world has a civilized section of mankind remained for so long cowering under the terror of superterrestrial forces; nowhere does man seem to have had a more tragic sense of the precariousness of his position in a world in which he feels an utter stranger. He is placed on earth simply to pay a toll of blood to divine powers who are athirst for it: even the sun must have a daily ration of human sacrifice if he is to consent to continue on his journey. Tlaloc, the god of rain, is no less exacting. The terrors of the year 1000 left memories that were not soon forgotten by this civilization. Try to imagine the state of mind of a people like the Aztecs, who every fifty-two years lived in the most fearful expectation of the end of the world. Death, violent death—the death gained in battle or from the sacrificial knife—was the only means of deliverance from such a hell on earth. The ritual sacrifice of young maidens, children, and prisoners of war that went on in the Aztec civilization—frequently the only reason for fighting was to replenish the altars with victims—has given it a sickening sort of notoriety. On certain feasts the priests would disguise themselves with the remains of a human victim who had previously been flayed alive, and then paint the altars and sanctuaries with fresh blood, having first been sanctified with it themselves; meanwhile the whole assembly would partake of a kind of communion, eating the corpses that were thrown down in hundreds from the tops of the altars. The civilizations of Peru and Bolivia, too, though more humane and less abandoned in their behavior, performed similar ritual sacrifices. No doubt the Assyrians, the ancient Chinese, and the Christian conquistadors—who were more wantonly cruel than the Indians whose customs so deeply horrified them— showed even greater contempt for human life; but no other fully evolved civilization has made death the first principle of a whole system of cosmology, magic, and religion—as though the existence of the species could be ensured only in this terrible universe at the cost of sacrificing a large proportion of its representatives; even those who were destined to go on living being obliged to pay the same terrible toll by making blood gush from their ears or dragging a thin cord, covered with thorns, through a hole pierced in their tongue.

Peruvian works of art undoubtedly show signs of humanitarian influence. Even though the face of the lord of creation usually appears distorted and deformed on the Chimu potteries, there are some that achieve a nobility comparable to the finest portraits of the *quattrocento.* But no breath of humanity ever reached the images of Central America. The gods portrayed by the Mayas, the Toltecs, and the Aztecs are monsters, and the men are made in the image of the gods. No other art has managed to produce such powerful symbols of the inhumanity of a hostile universe, or created such images of the demonic power that for primitive man is the driving force of the world.

The strange formal structure in pre-Columbian works provides a mixed conglomeration of elements, overlapping one into another without any sort of continuity. The key to all this is to be found in the Aztec system of hieroglyphics. Mexican writing was quite different from the Egyptian system, with its rows of picture words and ideograms arranged in a rational sequence, for the former combined all these signs together in a way that produced veritable conundrums. This kind of writing is typical of the "prelogical" stage of primitive thought, when the mind, still incapable of the deductive process that breaks things down by analysis and then reconstructs them into a synthesis, can apprehend the world in a sort of global fashion only as a complex of events that are unconnected and yet simultaneous. The introduction of a principle of continuity, an order of succession, into the chaos of phenomena is an achievement of rational thought, with its power of projecting intellectual lines of force into the discordant multiplicity of the world. This intellectual gift—which constitutes the divine element in man—is to be found in the Egyptians and Chaldeans; it is manifested in their art quite unconsciously. With the Greeks it became conscious—as a realization of certain unifying principles governing the various structural elements that determine the composition of a work of art and ordering them according to the laws of rhythm and harmony and balance. In an Egyptian bas-relief all the various poses are linked together to give them the continuity of an arabesque; even the shapes of Egyptian and Sumerian monsters are the result of a rational choice, their arrangement being decided, in the case of the Egyptians, in accordance with an architectural principle of proportion and, for the Mesopotamians, by an internal formal law. There is no linear continuity for the eye to follow in an Aztec bas-relief: its unity is continually being destroyed by sudden breaks which turn it into a chaotic medley of forms taken from every order of nature, the only rhythm running through these forms being like the rhythm of certain savage dances that are made up of a series of frenzied tremblings of the body—a kind of "seismic" rhythym, brute energy in action, ungoverned by any intellectual principle. We know enough about Mexican cosmological thought to realize that for the Aztecs the universe was a truly demonic medium of existence with no organic homogeneity. Consequently for them evolution did not take place as the result of any process of becoming but simply through sudden, quite arbitrary changes. It is obvious how easily such a conception could lead to pessimism (the oration made to celebrate the birth of a man into the world was always a chant of woe), for optimism develops in man when he feels it possible to order his life in a settled environment in which a periodic repetition of events occurs according to fixed laws.

There is nothing analogous to this strange art of the America of pre-Columbian times except in early Chinese bronzes. The similarity is indeed puzzling, for at times the two become absolutely identical—thus raising one of the most mysterious problems in the history of art. Some people have tried to find historical or ethnological reasons for this aesthetic parallel, but in the present embryonic state of our knowledge about the American continent—whose archaeological sites were until recently continually being ransacked by treasure hunters, to the great detriment of science—most scientists have wisely abandoned the attractive hypothesis of a "wrecked junk" or the idea of an Asiatic migration by way of the Bering Strait. In any case—and this fact is often forgotten—the artistic works of the two civilizations, though they manifest such strong affinities, are separated by several centuries. Possibly the simple truth is that similar conditions of life—and also, perhaps, a common remote ancestry—may have created similar effects at different points in time and space.

In our comparison of the various artistic civilizations we have seen that those of the West have been less dominated by the diabolic style than any of the others. Occasionally, however, Western artists have adopted this style by instinct, in order to represent hell as a sort of chaos. There is the unknown person, for instance, who, toward the end of the thirteenth century, created the wonderful mosaics in the Baptistery at Florence, far more important as the precursors of a new art than the work of Cimabue, which is still totally involved in Byzantine formalism.

The West having shown so little aptitude for demonology in art, its sudden reappearance in our own time is a matter of particular concern. In the early years of the 1900's, in the middle of the triumphant festivities and noisy jubilations of the peoples of the West, all quite intoxicated at the thought of the coming Century of Progress in which man's final happiness was to be realized, the authentic face of the Prince of Discord appears with the effect of a thunderclap. This time Satan chooses to make his appearance in Negro masks, and in Picasso's *Demoiselles d'Avignon* (1907) his grin leers out in prophecy of the bestiality that was to be unleashed upon the world a few years later. But in those days nobody took any notice; the picture was looked upon simply as an artistic joke, or even as a piece of intentional mystification. Thirty years later, the same prophetic genius, inspired by the civil war that was devastating his own country, Spain, conceived, in *Guernica* (1937), the callous disintegration of the human countenance that preceded in painting the frightful outrage that man was about to perpetrate upon himself in fact. Those pictures by Picasso, which took people by surprise and even caused a great deal of scandal, bear all the marks of the diabolic spirit, now engaged in an attack on the masterpiece of Creation itself. Picasso takes all the separate features of the human face, which has burst into fragments as though under the effect of a high explosive, and puts them together again, but according to no principle except that of incongruity. These leering puzzles are perhaps the most typical examples that can be found of that chaotic discontinuity, that hatred of all unity, which seems to be the very essence of the demonic style. I know that if Picasso were asked about this he would maintain that he had been guided in these works by one consideration only: the search for beauty. But that is exactly the diabolic claim. "Who is like to God?" cried St. Michael, felling the Prince of Pride with a sudden flash of light.

Moreover, there is a whole area of modern art with its own special idiom, and this idiom is the stylized chaos that is typical of the demonic. The originators of this destructive process believed in all good faith that they were being guided by a "constructive" instinct—but is not this very deception one of the evil spirit's well-known ruses? As for diabolic imagery, it flourishes again in surrealism, which, far more adeptly than Bosch, produces monsters from separate bits and pieces taken from every branch of the natural order and every element in human industry. Unnatural creation is Satan's prerogative.

After the idyllic naturalism of the nineteenth century, artists have unconsciously been driven to express the anguish of a world shaken by one of the most violent onslaughts of evil that mankind has had to endure. The red constellation that is the sign of Satan has reappeared on the horizon. The death roll of Assyria, China, and the Aztecs has been passed, and now bodies are being heaped up in millions round the altars to the Evil One. Modern man has outdone his predecessors in ferocity. The lampshades made from human skin that were found in Buchenwald are more devilish than the human brew on which the Ts'in generals feasted or the flayed remains with which the Aztecs disguised themselves; these had at least the excuse that they formed part of a magic ritual. Never before has Satan had such powerful means at his disposal; he now has his death factories, laboratories of suffering in which human nature can be tortured, disfigured, and degraded—that human nature which, like him, was created in the image of God, but which, unlike him, has kept the faculty to aspire toward the supreme Good, the divine Unity.

Primitive man lived in terror of cosmic forces that were always about to be unloosed upon him. Modern man, having, thanks to science, mastered nature, has freed himself from fear. But it is a brief illusion, for now we are entering upon a time comparable with the darkest periods of human history; and we tremble with anxiety under the threat of a catastrophe whose cause no longer lies in the nature of things but in ourselves. Dispossessed of nature, his former kingdom, Lucifer now seems to have installed himself at the very center of human intelligence, which has been far too ready to put itself on a level with God, playing with the forces it has mastered without having the humility to admit that the total chain of cause and effect must always remain beyond its comprehension. Modern science is many-sided and the knowledge it embraces far greater than any single human being could ever possibly absorb. The question is, does this prodigious sum of knowledge bring us nearer to God, or does it take us further away from him, and from that Unity, that state of Absolute Being, from which Satan, the Archenemy, has forever been excluded?

A Note on Hieronymus Bosch
and Brueghel the Elder

Emile Brouette

In pictorial art, where ever since the thirteenth century the fertile imagination of the illuminators has exercised itself on the subject of hell, two great names represent and synthesize the popular tendencies: Hieronymus Bosch and Pieter Brueghel the Elder.

Bosch's famous *Temptation of St. Anthony* in Lisbon does with the visual image what the contemporary *Hammer of Witches* does with words. In it we see the invasion of the ruined fortress where, according to tradition, St. Anthony sought solitude; there are the episodes of the witches' Sabbath, flights through the air, meetings of Satanists by the edge of a lake, the Black Mass, the devil pact, etc. In the same representational vein is the triptych *The Last Judgment,* in the Vienna Academy of Fine Arts, illustrating certain medieval themes that particularly bear out the fantastic element of chosen passages from the Apocalypse. At first glance, the composition seems a chaotic jumble: the earth is given over to infernal monsters, the background is a sky of horror lit up with flaming houses and towns, and all hell rushes out hungrily to seize its prey. Here is a man being burned alive, there hanged, there throttled, there quartered. The water torture, the wheel, the millstone heap on the agony. A devil flies on the back of a witch; lemurs, horrible creatures from the depths of Erebus and Avernus, hurl themselves upon a stricken and shaking humanity.

The masterpieces in the fantastic style of Brueghel the Elder are the *Fall of the Rebel Angels* in the Musée des Beaux-Arts in Brussels and the *Dulle Griet* in the Musée Mayer van den Bergh in Antwerp. Both are filled with the morbid unrest of Bosch. The first picture, which contains the apparition of a nightmare faun and of creatures with mollusk bodies and bat wings, represents the hurling of the damned from the heights of heaven to the burning floor of hell. The armed and helmeted amazon who flings with huge strides across the land of hell in the *Dulle Griet (The Enraged Amazon)* recalls the *Triumph of Death* in the Prado, a work with the same wealth and welter of macabre details: the ravages of a pitiless mower, with here an assassin, there a gibbet, and farther back the plague-stricken groups locked in battle, and on the horizon a shipwreck.

With the iconography of Bosch and Brueghel should be linked the popular art of the *danses macabres* and of the *ars moriendi,* which the xylography of the last years of the fifteenth century multiplied among the people. The sixteenth century—obsessed with the thought of death and of the last things, of hell and the devil—saw a flourishing imagery of sheerest terror. In its naïve symbolism, the *Ars moriendi* of Verard reproduced the common fear of what comes after death. These images, which are often very crude, depict numerous demons attacking the dying, and their grimacing, howling presence is much more frequent than the image of peace and the haloed head.

Balzac and the "End of Satan"

Albert Béguin

It would be surprising if Balzac had never evoked the figure of Satan. There was every reason for him to tackle it: his reading of occult writings; his susceptibility to literary fashion, which made him take up, and really get to the bottom of, all the themes of his time—most of all, however, the nature of his more intimate personal anxieties. It was not for nothing, nor without some inner compulsion, that throughout his entire work he built up—more even than a psychology or a sociology—a complete mythology of man. The Balzacian character is not shut in within himself, nor even reduced to his social coordinates; on every side he is open to influences, to calls, to supernatural forces, or at least to forces that tend to become supernatural as a result of a curious imaginative rhetoric. These forces, when named, are given the capital letter that turns them into active persons, protagonists in a struggle waged over each soul, over every destiny. They are called Money, Power, Passion; they are paired off as opponents—Matter and Spirit, Energy and Exhaustion, Hell and Paradise. They are the promise of Felicity or the threat of Sorrow around the living being; they form the immense confederacy of Destiny, and through them our brief existence opens out into the limitless distance of mysterious origins, of ancestral transmissions, of projections into the future toward generations to come.

And yet Satan is explicitly invoked by Balzac only once, and the polarity does not seem to be that of good and evil. We may guess at the conflicts between the spirits of energy and sluggishness; at the strong downward pull that opposes itself to the flights of the spirit. But these contrary tendencies receive no moral qualification, and the spiritual combat seems to be waged in the opaque dullness of the flesh; the desire which seeks temporal satisfaction in a thousand shapes through the heavy earthly dough is the same desire which calls us to immaterial joys of knowing. Thirsting after the absolute, Balzac had come to believe—and in this he was influenced to some extent by the occultists—that all life, whether spiritual or corporeal, sprang from one sole Energy, but was maintained by teeming antagonisms, by conflicts that generated its motion. Not only do the maxims of *Louis Lambert* assert the continuity and equal nature of the vital urge and of spiritual effort; the love episodes in Balzac's work would all have us believe that the exaltation of the senses, without the intrusion of any other element, leads to a transfiguration and brings carnal man to the threshold of angelic purity. Does not Louis Lambert go so far as to reverse the sense of the "Et Verbum caro factum est" and declare that the Gospel of the future will teach "And flesh shall be made the Word, it shall become the Word of God"? In the same way, do we not read in *Séraphita* that "the earth is heaven's nursery garden"? And does not Madame de Mortsauf declare in *Le Lys dans la Vallée* that we must "pass through a red melting pot [red is terrestrial, carnal passion] before we can arrive, saintly and perfect, in the higher spheres" ?

Yet this Balzacian angelism, which found its most complete expression in the character of Séraphita—an angel born of the perfect love of two fleshly creatures—came up against certain limitations which had to be recognized. The epilogue of *Séraphita* is the realization of an inevitable failure; the transformation of terrestrial man into a creature of light is impossible, or at least reserved to the rare elect. Humanity is seen once more to be fettered by time, confined within the limits of imperfection. With the consciousness of suffering —which Balzac has the courage not to turn away from when he is brought up against it in his work—he rediscovers tragedy. And this tragedy naturally finds expression as a grief connected with the concepts familiar to him; he is obsessed by the thought that forms the theme of *Peau de chagrin*—the thought of the inevitable using up of energy, of life consuming itself. The common norm demands that man, who is subject to the law of devouring time, should exhaust his strength in proportion as he uses it in the attempt to vanquish time. And this norm is valid for the spiritual man thirsting for truth—the man personified by Balthasar Claës in *La Recherche de l'Absolu*, or the painter Frenhofer in the *Chef-d'oeuvre inconnu*—just as much as for the ambitious man seeking power or wealth—Rubempré, Rastignac, Grandet, Nucingen.

One might ask oneself where Satan will find a crevice to slip through into this Balzacian universe—a universe from which the dualism of good and evil has been so successfully kept out that the greatest criminal, as long as he has imagination, appears as a wholly admirable being, quite on a level with the most distinguished minds.

In a world such as the world of the romantics, which had stepped outside the framework of Christianity, the devil assumes a thousand different aspects, according to the preferences and idiosyncrasies of each individual. The poets of the period all dreamed more or less of a reconciled universe, a restored cosmic harmony, and thus of an "end of Satan"; each imagined it in his own way and according to the law of his own vision of things. Toward 1830 the tinsel devil, which as a literary and theatrical figure had sent agreeable shivers down the spine throughout the eighteenth century, no longer interested anyone. The not very wicked devil whom first

Lesage and then Cazotte had put into circulation—a devil at best capable of helping out the plot of a novel or deceiving the credulous—was relegated to the junk pile. Byron now tried his hand at Satan; Hoffmann mixed his devil's brew; Goethe's Mephistopheles had his faithful, who failed to see how much of the purely literary and the faked there was in him. Lucifer won back his old prestige, and once again his sinister designs appeared perfectly credible. The declamatory writers of the time liked to pose as little Satans, and put on airs that they imagined to be the defiant gestures of great rebels. They admired the stubborn negation of the angel in exile, or else, out of sympathy with the sufferings of this exile, they became his champions, pleaded his cause, and dreamed of the hour when God should forgive him—the hour that was to usher in a golden age after the long centuries of darkness. The romantic period was essentially inconsistent, torn between pose and sincerity, wearing a mask, yet believing itself to be entirely open; it was an age that loved misfortune, extolled the victims of fate, and was a little inclined to confuse Lord Byron with Satan; but at the same time it tried to persuade itself that evil and suffering would one day be overcome. Satan, in this unreal literature which was nevertheless full of a very real anguish, became a symbolic figure, filled with the splendor of evil: but nonetheless he was to be one day reintegrated into shadowless light.

De Vigny played for some time with the idea of writing a *Satan Pardonné*, which much later was indeed to be written, but by Victor Hugo. The fallen angel of *La Fin de Satan* bears a family likeness to the poet who invented him; he carries on him the fatal marks of genius—loneliness, wounded pride, the despairing cry to an unresponsive heaven. The strife between God and Satan, which continues throughout the centuries, and will continue as long as the human history of which it is the true secret, here assumes the forms that are natural to Hugo's imagination. The entire myth of this prophetic epic is built up on the symbolism of light and shadow. Lucifer has descended into the kingdom of night—that is, into the absence of being, since being is light. Evil is only privation; it has no more than a negative existence. It is not Satan himself who is total night, the source of evil; born as he was in heaven, he still retains a luminous nature, even after his fall. It is his nocturnal daughter Lilith who is absolute evil, and she lives by his side in the chasm of a lifeless life. Forgiveness and the reintegration of Satan become possible in this way: his other daughter, Isis or Liberty, formed at the moment of his fall by a feather of his wing, has only to descend into the dark abyss and, being Light, she will disperse the shadows. Lilith will not even die at her approach: she will reveal herself as what she is—pure nullity. Then Satan, finding Liberty once more, in his daughter will see the fulfillment of his long-felt desire—the desire for the forgiveness of God.

Hugo's myth satisfied its author and seemed to him a valid solution of the problem of evil, because this problem was set in the particular coherence of his world of imagery. The Balzacian myth of the end of Satan is no less related to the physics and metaphysics of the *Comédie humaine.* In the tale called *Melmoth réconcilié,* written in 1835, Balzac retained almost nothing of the character he borrowed from Maturin's novel. He did not merely transfer the adventure to the Parisian setting of his novels; he also imagined the annihilation of evil in accordance with his own belief in vital energy and its irremediable exhaustion.

The plot unfolds in the Paris of the restored monarchy and in the world of the Stock Exchange. The offices of the Nucingen bank, the Gymnase Theater, a courtesan's flat— these form the scene of the last years of Satan's life. The strangeness of the events is all the more disturbing because they take place in an everyday setting, among such characters as an English aristocrat—more English than the English—a debauched bank clerk, formerly an officer of the Grande Armée, a young woman with a dubious reputation and a warm heart, and one or two shady characters from the financial demimonde. In this modern society, which has abjured the ethics of honor, everything is subjugated to the evil rule of money, and the devil has no difficulty in finding his instrument of perversion.

In his quest of souls for sale, Satan has fixed his choice upon the Englishman, Melmoth. He has given him supernatural powers, and turned this icy, rigid, black-clad figure, with his expressionless face and daggerlike eyes, into a patented instigator of evil upon earth. His powers are not indeterminate, but selected according to Balzacian optics: John Melmoth has the faculty of infallible action and, more fearful still, the gift of absolute knowledge. This choice of the benefits conferred by a pact with Satan reveals—without the author's knowledge, perhaps—certain of the anxieties that are often to be seen in his works. Thanks to the gold that is one of the material aspects of evil, Gobseck, the usurer, also enjoys a kind of possession which he imposes on others, and a diabolical clairvoyance which enables him to read souls and to force out their secrets. Is not this knowledge closely related to the "second sight" which Balzac attributed to the novelist, and which he always feared might lead to madness? The alchemist in the *Recherche de l'Absolu*, the artists of *Gambara*, *Massimilla Doni*, the *Chef-d'oeuvre inconnu*, are all victims of the same passion to know, which places them on the brink of universal knowledge. Ultimately, however, this passion is seen to be a curse, which destroys life, ruins the individual, and brings tragedy in its train.

Melmoth cannot fail to be aware of this cruel ambivalence of his power, and Satan has foreseen that he will not be able to bear its crushing weight for long. So he has granted him in addition the license to resell his privilege to anyone who will take it in exchange for his eternal salvation. The seduced man has thus become like his seducer. When he tires of his demonic role, he will be able to find a successor without any difficulty, for with his power to read souls, he can always discover someone who is ready to succumb.

Except for the period scenery, everything in the account is so far traditional, and although Balzac significantly insists on the gift of demoniacal knowledge, he has drawn his inspiration from the many conventional stories of Satanic pacts in popular literature, which was a happy hunting ground for the romantics where this theme was concerned. It is only later that the really Balzacian elements of the tale become apparent in the description of the powers of Satan and of their major deficiency; in the methods used by grace to save Melmoth's first successor; finally, and especially, in the end of the story itself, which turns on the curious idea that time wears away evil and causes its gradual devaluation.

Melmoth, then, catches the cashier Castanier red-handed, at the very moment when he is committing a forgery in order to be able to run off with the beautiful Aquilina; and he forces him to accept the pact. The pages in which Balzac describes the cashier's interior experiences and his sudden superhuman lucidity are written in that exalted yet precise style which, in the *Comédie humaine*, always marks the intoxication of discovery and the rapture of intelligence. When Balzac is carried away in this manner, we may be sure that he is touching upon a subject near to his own intimate preferences or his secret fears. The state of sovereign knowledge in which Castanier suddenly finds himself, with his thought encompassing the world "from a prodigious height," is like a hypostatic evocation of the dangerous privileges granted to men of genius, to great artists, to Balzac himself. Castanier has received from Satan the ability to satisfy all his desires, but the real gift, the gift that counts, is the omniscience that places him beyond time and space. "You shall be as gods."

It is possible that Balzac, in thinking out these moments of accursed ecstasy, had at the back of his mind some memory of *Faust*, which Nerval had translated a few years earlier. But there is in this episode an unmistakable personal note, which becomes even more striking later, when Castanier discovers—as he does very soon—the bitterness of the deception practiced on him. Gifted though he is with the unlimited power which Balzac had always dreamed of possessing, and which Louis Lambert thought he could acquire by method, the poor fellow soon comes to see that he has been duped. He has enjoyment and knowledge, but in exchange for them he has renounced love and prayer. "It was a terrible condition. . . . He felt within himself something vast which earth could never satisfy." His worst suffering is to have an intelligence which has assimilated everything, together with a desire which nothing can ever slake. Knowing all that is knowable, he "pants after the unknown"; and Balzac, returning to his ever significant image of the angel, writes: "He spent the whole day spreading his wings, longing to traverse the shining spheres of which he had a clear and despairing intuition."

"A clear and despairing intuition" of the universal mystery—such is the fruit of the Tree of Knowledge once it is possessed. Castanier discovers that he has cut himself off from other human beings and has bidden "a lamentable farewell to his human condition," without ceasing to be a temporal creature. He sinks into "that fearful melancholy of supreme power which Satan and God can remedy only by an activity known to no other." His misfortune is to be all-powerful without finding any object that appears worthy of the application of this power, and without any divine or demoniacal discernment to show him its possible use. For in the Balzacian world, there is no other satisfaction than by the deed. Castanier cannot acquire the creative force of God, but neither can he feel the hatred that gives Satan the joys of destruction; these joys exist only for a being who knows them to be eternal, whereas Castanier "feels himself a devil, but a devil to come"—an unaccomplished devil. He is a creature in between—neither angel nor beast, but man—bored with all that he can possess, and more than ever tormented by the desire for something beyond his possession.

This analysis is fully valid only when it is referred to the central themes of Balzac's thought—the obsession with ambivalent knowledge, the myth of creativeness and action, the passionate longing for the infinite, as piercing as that of Baudelaire, and secretly accompanied by the anguished memory of an irremediable lack forever inherent in the human condition.

But the hope of salvation will yet find expression through a truly Balzacian device. It is the insatiability of Castanier's Faustian character that opens the crack in his hell through which grace can infiltrate. All earthly things seem to him petty and ludicrous, and with the desire of evanescent immensity planted within him, he can think only of what escapes his grasp. He has renounced the eternity of the blessed, and for this very reason he can think of nothing else. "He could think only of heaven," says Balzac, rather as if the accursed desire for power had, in tricking him, hollowed out within him a space which only the presence of God could fill.

Driven half-mad by his sufferings, Castanier rushes to Melmoth, only to find that his predecessor in damnation has made an edifying end the day before, and to attend his funeral at St. Sulpice. Then music intervenes, as it so often does in Balzac—especially liturgical music. In the very hour of his sin, Castanier has already heard for a brief moment the angelic harmony of Heaven, but he has *stubbornly* refused to listen. Now, however, the strains of the *Dies Irae* quite overwhelm him. His very simplicity and ignorance make him all the more profoundly affected by the music, and help him to open his heart to the message of grace. Instinct, even more than intelligence, clears the way for the reception of this message, and Castanier, enlightened by a real revelation and once more conscious of his human insignificance, accepts the truth. Balzac comments somewhat strangely on this sudden conversion. The cashier, he says, had "soaked himself in the infiniteness of evil" and from it had retained the thirst for the infiniteness of good. "His infernal power had revealed the divine power to him."

The comment is brief, but we may well believe that Balzac's unexpressed mediations carried his mind much further, forecasting the profound intuitions of Bloy, the paradoxical experiences of Dostoevski's heroes, and the very substance of the work of Bernanos. What Castanier has just seen in a flash is that hell—to quote the astonishing saying of Barbey d'Aurevilly—"hell is heaven hollowed out."

It is not yet the end of Satan. The man who has been his instrument is saved, but he still has to get rid of the accursed burden by laying it on someone else. The denouement of *Melmoth réconcilié* is hasty, obviously scamped, yet brought about with a *coup de théâtre* that is not wholly gratuitous. Castanier sells his powers to a ruined financier, who keeps them only for a moment and makes them over at a loss, like falling shares. The evil one's gift keeps changing hands for a lower and lower price, until that evening it falls first to a house painter who hardly knows its value, and then to an amorous clerk. This last owner uses up its remaining force in an orgy that kills him before he can find a new buyer.

Thus evil is devalued like a currency, rubbed and worn away by use like an old coin, weakened as if by a gradual loss of energy. There is comedy in this epilogue, which shows the absolute power of Satan as something ludicrous, exhausted, limp, and done for as it now is. What was once sovereign knowledge has deteriorated into the commonplace instrument of sensuality. Omniscience becomes no more than a kind of aphrodisiac, and its last users are unaware of its origin.

No doubt this extremely original version of the end of Satan, dying of autoconsumption, has its own problems. If one tried to make it too coherent, one would run up against a blank wall of logical difficulties. Balzac, however, was not the man to let this trouble him; he was always fascinated by the creation of a mythology, which set in motion his inventive brain and gave him the feeling that he was penetrating the dark heart of the mystery which tormented him. But this energy which maintained his enthusiasm was also subject to the laws of wear and tear. The transport, the ecstasy of the first inspiration, so palpable beneath the irony of the tale of Melmoth, exhausts itself toward the end. Balzac gets out of it with a pirouette; he ends the tale with a few dubious puns and with the grotesque intervention of a German scholar, a disciple of Jakob Boehme, a first-rate demonologist, whom facetious clerks turn to ridicule. One may find this epilogue in bad taste, or, if one is more familiar with the personal anxieties that tormented Balzac, one may prefer to believe that this final burst of laughter drowns a cry of terror. Balzac is the man who spoke the revealing words "Death is certain, let us forget it." The problem of evil and the problem of the limitations of knowledge tortured him no less than the awareness of death. By fixing his mind on them too intently, he was afraid, as was Louis Lambert, of passing beyond the frontier that separates reasonable vision from insane hallucination. If he laughs, his laughter has a very troubled, a very disquieting ring.

Satan does not again make a personal appearance in Balzac's work, but he assigns emissaries who all, more or less unmistakably, carry his credentials. Their master is Vautrin, who comes very near to being created in the image and likeness of the dark angel. Here we are no longer in the region of the fantastic tale, but in that social reality of which Balzac is always regarded as having been the close observer, careful to reproduce it "as it really is." Vautrin, at the center of this world of *Illusions perdues* and *Splendeurs et Miseres des Courtisanes,* is no more, perhaps, than a bandit and a police spy, who uses obscure but entirely human methods to obtain the pleasures conferred by occult powers. He launches a reign of terror, for he holds in his hand the threads of a thousand very real intrigues, by means of which he practices blackmail, backs his threats, and disperses his enemies. He terrifies and he also seduces, holding some through fear and others through the inexplicable spell he casts over them. He is not unnaturally mixed up in the affairs of Gobseck, the usurer whose gold is the instrument of power and knowledge, as it is also for Satan and for the seekers of the philosopher's stone. Vautrin changes his name, his face, and his appearance, and in his new "incarnation" he sets himself to seduce those who had distrusted him in his previous avatar. He is the impostor who takes in everybody and who is known as "Cheat Death," but we are never quite sure whether or not he is deceiving his favorites to guide them toward happiness—toward what he believes is happiness, but is in fact the sensuality of power carried to its extreme limits. When confronted with any other form of life, any other desire, any passion different from his own, he emits the horrifying laughter of Mephistopheles witnessing Faust's love for Margaret.

This demiurge, who in many ways is one of the mythical presentations of Balzac himself within his work, is constantly spoken of in terms applicable to Satan. His passion for Lucien de Rubempré is a desire for possession—an irresistible desire to break into a living soul, to determine its fate, and to make of it a second self. It is far more than a case of commonplace homosexuality. As Thibaudet points out, the *Comédie humaine* could be called the Imitation of God the Father, and the paternity myth is central to it, from the tragic fatherhood of Goriot to the monstrous fatherhood of Vautrin—with Balzac himself always in the background, exalted by his paternal fertility, the father of his characters, and giving to each one of them a carnal, imaginative, or spiritual fertility as his chief resemblance to his progenitor.

But throughout the work, is it not rather a question of the imitation of Satan than the imitation of God the Father? Balzac, indeed, does not intend it to be so, and if he has considerable feeling for the great rebels of his Romanesque universe, he does not go so far as to extend this feeling to the Angel of Revolt. It is hard to imagine him writing Baudelaire's *Litanies de Satan*. On the other hand, we can easily imagine him questioning himself on his enterprise and perceiving its evil nature. Remaking God's world, re-creating a humanity to rival His, giving life to those children of imagination who are his fictional characters—is not this to imitate the Creator in His work—not in the mystical and devotional sense, but in that dangerous way in which he is imitated by Satan, "the ape of God"? If terror pursued Balzac into the nights that he spent "tearing the words out of silence," may we not believe that it was the terror of him who kindled the fire beneath the caldron of the sorcerer's apprentice and mixed the ingredients of which the Faustian homunculus was to be composed? One is reminded of the anguish of Achim von Arnim, who spent his days "in the solitude of poetry," clinging to the history of the golem—a creature that turned against the man who had been rash enough to give it life.

There is no "end of Satan" here; there is nothing more than the defeat of Vautrin-Balzac. The exhaustion of energy remains the irrevocable law, but it is the novelist who exhausts his strength and dies of having thrown the whole of his life's substance into his work, ruined by the ambition for absolute knowledge.

The Devil in Gogol and Dostoevski

Jacques Madaule

Why Gogol and Dostoevski? Because the one is, in a way, the father of the other. Both set themselves the Russian problem in the fullness of its implications; the problem that still troubles us, though in a different manner. What is Russia's place among the nations? What mission has Providence assigned to her? While yet hardly freed from her past, and hesitant about her future, the Russia of the last century was seeking herself through the voice of her great writers. Gogol and Dostoevski both dreamed of a Russia who would at last become fully aware of her Christian mission, who would know how to produce the lines of her future from her past, who would achieve heroism and harmony. They both tried to present her with this portrait of herself. But they both failed. Gogol was never able to finish *Dead Souls,* any more than Dostoevski could finish *The Brothers Karamazov.* Is not this double failure due to the fact that each of them became fascinated by the Russian devil?

Gogol, for example, dreamed of heroic and moving scenes, but wrote *The Inspector General.* This bitter comedy, in which the vices of the czarist bureaucracy are laid bare, is well known. A hive of thieves, swindlers, and extortioners in a distant provincial town is set buzzing by the prospect of an inspector's visit. This inspector, however—Khlestakov—is a practical joker, and the farce ends with the intervention of a real representative of the czar. It would not be forcing the author's intentions to see in this comedy some sort of symbol, not only of the Russian reality, but also of the author himself and of humankind.

Khlestakov here acts as a reagent. This society would not know its own rottenness if a Khlestakov had not appeared in its midst—an impostor who triggers off all the impostures around him. And is not Satan himself the impostor par excellence, who wishes to put himself in God's place? Milton could not help endowing him with greatness—a manifestation, perhaps, of British pride. An essentially insular soul was fired by the evocation of the celestial war which had all the appearance of a war for liberty. But the Russian soul is very different. It is acutely conscious of its essential degradation. That is why the Russian devil is a cheap cardboard "flat," devoid of all greatness.

Khlestakov is indeed the devil, around whom dance and crawl all the vices that he has himself unveiled. But he is fundamentally a mediocre creature, false and bragging. He appeals not to sentiments perverse yet sublime, but to whatever he finds most mediocre and most cowardly in us. The angel's apparition reduces him to dust. But until then he swaggers and preens himself. It is he who reigns in Russia, wherever the rays of grace do not penetrate. Russia is vast, flat, dismal, bored. The devil comes out of a yawn, one of those yawns that, according to Baudelaire, would swallow the world. Khlestakov is bored in this little provincial town where he has been compelled to stop through lack of money. How can he amuse himself? He will pass himself off as an inspector, and therein lies the whole comedy.

But was there not a Khlestakov in Gogol himself? One would have to be very ignorant of his life to deny it. Khlestakov haunted him, in the strongest sense of the word;

that is to say, he dwelled within him, and Gogol could not be rid of him until his death. Who among us is not a Khlestakov? That is the question which takes us by the throat, and which Gogol posed again, with even deeper anguish, in *Dead Souls*. This was to be a picture of Russia, the first part of which was to show the shadows, while the other two parts would lead us a little further toward the light. Unfortunately only the first two parts were written, and Gogol therein managed to construct a character even more diabolical than Khlestakov—the immortal Chichikov. He too was a mediocrity, perfectly versed in exploiting the mediocrity of others.

The strange theme of *Dead Souls* is familiar. The whole story turns on a gigantic and puerile swindle. Chichikov buys a number of serfs who still figure in the registers of the civil state, but who in fact are dead. He pretends to have transported them into barren regions which the government wants to cultivate. There the unfortunate serfs will officially die, and the crook will receive a large indemnity. Once again, it is impossible not to see a symbol, which is moreover stressed by the title of the book. Serfs were, no doubt, known as "souls" in Russia, and the title could just as well be translated "Dead Serfs." But surely the devil makes similar transactions with God and with men. He fights the Almighty for souls, but in reality he receives only dead souls, those which have lost all value. As for the souls themselves, he has previously deceived them, to be deceived in his turn by this harvest of nothingness.

Such, then, is the picture of the unctuous, mealy-mouthed Chichikov. His business does not hold together, any more than Khlestakov's imposture, but it is precisely in this that they are diabolical. He visits the owners, drinks and eats at their expense. He finds favor and inspires a certain confidence—after all, he dresses like everyone else, he endorses all the opinions he hears with remarkable impartiality. Who could distrust Chichikov? It is true that information about him is somewhat vague and uncertain. His origin is not unquestionable, and the business he proposes seems suspect.

Well, who cares? In the world of today one cannot be so fussy. Chichikov's dupes are also his accomplices. And Gogol ends his first part with those pages that I wish I could quote in their entirety. I shall give their conclusion, which was later to inspire Dostoevski.

And what Russian doesn't love it [the sleigh ride]? Could it be otherwise, when his soul longs to forget, to soar, at times to say: "The devil take all!" How could one not love this ride, when it produces such a wonderful intoxication? It is as if some unknown power had swept one up on his wing. One is flying, and everything else is flying too: the posts, the merchants sitting on the edge of their wagons, the forest on both sides, the dark stretches of pines and fir trees. The sound of the axes and the croaking of blackbirds; the entire road is flying and loses itself in the distance. There is something terrifying in these brief apparitions, when objects have no time to fix themselves; only the sky, the light clouds, and the moon appearing through them seem to be still. Oh! troika, troika bird, who invented you? You could be born only among bold people; upon that earth which has done nothing by halves, and which has spread like a pool of oil over half the world, so that the eyes would tire before they had counted the versts. It may be admitted that the vehicle is not a complicated one; it was not constructed with iron screws, but haphazardly put together, with the ax and the cooper's adze, by the skillful muzhik of Yaroslav. The driver wears no strong foreign boots; with his beard and his mittens he sits God knows how; and yet, as soon as he rises and gesticulates and begins to sing, the horses bound forward impetuously, the spokes become one continuous smooth surface, the earth trembles, the startled pedestrian cries out, and the troika flees, devouring space. . . . Already, far away, one can see something cleaving and piercing the air.

And you, Russia, do you not fly like the breathless troika which nothing can outdistance? You speed noisily by in a cloud of dust, leaving all behind. The spectator stops, astonished by this divine prodigy. Is it lightning fallen from heaven? What can this frantic and terrifying race mean? What unknown power lies hidden in these horses which the world has never seen? O chargers, sublime chargers! What whirlwinds stir your manes? Your trembling bodies seem to listen. Hearing the familiar song above them, they swell out their brazen breasts in unison and, hardly grazing the earth with their hooves, form but a taut line which cleaves the air. So flies Russia in divine inspiration. . . . Where do you run? Answer! But there is no answer. The little bell chimes melodiously; the troubled air flutters and eddies in gusts; everything on earth is overtaken, and with an envious look the other nations step aside to give it right of way.

(Dead Souls.)

This brilliant page is not as irrelevant to our subject as it appears, for it is after all Chichikov who has climbed into the troika, and when the prosecutor in *The Brothers Karamazov* takes up Gogol's image in the peroration of his indictment, it is with legitimate anxiety that he speaks of the bolting troika.

Gogol's devil is thus the product of a pent-up boredom born of the flat, vast wastes of land around. It is the same boredom that carries away the troika which delights Chichikov as much as it delights all Russians. The devil would not be so dangerous if he were not crouching in the inner core of our very selves. To quote the prince, who intervenes at the end of *Dead Souls,* just as he intervened at the end of *The Inspector General:* "The country succumbs already, not as the result of an invasion by twenty nations, but through our own fault." Gogol himself is Khlestakov; he is also Chichikov. He almost came to see it in the last years of his life, and that, fundamentally, is the reason why *Dead Souls* was never finished. There was no way of getting rid of the devil. In vain was he expelled into dry places; he would always reappear. In vain were beautiful and stirring literary works attempted; the best, artistically, were always those in which his grotesque grin had been captured and in which one could raise a laugh at his expense. Gogol was condemned to that very realistic observation from which he so much wanted to free himself. He could not help opposing the harmony of Pushkin (who had been his great model and who had even given him the themes of *The Inspector General* and *Dead Souls*) with a different music, no less powerful, but one that fixed the grinning image of the Reprobate over the threshold of Russian literature.

It is indeed impossible, where Gogol is concerned, to ignore the biographical element in an exegesis of his works. His case is unique in this sense: he was a writer who was naturally attracted by the most noble images and who was condemned to succeed only in the painting of vileness. Moreover, in order to depict the vices and blemishes of humanity with such force, it is necessary not only to have the roots of them within oneself, but also to oppose them violently from within. Gogol worked on *Dead Souls* during his stays in Italy, while he was in a state of enchantment over the light of Rome, and while Russia seemed to him a place of exile. But wherever he was, he could not wholly detach himself from his distant country. Although he refused to return to it, he had really never left it. It haunted him, and perhaps he never understood it better than when he was absent from it. Add to that the religious torments which filled all the latter part of his existence. He ended up by disowning the art which had been his whole life. And why? On the one hand because he felt a kind of powerlessness to realize his dream; on the other, because art seemed to him to be bound up with some diabolical influence.

I have purposely restricted myself to Gogol's two principal works, which are the least unknown to the Western public. But it would not have been difficult to make similar observations with regard to others: "The Nose," for example. Not only does the devil hold a preeminent place in Gogol's work, but the author's whole life represents a long and exhausting struggle against the inner demon: a kind of dialogue with this mysterious guest interrupted only by death. A careful search would reveal him in Pushkin also. Only there he is conquered and brought down. Evil, according to Pushkin, never totally destroys the essential harmony. But this triumph was not granted to Gogol. The czar's envoys who intervene both at the end of *The Inspector General* and of *Dead Souls* are to some extent "dei ex machina." They come from the author's will far more than from the nature of things.

The appeal to Good is a cry from the bottom of the chasm; but the vermin will crawl again as soon as the celestial messenger has turned his back. So much is this the case that Gogol's work ends in a poignant question: How can the devil be finally exorcised? How can man be given back his primitive nobility and purity? In no other literature perhaps is the nostalgia of the lost paradise so strong as in the Russian. We meet with it again in Dostoevski, who is, in many ways, Gogol's successor. But one factor is curiously absent from Gogol's work; this is the idea of redemption. The celestial envoys I mentioned do not bring redemption, and do not speak in the name of the Redeemer. They are rather the delegates of a higher and luminous world; they break into the darkness for a moment, only to let it close down again afterward. One might be under the ancient Law and in the time of the Promise. It was for Dostoevski to meet Christ and to suggest, in spite of a thousand difficulties, what His exorcism can do against the devil.

The role of the devil in Dostoevski's work is so central, so essential, that in order to keep this study to reasonable proportions, I shall limit myself to a rapid examination of a few principal works. Let us first consider *Crime and Punishment*. Everyone knows the story of how the student Rodion Romanovich Raskolnikov decides to murder an old woman usurer, not so much to escape from his great poverty—for there were other means of doing this—but to prove to himself that he is capable of living according to his own law. If that is the case, the world belongs to him, and here already is one of the three temptations later evoked in "The Legend of the Grand Inquisitor." As soon as the crime is committed—and it has not quite turned out as Raskolnikov had imagined it, since he had also to murder the usurer's sister, a pure and upright soul—the devil seizes the criminal and haunts him in the form of the Proprietor Svidrigailov. Svidrigailov is essentially an *ennuyé*, haunted by evil dreams: that, for instance, of the country house full of spiders which so curiously resembles hell. He lives in a room partitioned off from that of Sonia, and hears Raskolnikov confess his crime to her. For if Svidrigailov is the devil, Sonia is the angel. Each is installed in the soul of Raskolnikov, who has no secret from either.

Thus the whole drama of *Crime and Punishment* revolves around a struggle between two worlds: the higher and the lower. Raskolnikov has killed two women—one bad, the other good; the one (who may be said to animate the soul of Svidrigailov) able only to think of revenge; the other, who animates Sonia's soul, a forgiver of wrongs and an intercessor for the salvation of her murderer. Thus also Raskolnikov's soul is divided between good and evil. Sonia can only pray, but if Raskolnikov does not freely submit, if he does not humiliate himself as far as to confess his crime, and confess publicly, the angel's prayer will have been in vain. Sonia finally wins, and that is why she is allowed to accompany Raskolnikov to the place of punishment, which is at the same time that of redemption, while Svidrigailov, the vanquished devil, hangs himself.

In *The Idiot*, everything is more subtle and more obscure. No character is truly demonic, like Svidrigailov. Nevertheless the devil has already deeply ravaged the society in which Prince Myshkin finds himself, and always, as in Gogol, the devil is utterly insipid. It is he who jests with Ferdischenko, he whose ridiculous and sickly pride is found again in Gania; it is he who quickens the crawling and viscous baseness of Lebedev. But it is he especially who rages implacably against Natasha Filippovna. Prince Myshkin enters the lists to contend for this victim of his choice. Natasha Filippovna is known to be a creature of dazzling beauty, and this physical beauty is but the sign of an admirable spiritual integrity. But she has been corrupted in youth by the man who had established himself as her protector. Totski is the very type of emancipated nobleman of the forties who plays such a great role in Dostoevski's work. He has apparently seen nothing wrong in abusing a young orphan girl whom he has brought up especially for that purpose. But Natasha has been fatally injured. The prince has only to look at a photograph of the young woman to see this: "It is an extraordinary face! And I am convinced that this woman's destiny cannot be commonplace. Her expression is gay, and yet she must have suffered much, don't you think? It can be read in her look, and also in those two small protuberances that form two points under her eyes, on the verge of the cheeks. The face is excessively proud; but I cannot see if it is good or evil. Oh, that it could be good; all would be saved!"

Now that he has succeeded in bruising her, the devil uses Natasha as bait for the converging desires of General Epanchin, of Gania, and especially of Rogozhin, The last-named is, in certain ways, truly possessed. It is first by his eyes that Myshkin recognizes him. This is the first portrait of Rogozhin:

He was of small build, and seemed about twenty-seven years old; his hair was curled and almost black; his eyes were gray and small, but full of fire. His nose was flat, his cheekbones prominent; on his pinched lips was a continual smile that was impertinent, mocking, and even spiteful. But his broad and well-modeled forehead made up for the lack of nobility in the lower part of his face. What was particularly striking in the face was its pallor, and its look of utter exhaustion, although the man was fairly strongly built; one saw in it also something passionate, something suffering, which was in contrast with the insolence of the smile and the provocative self-conceit of the expression.

When, long afterward, Myshkin, returning from Moscow to St. Petersburg, arrived at the station without being met, "he suddenly thought he saw a pair of burning eyes which were staring at him very strangely in the crowd surging around the travelers. He tried to find where this gaze came from but could no longer see it. Perhaps it was only an illusion, but it left an unpleasant impression." Soon after, Myshkin visits Rogozhin in the dark house where he lives. And at the end of their conversation, Rogozhin cuts the pages of Soloviev's *History of Russia* with a little garden knife, brand new, which, later, he is to use to murder Natasha Filippovna, on the evening of their marriage. When Rogozhin sees the prince to the door, the latter stops for an instant before a copy of a Holbein representing the Savior after the Descent from the Cross. Rogozhin murmurs: "I like to look at that picture."

"That picture," cries the prince in sudden inspiration. "But do you know that a believer could lose his faith by looking at it?"

"Yes, one loses one's faith," agrees Rogozhin unexpectedly. Then Rogozhin asks the prince to give him his cross; he gets his mother to give him her blessing, and this is the end of this extraordinary scene:

"You see," said Rogozhin, "my mother understands nothing of what is said; she has not grasped the sense of my words, and yet she has blessed you. So she has acted spontaneously. . . . Come, good-by. For you, as for me, it is time to separate." And he opened the door.

"Let me at least embrace you before we part; how odd you look!" exclaimed the prince with a look of tender reproach.

He wanted to take him in his arms, but the other, who had already raised his, dropped them abruptly. He could not make up his mind, and his eyes avoided the prince. He could not bring himself to embrace him.

"Don't be afraid," he said, in an expressionless voice and with a strange smile, "even if I have taken your cross, I won't murder you for your watch."

But his face suddenly changed: a terrible pallor came over it; his lips quivered, his eyes blazed. He opened his arms, embraced the prince violently, and said in a strangled voice, "Take her then, if that is the will of Destiny. She is yours. I give her up to you. Remember Rogozhin."

And, turning from the prince without another glance, he went hastily back into his room and slammed the door.

The prince, however, is haunted all day by that look of Rogozhin's, which he had noticed on arriving at the station, met again in the street, and which seems to pursue him; he comes across it again while roaming through St. Petersburg, until at last he finds Rogozhin waiting for him, hidden in an alcove in the dark entrance to his house, and holding some shining object in his hand—the same knife he had used to cut the pages of *The History of Russia;* Rogozhin is lying in wait to kill him. The prince, thereupon, has an attack of epilepsy, which saves him from the dagger thrust. Rogozhin runs away like a madman. It is not the prince, but Natasha Filippovna who is to fall by that knife.

If I have dwelt rather long on this episode of *The Idiot*, it is because it shows vividly the warfare between good and bad spirits. Rogozhin is not wholly bad, any more than Myshkin is wholly good. If the prince had not, in spite of himself, ascribed to Rogozhin the intention of killing him, perhaps that intention would not exist. As for Rogozhin, he struggles fiercely with his own temptations. Myshkin himself recognizes it, when he remembers Rogozhin's strange remark about the Holbein picture: "That man must suffer terribly. He says he 'likes to look at this picture of Holbein.' It isn't that he likes looking at it, but that he needs to look at it. Rogozhin is not only a passionate soul, he has also the fighter's temperament: he wants at all costs to regain the faith he has lost. He feels the need of it, and is suffering. . . . Yes, to believe in something! To believe in someone!" As we can see, the devil is everywhere here, and we would be very much mistaken if we thought him to be wholly absent even from the soul of Myshkin.

Natasha Filippovna would not have so completely bewitched them both if she had not herself been, in her own way, possessed—possessed by her own shame, which she is unable to accept. And it is from perversity, as Rogozhin himself observes, that she finally decides to marry him, and that to do so she avoids the prince. It is not to her wedding that she flees, but to her death, to that ineluctable death which Rogozhin has long prepared for her and which she prefers to life itself. Her death means checkmate to Myshkin, and plunges him back into that idiocy from which he had emerged only for a while to accomplish a task that he was incapable of carrying through to the end. Moreover, it must not be forgotten that Rogozhin's father was a merchant who belonged to that sect of Old Believers that continued in Russia till the end of the old regime, and that Rogozhin himself, in the opinion of Prince Myshkin and Natasha Filippovna, would have been in every way like his father, had he not encountered the strange creature who was no longer capable of anything but self-destruction, and the destruction of others. I must leave aside the large group of secondary characters, although they are closely connected with the central drama, some of them—especially the young Hippolytus—being exceptionally interesting in relation to our theme.

But now we come to *The Possessed*, or rather, *The Demons*, to translate the Russian title literally. Dostoevski headed his work with two epigraphs, one of them a quotation from Pushkin:

> We have strayed, what shall we do?
> The devil is dragging us through the fields
> Making us turn in all directions.
>
> . . . .
>
> How many are they, where are they driven?
> What can their mournful chanting mean?
> Are they burning a goblin
> Or marrying a witch?

The other text is simply Luke 8 : 32–37, and tells the story of the evil spirits entering the swine.

The author's intentions are thus particularly clear. It is also easy to say that the demons are the companions of Pyotr

Stepanovich Verkhovenski. But who is the man out of whom these demons came in order to enter the swine? There can be no question: it is Nikolai Vsevolodovich Stavrogin. But in spite of what has happened, he himself has not been delivered: he is the archdemon among these demons. Motionless and empty, like the spider in the middle of her web, he animates all the others. His own pact is anterior to the story. We learn something of it only when we listen to his confession. What is interesting is that he has been the pupil of Stepan Trofimovich, who is himself the father of the horrible and shallow Pyotr Stepanovich who leads the hideous gang for the benefit of Stavrogin and under his soulless eye. Here the theme of *Dead Souls* is taken up again, with more depth. It is that of the tragic contest between Russia and the West which has continued ever since Peter the Great. Stepan Trofimovich is an "Occidental," pedantic, pretentious, hypocritical, and a little ridiculous, something like the great critic Belinski, who flourished in the same period. He is filled with noble and humanitarian ideas, which he tries to impart to his pupil. As for his son, he takes little interest in him. From his mildness, his helplessness, and his misunderstood soul were born the furious demons that ravage Russia.

This is not the place to discuss the validity of this viewpoint. It was, at any rate, Dostoevski's. The demons are more interesting because they are authentic. At the center of the work there is the fascinating character of Stavrogin. He is not mediocre; on the contrary, he is a man endowed with very great gifts. He can hardly be said to be haunted, except perhaps by nothingness. It is the vacuity of this soul which draws like an abyss and causes a kind of giddiness. Stavrogin is bored, not as Svidrigailov is bored, but with a metaphysical ennui. He is seeking the limit of his power, and all the experiments he undertakes seem to him vain. Out of pride, he tries to degrade himself, for, he thinks, his essence is such that no humiliation can really touch him. Nevertheless, he is seized at times by attacks of genuine possession. One such occasion

JACQUES MADAULE *Gogol and Dostoevski* 195

is when he leads a very respectable gentleman around the room holding him by his nose; another, when he savagely bites the ear of the provincial governor, after pretending that he wanted to whisper a secret to him. At such moments he is very pale, and those standing around wonder if he is in full possession of himself. But the point is never elucidated. In Stavrogin, we puzzle over the very mystery of evil, which seems to be loved and cultivated for its own sake, quite disinterestedly. It could be said of Stavrogin, as of Lucifer, that he has made a value of evil. All victims are acceptable to him, whether it is the unfortunate young girl who hangs herself after he has dishonored her, or Chatov, whom he leads to death after having deceived and betrayed him, or lame Marya Timofeyevna, whom he marries one day as a mockery and whom he later has murdered by the bandit Fedka; or Lizaveta Nikolayevna, his fiancée, who crawls at his feet while he gazes at the city in flames; or even Dasha, the devoted girl who would like to be his guardian angel, and yet cannot prevent him from hanging himself ignominiously in an attic. Stavrogin cannot be interested in his victims because he is incapable of loving. Love is so entirely dead to him that he no longer loves even himself.

I must leave aside the secondary demons who fill the novel—even the agitated and self-sufficient Pyotr Stepanovich, who seems to be the leader of the infernal band. He is nothing more than the reflection of Stavrogin, and it is perhaps the latter's deep thought which he one day suggests to the engineer Kirilov, convincing him that if man can once and for all master his own death, he will have killed God and replaced him, for there are only two possibilities: either God becomes man to save us, or else man becomes God and saves himself. Stavrogin knows the vanity of such ambitions. He himself, like the guilty archangel, believes in God, and admits it in his confession. But he has placed himself against God, as an adversary whom the Almighty may vanquish, but not subdue.

It is not impossible, I know, to find some sort of Byronic

romanticism in a character such as Stavrogin. The narrator himself is fascinated by his presence. Marya Timofeyevna calls him an impostor, but she is under his influence, and one of the most significant scenes is that in which the half-mad lame girl tells Stavrogin what he was and is:

"You are like him, you are very like him. Perhaps you are related. Oh, the cunning creatures! . . . Only mine is a radiant falcon and a prince, while you are only a bat, a little shopkeeper. If he likes, mine will bow before God, and if he doesn't, he won't. And Chatuchka, my darling, good, and dear Chatuchka, has struck you full in the face. Lebyadkin told me about it. What were you afraid of when you came in? What had frightened you? When I saw your common face—when I fell down and you picked me up—I felt as if a worm had climbed into my heart. That's not *he*, I thought, no, that's not *he*. My falcon would never have been ashamed of me in front of a young society woman. My God! The one thing that has kept me happy throughout these five years is the thought of my falcon living there, across the mountains, where he floats in the air and gazes at the sun. Tell me, impostor, were you paid a lot? Was it for the large sum of money that you gave your consent? I wouldn't have given you a penny. Ha, ha, ha. . . ."

And in the end, as he flees from her insults, she shouts to him: "Grishka Otrepiev, a-na-thema." Moreover, it is sufficient to observe the titles Dostoevski has given to certain chapters—all of them about Stavrogin—to grasp his intention. There is the chapter called "Prince Harry," that is to say the proud Henry V of England, the man of Falstaff and of Agincourt; there is "The Sins of Others," the sins for which Stavrogin makes the innocent Chatov pay; there is "The Subtle Serpent," obviously that of Genesis; there is "Ivan Czarevich." This mingling of grandeur and imposture, this glimpse of the archangel behind the archfiend, the sinister bat that takes the place of the falcon in the sun—all this characterizes Stavrogin, a unique person who had to be placed as a sort of model at the center of this study, and who cannot be outdone in grandeur any more than in baseness. Perhaps he is even too great to be real; too great not to be somewhat theoretical.

We return to earth with *A Raw Youth,* which contains the split character of Versilov, on whom I ought to dwell longer. But I wish to press on to *The Brothers Karamazov,* in which Dostoevski poured out all he knew of this and the other world. It is the entire Karamazov family which is at the same time angelic and demonic. The father, Fyodor Pavlovich, a Russian gentleman by birth, and a parasite, a professional buffoon, belongs to the same category as Svidrigailov. He degrades himself with apparent cheerfulness, but occasionally he gets pathetic in his cups, and asks his son Ivan if God really does not exist. He is vaguely tinged with Western ideas, just enough to hold monks, and old customs, in derision. He is possessed by the devil of sensuality—the especial devil of the Karamazovs. We need not discuss his first wife, who gave him Dmitri, nor Dmitri himself, in whom the demon of sensuality has had to struggle against a fundamentally good and generous nature, which, in the end, is to win.

But the second wife of Fyodor Pavlovich is a saint and martyr; she has opposed her purity to her husband's sensuality, her spirituality to his materialism. She has consoled herself for his ill treatment by praying before holy images. She has given him two sons, Ivan and Alyosha. In each of them there remains something of their mother's angelic nature. But Ivan, the university student, has been bitten by the demon of knowledge; in addition to pride, he has acquired a deep hatred and scorn for his father. He is his father's true murderer. Now, however despicable this father may be, he still retains, in spite of himself, the sacred stamp of fatherhood. To raise a hand in cold blood against one's father is of all acts the most diabolical. Ivan dares not do it, but he incites to it the infamous Smerdyakov, who is the fourth Karamazov brother. His mother was a wretched idiot whom Fyodor raped out of bravado and some extraordinary refinement of sensuality. Smerdyakov feels the double humiliation of his birth and seeks revenge. It is impossible to exaggerate the part played by humiliation in Dostoevski's work. If the humbled one accepts his humiliation, he may rise very high in sanctity; but if it provokes only the reaction of hurt pride in him, he is lost: let us remember Natasha Filippovna. Smerdyakov is no less proud than Ivan, and far more humiliated. Henceforth the two men understand each other's hints, and the one can carry out what the other has conceived. Alyosha, on the other hand, although he does not altogether escape from the demon of sensuality which haunts his family, has received an almost wholly angelic nature from his mother, as Romano Guardini has pointed out. Had the novel been completed he would have played the role of a Myshkin, but a Myshkin who succeeded and became the regenerator of Russia. Thus it can be seen that the aim of *The Brothers Karamazov* is not so far removed from that of *Dead Souls*, which was not finished either. And it can also be seen that Dostoevski's entire work is nothing but a combat between angels and devils, a combat whose outcome is often uncertain, as Milton says.

Moreover, these are not the only diabolical characters in *The Brothers Karamazov*. Mention must also be made of the young Liza, who tempts Alyosha, and of the horrifying seminarist, who mocks him. But the character who absorbs our attention even more is Ivan. He has an acute sense of the evil which reigns on earth, and it is by asking Alyosha for some explanation of this evil, and especially of the suffering of the innocent, that he attempts one day to shake his faith. Yet a little before that he says: "I must confess something to you; I have never been able to understand how one can love one's neighbor. To my mind it is precisely one's neighbor whom one cannot love; at any rate, one can only love him at a distance. . . . A man must be hidden before one can love him; as soon as he shows his face, love vanishes." So we find again in him the absence of love which characterized Stavrogin. But he is a much younger and very much more human Stavrogin. For while the latter coldly declares to Chatov that whatever he does, he cannot love him, Ivan on the contrary finds it extremely difficult not to love Alyosha, and he certainly does love Katerina Ivanovna, who was Dmitri's fiancée.

It is because Ivan's soul is still fresh, though corrupted by pride, that he cannot bear the thought of being his father's murderer, and this thought brings on an attack of fever, during which he has an interview with the devil in person. This is the only time that Dostoevski brings the evil one directly on the scene, and an analysis of their dialogue may conclude this all too brief study, for the devil of Ivan Karamazov is very close to that of Gogol. Here, first, is his physical appearance:

He was a gentleman, or rather a peculiarly Russian sort of gentleman, *qui frisait la cinquantaine,* going a little gray, with long thick hair and a pointed beard. He was wearing a brown jacket, well cut enough but already rather the worse for wear, at least three years old and thus completely out of fashion. His linen and his long cravat all spoke of the well-dressed man, but on closer inspection the linen revealed itself as of a dubious cleanliness, and the cravat as much soiled. His check trousers sat well on him, but they were too light and too close-fitting—the sort that nobody wears nowadays: his hat was a white felt one, quite out of keeping with the season. In short, a dandy fallen on bad times. He looked like one of those landed proprietors who flourished during the days of serfdom; he had lived in good society, but bit by bit, impoverished by his youthful dissipations and the recent abolition of serfdom, he had become a sort of high-class sponger, admitted into the society of his former acquaintances because of his pliable disposition, as a man one need not be ashamed to know, whom one can invite to meet anybody, only fairly far down the table. These hangers-on—compliant characters, good raconteurs, handy at the card table, unwilling social errand boys—are usually widowers or bachelors: Sometimes they have children, always brought up somewhere else, usually with some aunt or other whom the gentleman concerned never mentions in good company, as if the relationship embarrassed him. He ends up by losing contact with his children, who write to him from time to time (for his name day or Christmas) letters of congratulation which he sometimes answers and sometimes doesn't.

The expression of this unexpected guest was affable rather than friendly and obviously prepared for whatever politeness the situation might demand. He had no watch, but carried a tortoise-shell lorgnette on a black ribbon. A massive gold ring with a cheap opal adorned the middle finger of his right hand. Ivan Fyodorovich kept silent, determined that he for his part would not start the conversation. The visitor waited, like a poor relation who, arriving at teatime to provide company for the master of the house, finds him preoccupied with his thoughts and remains silent, ready nevertheless for polite conversation if his host initiates it.

Does not this description irresistibly remind one of a character such as Versilov, for instance? In Ivan's devil there is nothing left of that grandeur that we noticed in Stavrogin. He himself admits, with perfect simplicity, that if he is a fallen angel, he has completely forgotten it and has henceforth only one modest ambition: that of passing for a well-bred man. He does not like the fantastic, and he does not mind terribly whether people believe in him. He complains of rheumatism contracted in interstellar space where, as we know, it is very cold. When Ivan is astonished to hear that he suffers from such a human infirmity, the devil replies: "If I become incarnate, I must suffer the consequences—Satanas sum et nihil humani a me alienum puto." The devil then chats for a long time and gets himself insulted by Ivan, who feels that he is the victim of a hallucination but lets himself be taken in. The devil is, of course, also Ivan himself. His progressive and liberal ideas are those of Ivan. His system of future happiness for humanity is that of the Grand Inquisitor, or of Chigalev in *The Possessed*. Listen to him:

"Once the whole of humanity professes atheism—and I believe that this epoch will come in its turn, as inexorably as a geological period—then the old conception of the world will disappear of its own accord, without any cannibalism; and with it the old morality. Men will join together in drawing from life every possible enjoyment, but in this world alone. The human spirit will rise to a titanic pride, and this will be the deification of humanity. Triumphing ceaselessly and limitlessly over nature, by virtue of his knowledge and his power, man will experience thereby a joy so intense that it will replace for him the hope of heaven. Each will know that he is mortal, without hope of resurrection, and will resign himself to death with proud tranquillity, like a god. He will scorn in his pride to murmur at the shortness of life; he will love his brothers with an entirely disinterested love. Love itself will bring only passing joys, but the very knowledge of its transiency will deepen its intensity in proportion as it was once diluted by the hope bf an eternal love beyond the tomb. . . .''

It is the return of the golden age, of which Versilov also dreams. It is above all the ultimate outcome of that liberalism of the forties, which Dostoevski never tires of attacking. Gogol's devil, and even Dostoevski's, do not consider it beneath them to be commonplace. The devil repeats several times to Ivan: "Do not demand 'the great and the beautiful' from me." He even styles himself Khlestakov grown old, and here the reference to Gogol is direct. Nevertheless he is always the Tempter of Genesis, who promises man: "And you shall be as God." Dostoevski's glory lies not only in having lit up these troubled depths, but in having shown that the unfolding of a certain history has no other end than the disappearance of humanity itself from this earth. The devil is more present than ever, and I shall not insult the reader by stressing the analogies constantly suggested by the great Russian writers of the last century. In their country they diagnosed a disease that was not specific to it but was singularly virulent there. Perhaps indeed, it was for Russia, of all nations, to have both the secret of the disease and its remedy. That remedy is love—the love which Alyosha shows, and which he makes his young friends show, to poor Ilyusha: "Is it true," asks Kolya on the day of the child's burial, "what religion says, that we shall rise from the

dead, that we shall all see each other again, us and Ilyusha?''
''Certainly, we shall rise again, we shall see each other again,
we shall tell each other everything that has happened,'' replies
Alyosha.

POSTSCRIPT

Dom Aloïs Mager, O.S.B.

In literature, notably the literature of the novel, it is preeminently the French and Russian writers who confront us with a new inner reality: demonism. It is true that Nietzsche before them had uncovered the Satanic depths; nevertheless it was the men of letters, the masters of living psychology, whose shrewd prevision foretold what has become an immediate reality to the world of today. No one has revealed the human soul more penetratingly than the French and the Russians, and in making any analysis of their work we are fully entitled to speak of demonism. With an extraordinarily sensitive touch, they were able to reach those extremities where the influence of Satan seeps through. They smelled out the demon's breath and realized what a compelling motive power it might be; they then attempted to translate the demonism into literary form, that the general public might focus its attention on the reality that had just been brought to light. One may here recall the novels of Bernanos: *Sous le Soleil de Satan* and *Le Journal d'un curé de campagne*.

Du Bos, in his *Dialogue avec André Gide* (Paris, 1929), traced the lines of "demonism" in Gide and Nietzsche, nor did he forget Dostoevski, whose *Notes from the Underground* shows demonism in its naked form. Dostoevski's expositions are so realistic that Du Bos believes that he was in direct cooperation with Satan. And Karl Pfleger justly observes: "The demonic figures produced by Dostoevski—Raskolnikov, Svidrigailov, Kirilov, Verkhovenski, Ivan, Dmitri, Smerdyakov, and the father of the Karamazov brothers—are not mere creatures of the imagination: they are born of what he himself had experienced inwardly." No writer before Dostoevski has ever shown such realism in his portrayal of demonism in the infrahuman, the suprahuman, and the infrasuprahuman. These demons with human faces think unreally. They are pure visionaries. Their analytical reason or their fleshly voluptuousness loses all contact with "living life." At times they seem powerful and of great weight, but they are so only in destruction. Whatever they do, their work ends only in destruction, because it comes forth from men who are already destroyed to the depth of their souls (Pfleger, *Die Geister, die um Christus ringen*, pp. 208–21). Pfleger has a strong inkling, though he is not consciously aware of it, of the origins of demonism in Dostoevski when he writes:

> The lower regions are nothing but the anthropological secret of liberty and trial in liberty. They are not in themselves Satanic, but demons emerge from them. Man who is from birth destined to liberty becomes a demon if he abuses liberty.

> (Pp. 208–209.)

In theological language we would say that the consequences of original sin are not in themselves demonic; they are human: but they are points of entry for demons. These doors are set open when man, consciously and experimentally, lets himself be guided by the impulse of the triple result of original sin in his thought, his will, and his action. This is what makes man a slave; this is what fetters him in the use of his liberty. It is possible for him to become and to remain free of the slavery of triple concupiscence; but it is also possible for him not to become and not to remain free of this slavery. The man who chooses the second possibility gives himself up to the action of Satan and himself becomes, gradually, a demon.

Black Mass in Paris

From *Là-Bas* by J.-K. Huysmans
Translated by Maisie Ward

"Listen," said Hyacinthe, "I still hold to my decision of the other evening: I will not let you get mixed up with Canon Docre. I can, however, arrange for you to be present, without actually meeting him, at the ceremony you so crave to learn about."

"The Black Mass?"

"Yes, within the next week Docre will have left Paris. Before he leaves, you shall see him once with me but never again. Keep your evenings free for a week, and I will give you a signal when the moment comes. You owe me your best thanks, my friend, for I am defying my confessor's orders—I shall never dare see him again and I am damning my soul to hell."

. . . .

"*You* have taken part in a Black Mass?"

"Yes, and I can tell you now how you will regret having seen anything so strange, so ghastly. It's an unfading memory with horror in it, even—in fact, especially—when one has taken no personal part in the ceremonies."

He looked at her—how pale she was, how clouded and vague her eyes.

"It's your deliberate choice," she went on. "You cannot complain if the ceremony horrifies or disgusts you."

The deep melancholy in her voice shook him a little.

"But this man," he asked, "this Docre, where does he come from, what has his past been, how did he become a master of Satanism?"

"I have no idea. I knew him as a priest settled in Paris who became the confessor of a queen in exile. Horrible stories were told about him, but thanks to his supporters these were kept dark during the period of the Empire. He was sent by his bishop to La Trappe, then driven out of the clergy, excommunicated by Rome. I have heard too that he has several times been accused of poisonings, but acquitted for lack of proof. Today he lives comfortably—how I don't know—traveling a great deal with a woman whose preternatural insights he finds useful. The world classes him as a criminal. He is learned, he is depraved—and utterly charming!"

"How your voice changes—and your eyes! Admit you are in love with him."

"No longer—but I don't mind owning to you we were once madly in love."

"And now?"

"That is all over, I swear. We are now nothing more than friends."

"But at that time you must often have gone to his place. How strange was it? Would you describe it as abnormal?"

"No, it was comfortable and clean. He had a chemist's outfit and an immense library. The only odd book he showed me was the office of the Black Mass written on parchment. The book was most beautifully illuminated. Its binding was made from the dried skin of an unbaptized baby! A large host consecrated at a Black Mass was the design stamped on the cover."

"And what of the manuscript itself?"

"I did not read it."

. . . .

They went up the Rue Vaugirard in a cab. Hyacinthe Chantelouve muffled up in her corner spoke not a word. As they passed a street lamp Durtal looked at her but could see only her veil. In her silence he sensed agitation and fear. She let him take her hand, but through her glove he felt its icy cold. For once her blond hair was unbrushed, and struck him as drier and coarser than he had known it.

"Are we nearly there, my dear?"

But in a low, agonized voice she answered, "Please don't talk."

He began to look through the cab windows and note where they were going. The road stretched ahead—endless, already deserted, so badly paved that the axles groaned at every turn of the wheels. The gas lamps, giving a poor light from the first, grew more and more scarce as they approached the city walls. Her cold, withdrawn expression bothered him, made him realize the weirdness of what they were doing.

At last the carriage turned abruptly into a dark street, made another turn, and stopped.

Hyacinthe got out, and Durtal, waiting for his change from the cabman, gave a quick glance at their surroundings. They were in a sort of blind alley. Low, depressing houses stood on each side of a path badly paved and with no sidewalks. He turned when the driver had gone and found himself facing a long, high wall above which he could hear the rustle of leaves in the darkness. A small door with a peephole was set in the thickness of the wall, its dense black broken by great white patches of plaster filling the holes in it. Suddenly a light shone from a front window, and a man leaned out and spat on the doorstep.

"Here we are," said Madame Chantelouve. She rang and the little window opened. She lifted her veil, the light was turned on her face. The door opened noiselessly, admitting them into a garden.

"Good evening, madame."

"Good evening, Marie. Is it in the chapel?"

"Yes, madame, shall I take you there?"

"No, thanks."

The woman holding the lantern looked hard at Durtal. And he saw under a hood tumbled gray hair over an aged face. She did not give him much time to inspect her but disappeared at once into a building near the wall—evidently her lodge.

He followed Hyacinthe through a dark path winding through trees to a building with a porch. She, evidently at home in the place, pushed open the door; her heels rang on a stone pavement.

"Watch out," she said, "there are three steps."

They emerged into a court, stopped in front of an old house. She rang the bell, a little man appeared, bowed, asked her how she was in an affected singsong. She greeted him briefly and moved on. Durtal became aware of eyes, damp and gluey, cheeks plastered with rouge, painted lips. He had fallen, he felt, into a den of sodomites.

"You didn't prepare me for such company," he said to Hyacinthe as he caught up with her at a turning in the passage, lit by a lamp.

"Did you think you would meet saints here?" she asked with a shrug as she opened a door. They were in a chapel with a low ceiling, crossed by beams smeared over with pitch, windows hidden by heavy curtains, walls stained and crumbling. At the first step Durtal recoiled. The hot air from the radiators, the atrocious smell of damp and decay, were too much for him. His throat was choked and his head ached.

He felt his way forward, exploring the chapel, dimly lit by hanging sanctuary lamps of rose-colored glass and gilded bronze. Hyacinthe signed to him to sit down while she moved over toward a group of people on divans in a dark corner. Annoyed at being thus put on one side, Durtal noted that there were very few men in the congregation and many women, but his efforts to distinguish their features were vain. Here and there, however, when the lights momentarily brightened, he noted a large Junoesque brunette and the face of a man, clean shaven. Watching them, he was certain that the women were not chattering with one another—their conversation was serious, they were nervous: never a laugh, never a loud voice, only vague, furtive whispering with no illuminating gesture.

"*Sapristi*," said he to himself, "it doesn't look as if Satan made his faithful happy."

An altar boy dressed in red came forward and lit a row of candles. And now the altar was visible, an altar like that of any church, crowned by a tabernacle above which appeared the figure of Christ—but a Christ base and despicable. The neck had been stretched upward; on the agonized face the mouth had been twisted into a sneering smile. He was naked, but in place of the usual linen around his waist, the signs were visible of a man sexually stirred. In front of the tabernacle was placed a veiled chalice. The altar boy smoothed the altar cloth with his hands, waggled his hips, drew himself up on one foot as if to fly, gestured obscenely as he reached to light the black candles, whose smell of bitumen and resin increased the stifling foulness of the atmosphere. Durtal recognized the "altar boy" as the elderly homosexual who had charge of the gate through which he had entered, and realized the symbolism of the substitution.

And now a really hideous altar boy came into view. Of skeleton thinness, shaken with coughing, dolled up with rouge and cosmetics, he limped forward singing. Reaching the tripods which flanked the altar, he stirred up the heat still alive in the ashes, throwing into it leaves and fragments of resin.

Durtal was getting bored by the time Hyacinthe came up. She apologized for having so long deserted him, suggested that he move, and led him into a remote corner, far behind the rows of chairs.

"Are we really in a chapel?" he asked.

"Yes. This house, this church, the garden through which we passed, are the remains of an old Ursuline convent, now a ruin. For a long time fodder was stored in the chapel, the house belonged to a man who rented out carriages—and he sold it to that woman." She pointed out as she spoke the statuesque brunette Durtal had already noticed.

"She is married, is she?"

"No, she was once a nun—violated by Canon Docre."

"And what about those men who seem to prefer the dark?"

"Those are Satanists. . . . One of them was a professor in the School of Medicine; he has a chapel in his house where he prays to the statue of Venus Astarte enthroned on his altar."

"Bah!"

"Yes, he is getting old but his Satanist prayers double the strength he concentrates on creatures of that sort"—and she pointed to the choirboys.

"You can swear to the truth of all this?"

"So little am I inventing that you can read it all in a religious paper, *Annales de la Sainteté.* Though the article was unmistakably about him, the gentleman did not dare to prosecute the paper for libel— Hullo, is something the matter with you?" she asked suddenly looking at him.

"I . . . I'm stifling. The stink of those incense burners is nauseating."

"You'll get used to it in a few minutes."

"But what on earth are they burning that stinks like that?"

"All sorts of plants with scents agreeable to Satan our master." Her voice had suddenly become unlike her own, harsh and guttural—he had heard it once or twice in bed with her.

He looked at her: she was pale, her lips compressed, her eyes blinking back tears.

"Here he is," she whispered suddenly, as the women hurried ahead of them to kneel on their chairs.

The canon came in, preceded by the two altar boys and

wearing a soiled biretta on which two buffalo horns had been sewn.

Durtal looked closely at him as he approached the altar. He was tall but badly built. His forehead went in a straight line to his nose, his lips and cheeks bristling with the stiff dry hairs which with old priests often result from long years of shaving. His features were heavy and deeply lined, his eyes like apple pips, small and dark, set close to the nose, phosphorescent, like those of cats. The general effect was evil but dynamic, while his hard, steady eyes had none of the shiftiness and cunning Durtal had expected.

He bowed solemnly before the altar, went up the steps, and began his mass.

And then Durtal realized that except for his vestments the man was naked. The ridge made by his garters showed above his black stockings. The chasuble was of the usual shape, but its color was the dark red of blood. In a central triangle a black goat reared its horned head, surrounded by a growth of meadow saffron, pine cones, deadly nightshade, and plants with poisonous roots.

Docre genuflected and bowed as the ritual directed, the altar boys on their knees made the responses in Latin, their clear voices seeming to sing on the final syllables.

"But it's just an ordinary low mass," said Durtal.

Madame Chantelouve gave him a negative sign. And at that moment the altar boys were filing behind the altar, one carrying copper heaters, the other thuribles, which they distributed among the worshipers. The women were wrapped in the smoke; some bending their heads down over the thuribles drew in the smoke through nose and mouth, then groaning close to collapse, ripped open their dresses.

At this point the sacrifice was halted. The priest came down the steps backward, knelt on the lowest, and in a high trembling voice cried out:

"Master of all Slander, Dispenser of Crime's Rewards, Lord of Magnificent Sins and Mighty Vices, Satan, it is you we adore. God of Right Reason, receive the falsity of our tears. You save family honor by abortion in wombs made fruitful in heedless moments, you tempt to early miscarriages, your midwifery saves the unborn from the agonies of growing up, from the misery of failure.

"Support of the poor man strained beyond endurance, tonic of the defeated, you bestow on them gifts of hypocrisy, ingratitude, and pride wherewith to defend themselves against the attacks of those children of God, the Rich.

"Lord of the Despised, Satan, Reckoner of Humiliations, Maintainer of Age-Long Hatreds, you alone can stir to action the mind of a man crushed by injustice. You whisper to him well-laid plans for revenge, crimes certain of success, you push him into murders, fill him with the delight of revenge, with intoxication over the sufferings he has brought about, the tears he has caused to flow.

"O Satan, Hope of Virility, Anguish of Empty Wombs, you do not vaunt the negativeness of Lenten fasts, you alone receive the entreaties of the flesh, the petitions of families poor and greedy. You lead the mother to sell her daughter, to part with her son. You help loves sterile and forbidden. You bring men to screaming neuroses, you are a leaden weight around the neck of hysteria, the bloodstained inspirer of rape!

"Master, your servants beseech you on their knees. They entreat you to secure for them the exquisite joy of crimes undiscovered by the law, to help them with evil deeds of which the secret paths bewilder the mind of man. They entreat you to hear their desire for the agony of all who love and serve them. From the King of the Dispossessed, the Son whom the inflexible Father drove away, they demand glory, wealth, and power."

And now Docre rose to his feet and arms spread out shouted in a clear voice filled with hate:

"And you, Jesus, Artisan of Frauds, Stealer of Worship you have no right to. As a priest I can force you, with or against your will, to come down into this host, to take flesh in this bread. Thief of Love—listen to me! From the day you came forth from a virgin's womb, you have broken every pledge, lied in every promise. Centuries wept as they awaited you—God who has fled, God who stays silent! You were pledged to redeem men and they are unredeemed, to appear in your glory and you are asleep. Lie on, tell the unhappy man who calls on you, 'Have hope, be patient, suffer on, the hospital for souls will welcome you, the angels will come to your assistance, Heaven is opening for you.' Impostor! You know very well that the angels are leaving you, disgusted by your inertness! You who should be the spokesman for our laments, the ambassador of our tears, bringing them to the Father. But you have failed to do it—because it seems this act of intercession would disturb the slumber with which you are satiated in your happy Eternity.

"You have forgotten the poverty you preached, beloved servant of the banks! You have witnessed the feeble ground down by their extortions, you have listened to the death rattle of the fainthearted paralyzed by famines, women torn apart for a piece of bread. From the chancery of Simon Magus, your followers, your trade representatives, your Popes, all you have given them is excuses for delay, evasive promises, you cheap sacristy lawyer, you god of Big Business!

"Monster, whose inconceivable cruelty inflicts life on the innocent whom you dare to condemn in the name of some nameless original sin, to punish for unknown rules broken, we are determined to force on you the confession of your shameless lies, your unforgivable crimes! We want to drive deep your nails, to press the thorns into your forehead, to bring the agony of blood pouring back into your dried wounds!

"All this we can do and will do by desecrating your Body—cursed Nazarene, Profaner of Generous Vices, Distiller of Idiot Purity, cowardly King of Cowards, base poltroon of a god."

"Amen," chorused the altar boys in voices crystal clear.

Durtal, listening to this torrent of blasphemies and

insults, was stupefied by the filth the priest poured out. Silence followed his howls, smoke from the censers befogged the chapel. The women, hitherto still, began to stir, when the canon, turning in their direction, blessed them with a sweeping gesture of his left hand.

And suddenly the altar boys set the bells ringing.

It seemed a signal—the women threw themselves down and rolled on the carpet. One of them, as if moved by springs, threw herself on her stomach and beat the air with her feet, another squinting hideously, first made a clucking noise, then became voiceless—her jaws wide, her tongue sticking to the roof of her mouth. Another, her face swollen, the pupils of her eyes dilated, let her head fall on her shoulders and then, lifting it abruptly, began to tear her throat with her nails. Yet another stretched out on her back, undid her skirt, showing a naked stomach, huge with flatulence, twisted her face into hideous grimaces: from her blood-filled mouth she thrust out her tongue, bitten at the edges, and could not get it back in!

Durtal stood up to get a better view of Canon Docre.

Gazing at the Christ whose image stood above the tabernacle, he spread out his arms and spat out the foulest insults, shrieking at the top of his voice, cursing like a drunken cabman. One of the altar boys knelt in front of him, his back to the altar. A shudder ran through the priest as solemnly he intoned: "*Hoc est enim corpus meum.*" Then, instead of kneeling after the consecration before the sacred host, he turned to the congregation, his face swollen, steaming with sweat.

He stood staggering between the two altar boys, who lifted his chasuble, revealing his naked stomach, and supported him while the host he was carrying shot out of his hands onto the steps, broken and soiled.

Durtal shuddered as a wave of madness shook the room. Sheer hysteria overwhelmed the women. While the boys incensed the naked priest, they threw themselves flat down at the foot of the altar, tearing at the Eucharistic bread, breaking off damp fragments and swallowing them.

One woman, crouched over a crucifix, laughed heart-rendingly and cried out: "My priest, my priest!" An old woman tearing out her hair sprang up, spun around on one foot, and threw herself down next to a girl who crouched close to one wall, shaking convulsively and weeping as she spat out blasphemies. Through the smoke from the incense, Durtal could see Docre's red horns. As he sat there raging, he chewed the consecrated wafers, spat them out, divided them among the women who yelled as they stamped them underfoot or collided with one another to snatch at a host to profane it.

It was like the padded darkroom of an asylum, a monstrous hot bath of prostitutes and lunatics.

And now while the altar boys gave themselves to the men, and the lady of the house climbed onto the altar and placed the chalice under the naked legs of the Christ figure, a small boy at the back of the chapel, who up to then had not moved, suddenly threw himself forward howling like a dog. Half-stifled and utterly sickened, Durtal longed to escape. He looked for Hyacinthe, but she was beside him no longer. At last, seeing her near the canon, he stepped over the tangle of bodies on the floor and managed to get close to her. Her nostrils quivered as she breathed in the compound of foul scents and coupled bodies. "The odor of the Sabbath," she whispered between clenched teeth.

"Will you come away now?" he asked.

At this she seemed to wake up, and after a moment's hesitation she followed him without a word. He shouldered his way through the women, and thrust Hyacinthe to the door, crossed the court, passed the porter's lodge, now empty, and reached the street. There he stopped and breathed deep lungfuls of air; Hyacinthe, motionless, her mind far away, stayed by the wall. "I suppose you want to go back in," he said, contempt in his voice.

"No," she said, "but those scenes shatter me. I am utterly exhausted. I must have a glass of water."

She moved up the street, leaning on him, to the wineshop. It was a miserable hole, a tiny room with wooden tables and benches, a zinc counter. Two laborers were playing cards—they turned to look and laughed. The owner drew the pipe from his mouth and spat, seeming in no way surprised to see a lady of such elegance in his rat hole. Durtal thought he even caught a knowing wink given and returned. The owner lit a candle and murmured to Durtal: "You can't drink with these people. It would look odd. I'll take you to a private room."

"Seems to be a lot of fuss about a glass of water," Durtal said to Hyacinthe, who had started up a spiral stair. But she had already entered a bedroom, with torn wallpaper, damp smelling. Pictures from magazines were pinned to the walls, the floor was a mess. For furniture there was a bed, a cracked chamberpot, a table, a basin, a couple of chairs. The owner appeared, deposited a bottle of whisky, sugar, glasses, and departed.

Suddenly Hyacinthe's arms were round Durtal, gripping him tight.

"Oh no!" he cried, furious with himself for having fallen into the trap. "I've had enough of that! Anyhow it's getting late, your husband will be waiting for you. . . . "

She wasn't listening.

"I've got to have you," she insisted, and she had him on the bed, forcing his lust. She was in a frenzy, showing him sexual horrors he had never dreamed of. When it was over, he had his last shock, for he saw on the bed what seemed to be fragments of a host.

While she was putting on her clothes, silent and lost in her thoughts, he sat down on a chair and the stink of the room almost overcame him. He was not absolutely convinced of transubstantiation, was not at all sure that the Savior was really present in that dirty bit of bread. But the sacrilege in which he had unwittingly been involved depressed him immeasurably.

"If it's true!" he said to himself, "Hyacinthe and that wretched priest certainly are a kind of evidence for the real Presence. No, I've had all the filth I can stand. I'm through with her. After all, it was only at our first meeting that I actually wanted her."

On their way out he had to endure the knowing smiles of the laborers; he paid his bill and almost ran out of the place without waiting for his change. In the Rue Vaugirard he hailed a cab. They rode on, not so much as glancing at each other, wrapped in their own thoughts.

Hyacinthe got out when they reached her door. "Let us meet soon," she said. There was a touch of uncertainty in her voice.

"No," he answered, "let's break it off now. It wouldn't have worked anyway. You want everything, I want nothing. And after what's happened tonight— No, definitely."

He gave the cabman his address and sank back into the depths of the cab.

The Hint of an Explanation

Graham Greene

A long train journey on a late December evening, in this
new version of peace, is a dreary experience. I suppose that
my fellow traveller and I could consider ourselves lucky to
have a compartment to ourselves, even though the heating
apparatus was not working, even though the lights went out
entirely in the frequent Pennine tunnels and were too dim
anyway for us to read our books without straining the eyes,
and though there was no restaurant car to give at least a change
of scene. It was when we were trying simultaneously to chew
the same kind of dry bun bought at the same station buffet that
my companion and I came together. Before that we had sat at
opposite ends of the carriage, both muffled to the chin in
overcoats, both bent low over type we could barely make out,
but as I threw the remains of my cake under the seat our eyes
met, and he laid his book down.

By the time we were half-way to Bedwell Junction we
had found an enormous range of subjects for discussion;
starting with buns and the weather, we had gone on to politics,
the Government, foreign affairs, the atom bomb, and by an
inevitable progression, God. We had not, however, become
either shrill or acid. My companion, who now sat opposite me,

leaning a little forward, so that our knees nearly touched, gave such an impression of serenity that it would have been impossible to quarrel with him, however much our views differed, and differ they did profoundly.

I had soon realized I was speaking to a Catholic—to someone who believed—how do they put it?—in an omnipotent and omniscient Deity, while I am what is loosely called an Agnostic. I have a certain intuition (which I do not trust, founded as it may well be on childish experiences and needs) that a God exists, and I am surprised occasionally into belief by the extraordinary coincidences that beset our path like the traps set for leopards in the jungle, but intellectually I am revolted at the whole notion of such a God who can so abandon his creatures to the enormities of Free Will. I found myself expressing this view to my companion who listened quietly and with respect. He made no attempt to interrupt—he showed none of the impatience or the intellectual arrogance I have grown to expect from Catholics; when the lights of a wayside station flashed across his face that had escaped hitherto the rays of the one globe working in the compartment, I caught a glimpse suddenly of—what? I stopped speaking, so strong was the impression. I was carried back ten years, to the other side of the great useless conflict, to a small town, Gisors in Normandy. I was again, for a moment, walking on the ancient battlements and looking down across the grey roofs, until my eyes for some reason lit on one stony "back" out of the many, where the face of a middle-aged man was pressed against a window pane (I suppose that face has ceased to exist now, just as I believe the whole town with its medieval memories has been reduced to rubble). I remembered saying to myself with astonishment, "That man is happy—completely happy." I looked across the compartment at my fellow traveller, but his face was already again in shadow. I said weakly, "When you think what God—if there is a God—allows. It's not merely the physical agonies, but think of the corruption, even of children. . . ."

He said, "Our view is so limited," and I was disappointed at the conventionality of his reply. He must have been aware of my disappointment (it was as though our thoughts were huddled as closely as ourselves for warmth), for he went on, "Of course there is no answer here. We catch hints" . . . and then the train roared into another tunnel and the lights again went out. It was the longest tunnel yet; we went rocking down it and the cold seemed to become more intense with the darkness, like an icy fog (perhaps when one sense—of sight—is robbed, the others grow more acute). When we emerged into the mere grey of night and the globe lit up once more, I could see that my companion was leaning back on his seat.

I repeated his last words as a question, "Hints?"

"Oh, they mean very little in cold print—or cold speech," he said, shivering in his overcoat. "And they mean nothing at all to another human being than the man who catches them. They are not scientific evidence—or evidence at all for that matter. Events that don't, somehow, turn out as they were intended—by the human actors, I mean, or by the thing behind the human actors."

"The thing?"

"The word Satan is so anthropomorphic." I had to lean forward now: I wanted to hear what he had to say. I am—I really am, God knows—open to conviction. He said, "One's words are so crude, but I sometimes feel pity for that thing. It is so continually finding the right weapon to use against its Enemy and the weapon breaks in its own breast. It sometimes seems to me so—powerless. You said something just now about the corruption of children. It reminded me of something in my own childhood. You are the first person—except for one—that I have thought of telling it to, perhaps because you are anonymous. It's not a very long story, and in a way it's relevant."

I said, "I'd like to hear it."

"You mustn't expect too much meaning. But to me there seems to be a hint. That's all. A hint."

He went slowly on, turning his face to the pane, though he could have seen nothing real in the whirling world outside except an occasional signal lamp, a light in a window, a small country station torn backwards by our rush, picking his words with precision. He said, "When I was a child they taught me to serve at Mass. The church was a small one, for there were very few Catholics where I lived. It was a market town in East Anglia, surrounded by flat chalky fields and ditches—so many ditches. I don't suppose there were fifty Catholics all told, and for some reason there was a tradition of hostility to us. Perhaps it went back to the burning of a Protestant martyr in the sixteenth century—there was a stone marking the place near where the meat stalls stood on Wednesdays. I was only half aware of the enmity, though I knew that my school nickname of Popey Martin had something to do with my religion, and I had heard that my father was nearly excluded from the Constitutional Club when he first came to the town.

"Every Sunday I had to dress up in my surplice and serve Mass. I hated it—I have always hated dressing up in any way (which is funny when you come to think of it), and I never ceased to be afraid of losing my place in the service and doing something which would put me to ridicule. Our services were at a different hour from the Anglican, and as our small, far-from-select band trudged out of the hideous chapel the whole of the townsfolk seemed to be on the way past to the proper church—I always thought of it as the proper church. We had to pass the parade of their eyes, indifferent, supercilious, mocking; you can't imagine how seriously religion can be taken in a small town, if only for social reasons.

"There was one man in particular; he was one of the two bakers in the town, the one my family did not patronise. I don't think any of the Catholics patronised him because he was called a free-thinker—an odd title, for, poor man, no one's thoughts were less free than his. He was hemmed in by his hatred—his hatred of us. He was very ugly to look at, with one wall eye and a head the shape of a turnip, with the hair gone on the crown, and he was unmarried. He had no interests, apparently, but his baking and his hatred, though now that I am older I begin to see other sides to his nature—it did contain, perhaps, a certain furtive love. One would come across him suddenly, sometimes, on a country walk, especially if one was alone and it was Sunday. It was as though he rose from the ditches and the chalk smear on his clothes reminded one of the flour on his working overalls. He would have a stick in his hand and stab at the hedges, and if his mood were very black he would call out after you strange abrupt words that were like a foreign tongue—I know the meaning of those words, of course, now. Once the police went to his house because of what a boy said he had seen, but nothing came of it except that the hate shackled him closer. His name was Blacker, and he terrified me.

"I think he had a particular hatred of my father—I don't know why. My father was manager of the Midland Bank, and it's possible that at some time Blacker may have had unsatisfactory dealings with the bank—my father was a very cautious man who suffered all his life from anxiety about money—his own and other people's. If I try to picture Blacker now I see him walking along a narrowing path between high windowless walls and at the end of the path stands a small boy of ten—me. I don't know whether it's a symbolic picture or the memory of one of our encounters—our encounters somehow got more and more frequent. You talked just now about the corruption of children. That poor man was preparing to revenge himself on everything he hated—my father, the Catholics, the God whom people persisted in crediting, and that by corrupting me. He had evolved a horrible and ingenious plan.

"I remember the first time I had a friendly word from him. I was passing his shop as rapidly as I could when I heard his voice call out with a kind of sly subservience as though he were an under servant. 'Master David,' he called, 'Master David,' and I hurried on. But the next time I passed that way he was at his door (he must have seen me coming) with one of those curly cakes in his hand that we called Chelsea buns. I didn't want to take it, but he made me, and then I couldn't be other than polite when he asked me to come into his parlour behind the shop and see something very special.

"It was a small electric railway—a rare sight in those days, and he insisted on showing me how it worked. He made me turn the switches and stop and start it, and he told me that I could come in any morning and have a game with it. He used the word 'game' as though it were something secret, and it's true that I never told my family of this invitation and of how, perhaps twice a week those holidays, the desire to control that little railway became overpowering, and looking up and down the street to see if I were observed, I would dive into the shop."

Our larger, dirtier, adult train drove into a tunnel and the light went out. We sat in darkness and silence, with the noise of the train blocking our ears like wax. When we were through we didn't speak at once and I had to prick him into continuing. "An elaborate seduction," I said.

"Don't think his plans were as simple as that," my companion said, "or as crude. There was much more hate than love, poor man, in his make-up. Can you hate something you don't believe in? And yet he called himself a free thinker. What an impossible paradox, to be free and to be so obsessed. Day by day all through those holidays his obsession must have grown, but he kept a grip; he bided his time. Perhaps that thing I spoke of gave him the strength and the wisdom. It was only a week from the end of the holidays that he spoke to me of what concerned him so deeply.

"I heard him behind me as I knelt on the floor, coupling two coaches. He said, 'You won't be able to do this, Master David, when school starts.' It wasn't a sentence that needed any comment from me any more than the one that followed, 'You ought to have it for your own, you ought,' but how skilfully and unemphatically he had sowed the longing, the idea of a possibility. . . . I was coming to his parlour every day now; you see I had to cram every opportunity in before the hated term started again, and I suppose I was becoming accustomed to Blacker, to that wall eye, that turnip head, that nauseating subservience. The Pope, you know, describes himself as 'The servant of the servants of God,' and Blacker—I sometimes think that Blacker was 'the servant of the servants of . . .' well, let it be.

"The very next day, standing in the doorway watching me play, he began to talk to me about religion. He said, with what untruth even I recognized, how much he admired the Catholics; he wished he could believe like that, but how could a baker believe? He accented 'a baker' as one might say a biologist, and the tiny train spun round the gauge O track. He said, 'I can bake the things you eat just as well as any Catholic can,' and disappeared into his shop. I hadn't the faintest idea what he meant. Presently he emerged again, holding in his hand a little wafer. 'Here,' he said, 'eat that and tell me. . . .' When I put it in my mouth I could tell that it was made in the same way as our wafers for communion—he had got the shape a little wrong, that was all, and I felt guilty and irrationally scared. 'Tell me,' he said, 'what's the difference?'

" 'Difference?' I asked.

" 'Isn't that just the same as you eat in church?'

"I said smugly, 'It hasn't been consecrated.'

"He said, 'Do you think if I put the two of them under a microscope, you could tell the difference?' But even at ten I had the answer to that question. 'No,' I said, 'the—accidents don't change,' stumbling a little on the word 'accidents' which had suddenly conveyed to me the idea of death and wounds.

"Blacker said with sudden intensity, 'How I'd like to get one of your ones in my mouth—just to see. . . .'

"It may seem odd to you, but this was the first time that

the idea of transubstantiation really lodged in my mind. I had learnt it all by rote; I had grown up with the idea. The Mass was as lifeless to me as the sentences in *De Bello Gallico;* communion a routine like drill in the school-yard, but here suddenly I was in the presence of a man who took it seriously, as seriously as the priest whom naturally one didn't count—it was his job. I felt more scared than ever.

"He said, 'It's all nonsense, but I'd just like to have it in my mouth.'

"'You could if you were a Catholic,' I said naïvely. He gazed at me with his one good eye like a Cyclops. He said, 'You serve at Mass, don't you? It would be easy for you to get at one of those things. I tell you what I'd do—I'd swap this electric train for one of your wafers—consecrated, mind. It's got to be consecrated.'

"'I could get you one out of the box,' I said. I think I still imagined that his interest was a baker's interest—to see how they were made.

"'Oh, no,' he said. 'I want to see what your God tastes like.'

"'I couldn't do that.'

"'Not for a whole electric train, just for yourself? You wouldn't have any trouble at home. I'd pack it up and put a label inside that your Dad could see—"For my bank manager's little boy from a grateful client." He'd be pleased as Punch with that.'

"Now that we are grown men it seems a trivial temptation, doesn't it? But try to think back to your own childhood. There was a whole circuit of rails on the floor at our feet, straight rails and curved rails, and a little station with porters and passengers, a tunnel, a foot-bridge, a level crossing, two signals, buffers, of course—and above all, a turntable. The tears of longing came into my eyes when I looked at the turntable. It was my favorite piece—it looked so ugly and practical and true. I said weakly, 'I wouldn't know how.'

"How carefully he had been studying the ground. He must have slipped several times into Mass at the back of the church. It would have been no good, you understand, in a little town like that, presenting himself for communion. Everybody there knew him for what he was. He said to me, 'When you've been given communion you could just put it under your tongue a moment. He serves you and the other boy first, and I saw you once go out behind the curtain straight afterwards. You'd forgotten one of those little bottles.'

" 'The cruet,' I said.

" 'Pepper and salt.' He grinned at me jovially, and I—well, I looked at the little railway which I could no longer come and play with when term started. I said, 'You'd just swallow it, wouldn't you?'

" 'Oh, yes,' he said. 'I'd just swallow it.'

"Somehow I didn't want to play with the train any more that day. I got up and made for the door, but he detained me, gripping my lapel. He said, 'This will be a secret between you and me. To-morrow's Sunday. You come along here in the afternoon. Put it in an envelope and post it in. Monday morning the train will be delivered bright and early.'

" 'Not to-morrow,' I implored him.

" 'I'm not interested in any other Sunday,' he said. 'It's your only chance.' He shook me gently backwards and forwards. 'It will always have to be a secret between you and me,' he said. 'Why, if anyone knew they'd take away the train and there'd be me to reckon with. I'd bleed you something awful. You know how I'm always about on Sunday walks. You can't avoid a man like me. I crop up. You wouldn't ever be safe in your own house. I know ways to get into houses when people are asleep.' He pulled me into the shop after him and opened a drawer. In the drawer was an odd-looking key and a cut-throat razor. He said, 'That's a master key that opens all locks and that—that's what I bleed people with.' Then he patted my cheek with his plump floury fingers and said, 'Forget it. You and me are friends.'

"That Sunday Mass stays in my head, every detail of it, as though it had happened only a week ago. From the moment of the Confession to the moment of Consecration it had a terrible importance; only one other Mass has ever been so important to me—perhaps not even one, for this was a solitary Mass which would never happen again. It seemed as final as the last Sacrament, when the priest bent down and put the wafer in my mouth where I knelt before the altar with my fellow server.

"I suppose I had made up my mind to commit this awful act—for, you know, to us it must always seem an awful act—from the moment when I saw Blacker watching from the back of the church. He had put on his best Sunday clothes, and as though he could never quite escape the smear of his profession, he had a dab of dried talcum on his cheek, which he had presumably applied after using that cut-throat of his. He was watching me closely all the time, and I think it was fear—fear of that terrible undefined thing called bleeding—as much as covetousness that drove me to carry out my instructions.

"My fellow server got briskly up and taking the communion plate preceded Father Carey to the altar rail where the other Communicants knelt. I had the Host lodged under my tongue: it felt like a blister. I got up and made for the curtain to get the cruet that I had purposely left in the sacristy. When I was there I looked quickly round for a hiding place and saw an old copy of the *Universe* lying on a chair. I took the Host from my mouth and inserted it between two sheets—a little damp mess of pulp. Then I thought: perhaps Father Carey has put the paper out for a particular purpose and he will find the Host before I have time to remove it, and the enormity of my act began to come home to me when I tried to imagine what punishment I should incur. Murder is sufficiently trivial to have its appropriate punishment, but for this act the mind boggled at the thought of any retribution at all. I tried to remove the Host, but it had stuck clammily between the pages and in desperation I tore out a piece of the newspaper and screwing the whole thing up, stuck it in my trousers pocket. When I came back through the curtain carrying the cruet my eyes met Blacker's. He gave me a grin of encouragement and unhappiness—yes, I am sure, unhappiness. Was it perhaps that the poor man was all the time seeking something incorruptible?

"I can remember little more of that day. I think my mind was shocked and stunned and I was caught up too in the family bustle of Sunday. Sunday in a provincial town is the day for relations. All the family are at home and unfamiliar cousins and uncles are apt to arrive packed in the back seats of other people's cars. I remember that some crowd of that kind descended on us and pushed Blacker temporarily out of the foreground of my mind. There was somebody called Aunt Lucy with a loud hollow laugh that filled the house with mechanical merriment like the sound of recorded laughter from inside a hall of mirrors, and I had no opportunity to go out alone even if I had wished to. When six o'clock came and Aunt Lucy and the cousins departed and peace returned, it was too late to go to Blacker's and at eight it was my own bed-time.

"I think I had half forgotten what I had in my pocket. As I emptied my pocket the little screw of newspaper brought quickly back the Mass, the priest bending over me, Blacker's grin. I laid the packet on the chair by my bed and tried to go to sleep, but I was haunted by the shadows on the wall where the curtains blew, the squeak of furniture, the rustle in the chimney, haunted by the presence of God there on the chair. The Host had always been to me—well, the Host. I knew theoretically, as I have said, what I had to believe, but suddenly, as someone whistled in the road outside, whistled secretively, knowingly, to me, I knew that this which I had beside my bed was something of infinite value—something a man would pay for with his whole peace of mind, something that was so hated one could love it as one loves an outcast or a bullied child. These are adult words and it was a child of ten who lay scared in bed, listening to the whistle from the road, Blacker's whistle, but I think he felt fairly clearly what I am describing now. That is what I meant when I said this Thing, whatever it is, that seizes every possible weapon against God, is always, everywhere, disappointed at the moment of success. It must have felt as certain of me as Blacker did. It must have felt certain, too, of Blacker. But I wonder, if one knew what happened later to that poor man, whether one would not find again that the weapon had been turned against its own breast.

"At last I couldn't bear that whistle any more and got out of bed. I opened the curtains a little way, and there right under my window, the moonlight on his face, was Blacker. If I had stretched my hand down, his fingers reaching up could almost have touched mine. He looked up at me, flashing the one good eye, with hunger—I realize now that near-success must have developed his obsession almost to the point of madness. Desperation had driven him to the house. He whispered up at me, 'David, where is it?'

"I jerked my head back at the room. 'Give it me,' he said, 'quick. You shall have the train in the morning.'

"I shook my head. He said, 'I've got the bleeder here, and the key. You'd better toss it down.'

"'Go away,' I said, but I could hardly speak with fear.

"'I'll bleed you first and then I'll have it just the same.'

"'Oh no, you won't,' I said. I went to the chair and picked it—Him—up. There was only one place where He was safe. I couldn't separate the Host from the paper, so I swallowed both. The newsprint stuck like a prune skin to the back of my throat, but I rinsed it down with water from the ewer. Then I went back to the window and looked down at Blacker. He began to wheedle me. 'What have you done with it, David? What's the fuss? It's only a bit of bread,' looking so longingly and pleadingly up at me that even as a child I wondered whether he could really think that, and yet desire it so much.

"'I swallowed it,' I said.

"'Swallowed it?'

"'Yes,' I said. 'Go away.' Then something happened which seems to me now more terrible than his desire to corrupt or my thoughtless act: he began to weep—the tears ran lopsidedly out of the one good eye and his shoulders shook. I only saw his face for a moment before he bent his head and strode off, the bald turnip head shaking, into the dark. When I think of it now, it's almost as if I had seen that Thing weeping for its inevitable defeat. It had tried to use me as a weapon and now I had broken in its hands and it wept its hopeless tears through one of Blacker's eyes."

The black furnaces of Bedwell Junction gathered around the line. The points switched and we were tossed from one set of rails to another. A spray of sparks, a signal light changed to red, tall chimneys jetting into the grey night sky, the fumes of steam from stationary engines—half the cold journey was over and now remained the long wait for the slow cross-country train. I said, "It's an interesting story. I think I should have given Blacker what he wanted. I wonder what he would have done with it."

"I really believe," my companion said, "that he would first of all have put it under his microscope—before he did all the other things I expect he had planned."

"And the hint?" I said. "I don't quite see what you mean by that."

"Oh, well," he said vaguely, "you know for me it was an odd beginning, that affair, when you come to think of it," but I should never have known what he meant had not his coat, when he rose to take his bag from the rack, come open and disclosed the collar of a priest.

I said, "I suppose you think you owe a lot to Blacker."

"Yes," he said. "You see, I am a very happy man."

Variations on a Theme

F. J. Sheed

The Middle Ages, trying to make Satan a figure of horror—horns, tail, pitchfork—managed to turn him into a figure of fun. Our own age has turned him into a figure of speech—the personification either of the chaotic element in man or of the general bloodiness of nature. The only set of people now who can be counted on to take him seriously—seriously enough to crave contact with him—are the Satanists. One wonders how seriously Satan takes the Satanists.

What indeed do we know about him? If he is an illusion, he is an astonishingly persistent one.

Scripture, the New Testament especially, has demons in plenty, their "name is legion," multitudinous, anonymous. But one is their chief; Jesus speaks of "the Devil and his angels," Revelation of "the Dragon and his angels." This one, whom the Irish used to call the Abbot of Hell, is the only one given a name. As well as Devil—from the Greek word *diabolos*, an "enemy" or "accuser"—he is called Satan from a Hebrew word with roughly the same meaning; Apollyon, written in Greek as Abaddon, the Exterminator; Asmodeus, the husband-murdering devil of the book of Tobias; Belial, which means "useless," "unprofitable"; Beelzebub, the Canaanite Lord of the House or (in mockery, perhaps) Beelzebub, Lord of the Flies—one knows what flies mean in a hot climate.

We use other names for the Devil that Scripture does not give him, two especially, Lucifer (Light-Bearer) and Mephistopheles. This last appears in the Middle Ages as one of Satan's High Command, and is immortalized, if that be the word, by Marlowe and Goethe, Berlioz and Gounod. What his name means we do not know.

That Scripture takes the Devil seriously is not in doubt. But how does it view him—as a person, someone? Or as only the negative element in man or the universe? Is Scripture's Satan simply "Something in ourselves that makes for wickedness"?—counterweight to the "Something not ourselves that makes for righteousness," which was as far as Matthew Arnold cared to commit himself about God?

Like Adam, like Christ, the word Satan begins as a common noun preceded by "the"—"the satan," "the enemy"—before we meet it as a name. Only once in the Old Testament (1 Chronicles 21:1) is "the" omitted, and never in the New, save when Satan is directly addressed.

When we think of the Devil in the Old Testament, two episodes immediately occur to us, the tempting of Eve and the tormenting of Job. Eve's tempter is called only the Serpent, with no mention of the Devil or Satan. As a specimen temptation, a model of all the temptations that have ever been, the writer has given us a masterpiece—a forbidden action shown as alluring, the promise that the experience will be enriching, the insinuation that to refuse it would be to deny one's own maturity. How in the depth of his own mind the writer saw the Tempter, we can only guess; he certainly *shows* him as someone, a being with a mind and a will, and that will bent upon man's destruction.

That, too, is how "the satan" who tormented Job is shown. There are those who think the writer could not have meant him for our Satan but for an angel in good standing, who had either the function of public prosecutor or a natural pleasure in prosecuting. But the "good standing" is assumed only because he appears along with other angels and has to ask God's permission to test Job. Even in a theological treatise, which the Book of Job was not, the Devil might be shown as doing both these things. For the rest, Job's tempter is our Satan at his most vicious.

In the Gospels, Jesus acts and speaks as if Satan and the demons were real and personal. It is suggested that he did this merely to humor his hearers, who *did* believe in them. If so, he carried the humoring rather far—to the point of conversing with demons. And he was not much given to humoring his hearers. Considering how he upset the most cherished Jewish convictions—on the Sabbath, on the Temple, on his own power to forgive sins, on foods clean and unclean, on the Messiah—it would be odd if he pretended to believe in Satan merely because his hearers did.

After all it was to his own followers, the men he was training to carry on his work, that he said: "Satan has desired to have you that he might sift you like wheat"; and this was at the Last Supper, with no scribes or Pharisees there to be edified.

Matthew, Mark, and Luke all give the Testing of Christ by Satan in the desert. John, who does not, has the three passages in which, with Calvary almost on him, Jesus shows himself so preoccupied with Satan (12:31, 14:30, 16:11). And it is John who writes in his First Epistle, "The reason the Son of God appeared was to destroy the works of Satan" (3:8).

This fits with the reason that the risen Christ gave Paul on the road to Damascus for sending him to the Gentiles: "to open their eyes, that they may turn from the power of Satan to God" (Acts 26:18). We find Satan mentioned by Paul rather more often than by Christ. To the Ephesians he wrote of man's war with the Devil: "We are contending not against flesh and blood but against the world rulers of this present darkness ["the cosmocrats of the dark eon," the Greek reads], against the spiritual hosts of wickedness in the heavenly places" (6:11). That would be a curious description of a tendency to evil within our own souls! As indeed would Peter's "Your adversary the Devil prowls around like a roaring lion seeking someone to devour" (1 Peter 5:8).

To return to Jesus—if he did not believe that he was contending with minds and wills bent upon destroying men, his words and deeds in their regard are incomprehensible. The Christian who does not himself believe in a personal devil is faced with the question why Jesus should have been so grossly wrong on a matter of that spiritual importance.

But need he have been wrong? This is not the place for a metaphysical discussion. But the distinction between matter and spirit is not a meaningless product of superstition. Matter exists, so does mind. Within the realm of matter there is an almost infinite complexity, but the human mind is as complex. Man has in him both matter and spirit. Below man there are beings solely material. There is no obvious reason why there should not be solely spiritual beings higher than man. In the one spirit that we find available for experience and experiment—the human mind with its tie to the matter of the body—there are possibilities of evil which we have not finished exploring yet.

If there exist spirits not tied to matter, then it is not impossible, not even improbable, that some of them should choose evil. In our own experience of the power self has to distort life, there is nothing to make it hard to believe in spirit-selves grown monstrous. When we hear Christ speak of the Devil as "a murderer from the beginning, a liar and the father of lies," I cannot see why we feel that we can simply flip the words aside.

The one reason given for thus disposing of them is that the paganisms surrounding Israel had developed a demonology and that this had invaded Judaism between the two

Testaments. This is one of those arguments which prove too much. There is no single teaching of Christ or belief of Christians which we cannot find the great paganisms feeling toward. It is mere provincialism to assume that there were no valid insights in that vast welter of religions—Zoroaster's Ahriman, for instance. Pagans were men, man's mind thrusts and explores. Pagans were praying men; God loved them and did not ignore their prayers.

Certainly the main line of Christian thinking on the Satan we actually meet in the New Testament is not to be matched outside it. Satanism being the theme of this book, one wonders what that main-line Satan thinks of it.

Man's soul is a spirit, but it is a soul too: it animates a body and some of its energy has to be expended on the animating. Indeed so many and various are the demands made by the body, so urgent are its pleasures and pains, that our spirit hardly has time to live its spirit life! But Satan is sheer spirit, with no body to drain his vitality, no bodily pains and pleasures to distract his mind from its proper activity. His intellect towers over man's. By all the values he has, he must surely despise men. The one quality our main-line tradition is certain he has is pride—the self treating itself as God, "the world well lost for love," self-love.

None of this do I know, of course. I am just letting my mind run on, or my fancy rather. I cannot get rid of the feeling that Satan loathes having his human victims in Hell; they lower the intellectual tone of the place. Eagles don't catch flies. Satan would rather throw these lost souls back, as a big-game fisherman would throw back sardines. But in the war he wages against Christ men represent the only victories possible for him. And even if men mean nothing to him, for some reason that he cannot fathom, God loves them. Satan may feel it humiliating to have to live with them, but God's Son thought them worth dying for. So Satan can still in this sinner or that frustrate Christ, render his death fruitless.

On the same line of thinking, one suspects that he must be

torn two ways about Satanists. Insofar as they help to win his wretchedly small victories, they have their place. But they are such poor stuff mentally that he must cringe to have them wearing his name, representing him to the world.

Scripture does not suggest that those in Hell are tortured by Satan, or even by his demons. One feels that it would be beneath their dignity. To have snatched them from Christ's hands is sufficient victory; why should they soil their own hands with them? There may, of course, be a satisfaction in merely being the cause of suffering. Certainly men have found it so—why not demons? There are surely depths in diabolic psychology, or pneumatology, if you prefer, that we cannot know. One mysterious glimpse we have been given. When Jesus expelled the demons from a man in Gerasa—which we used to call Gadara—they begged to be allowed to enter a herd of swine, and not be sent back to the Pit. They preferred pigs to their own kind—but the pigs could not stand *them*.